A TIME TO LAUGH

(Ecclesiastes 3:4)

—

A BRIGGS FAMILY COLLECTION

Illustrated by Calvin Grondahl

·—

Salt Lake City
1987

First Printing, October 1987

ISBN No. 0-88494-649-5

Acknowledgements and Permissions

Calvin Grondahl's illustrations are from the books FREEWAYS TO PERFECTION and SUNDAY FOYER. Permission for their use has been granted by the Sunstone Foundation.

We also express sincere thanks to all those who have granted us permission to use their works in this publication. It is through their poems, stories, jokes, or interesting comments that we have enjoyed many meetings, roadshows, talent nights, etc.

Many sources attribute their stories to Mr. Anonymous, the famous unknown author. Who knows where these jokes originated? Old jokes never die; some disappear for decades, then come to life again. It has been said that "If Adam came back to earth, the only thing he would recognize would be the jokes." If you are the originator of any of the humor found in this collection, please accept our appreciation and apologies if proper credit has not been given.

DEDICATION

This book is dedicated to our children,
Jenny, Jeff, Robby, Lori and Danny....
without whose help it could have been
finished much sooner!

CONTENTS

ACKNOWLEDGEMENTS

This book is written in memory of three great literature teachers, Mrs. Chapman, Mrs. Biddulph, and Mrs. Price. They attempted to teach the humor of old English literature through Chaucer and Shakespeare. One day as we attempted to struggle through the prologue of Chaucer's Canterbury Tales in an old English brogue, Mrs. Chapman said, "Why is it that you remember every joke you've ever heard, but can't remember one line of Chaucer?"

Then this wise teacher answered her own question. "I'll tell you why. You repeat, time and time again the jokes you hear, but outside this room you wouldn't be caught dead repeating the words of Chaucer!"

So, in memory of these great teachers, let us share with you our collection of the Briggs' family humor file as enhanced, modified and adapted over the years through the art of repetition.

THE BRIGGS FAMILY

PROLOGUE

Attempting to write a humor book for a religious audience is like walking across the mighty Niagara Falls on a tight rope. The Lord commanded us to have "a glad heart and a cheerful countenance" and yet "not with much (excessive) laughter, for this is sin." (D&C 59:15)

We have therefore tried to carefully edit the humor found within this book so as to help the speaker, the listener or the casual reader relax and enjoy the message. Some may question if all the selections are indeed humorous. Good humor is really the refining of the heart as Thomas Carlyle stated, "True humor springs not more from the head than from the heart. It is not contempt. Its essence is love. Its issue is not in laughter, but in still smiles which lie far deeper."

Humor, anecdotes, testimonies and parables help make messages live within us. They are personal; we each take from them something different. Good humor can make people cry or laugh, often at the same time. Laughter is therapeutic. Even Christ's parables were often interpreted differently by his disciples, the Pharisees and the Romans. Similarly, good humor used by a speaker, whether at general conference, sacrament meeting, a fireside or to a friend in the hall, may teach a profound principle of truth or simply be worth a moment's laugh. Remember above all to keep your humor clean. A speaker is really hard up if he thinks a dirty remark is good humor.

True humor is interpreted in the heart and mind of the listener. It has been said, "Tell me what you laugh at, and I'll tell you who you are."

Hopefully the jokes, poems, stories and incidents contained here don't belittle or ridicule other people. They are not intended to reflect unpleasantly on politics, religious faiths, business or mannerisms of anyone. We should never lose friends in the efforts to win laughs. "What a man laughs at may well be the measure of his mind," said Richard L. Evans.

It has been delightful searching through old magazines, journals, books, conference addresses, newspapers, etc., to find the type of humor appropriate for religious use. Collect good stories and illustrations. When you find one, write it down for future use. If you don't already have a file, start one now.

HOW PROPHETS
AND GENERAL AUTHORITIES
HAVE USED HUMOR

THE PROPHET JOSEPH SMITH

"Joseph Smith interested and edified, while, at the same time he amused and entertained his audience; and none listened to him that were ever weary with his discourse. I have known him to retain a congregation of willing and anxious listeners for many hours together, in the midst of cold or sunshine, rain or wind, while they were laughing at one moment and weeping the next. Even his most bitter enemies were generally overcome, if he could get their ears."

Autobiography of Parley P. Pratt, p.45-46 Third Edition

BRIGHAM YOUNG

"How is it that Brother Brigham is able to comfort and soothe those who are depressed in spirit, and always make those with whom he associates so happy? I will tell you how he makes us feel so happy. He is happy himself and the man who is happy himself can make others feel so, for the light of God is in him, and others feel the influence, and feel happy in his society."

Journal of Discourses, 3:12

HUGH B. BROWN

"A wholesome sense of humor will be a safety valve that will enable you to apply the lighter touch to heavy problems and to learn some lessons in problem-solving that 'sweat and tears' often fail to dissolve."

Conference Report, April 1968 p. 100

J. GOLDEN KIMBALL

"I would like my preaching to have color, thrill, feel homelike, and revive old memories; and, if I can't feel that way among the Latter-day Saints, where on earth can I go to feel that free."

J. Golden Kimball, p. 91, Bookcraft, 1966

HEBER C. KIMBALL

Our leaders have demonstrated that one can enjoy both faith and humor. It has been said of Heber C. Kimball, counselor to Brigham Young, that he prayed and conversed with God "as one man talketh to another." However, on one occasion, while offering an earnest appeal on behalf of a certain one of his fellow creatures, he startled the kneeling circle by bursting into a loud laugh in the very midst of his prayer. Quickly regaining his composure and solemn address, he remarked apologetically, "Lord, it makes me laugh to pray about some people."

Life of Heber C. Kimball, p. 427, Bookcraft, Third Ed., 1967

BRIGHAM YOUNG

"I will take the liberty of suggesting to my brethren who address this congregation that our sermons should be short, and if they are not filled with life and spirit, let them be shorter."

Journal of Discourses, 12:27

SPENCER W. KIMBALL

The first time he spoke publicly after his throat operation, he started by telling the congregation that he had gone to New York and fallen among cutthroats and thieves who had slit his throat and stolen his voice. The audience laughed heartily and both he and they relaxed.

Spencer W. Kimball, p. 311, Bookcraft, 1977

JAMES E. FAUST

"For many years as I have blessed newborn children, including my own, I have blessed them with a sense of humor. I do this with the hope that it will help guard them against being too rigid, in the hope that they will have balance in their lives, in the hope that situations and problems and difficulties will not be overdrawn."

BYU Devotional, March 17, 1981

MARION D. HANKS

"What shall we give to the children? Pray for a sense of humor. 'Laughter leavens life' and brings a sunny spirit."

Conference Report, October 1968, p. 117

PAUL H. DUNN

I also heard about a mother and her young daughter who were listening to a public speaker when the child said to her mother, "Isn't that man happy?" The mother replied, "I guess so." To which the girl remarked: "Why doesn't he tell his face?"

The Ensign, December 1971, p. 120

LEGRAND RICHARDS

For several decades Elder LeGrand Richards brought humor, enthusiasm and a great missionary spirit to stake and general conferences. Shortly before his death, a stake president asked, "Brother Richards, how are you feeling?" The great apostle said, "Well, President, I'll tell you. My body, the house I live in, is getting old and creaky," and then he added with all of his ninety-five years of youth testifying, "but the real LeGrand Richards is still on fire."

James E. Faust, BYU Devotional, March 17, 1981

J. GOLDEN KIMBALL

"I was lying in the hospital waiting for an operation. I had been there six days in preparation and in nervous anticipation of the event. The operation was serious. The doctor said I needed "considerable fixing." Later, I learned that over twenty inches of incision was required, most of it in the bone.

The day before the dreadful ordeal, a mutual friend brought Brother J. Golden Kimball to administer to me. First, he talked and visited a considerable time and then blessed me. There was nothing frivolous about his talk, and yet he soon had me smiling. Later, the smiles were interspersed with laughter. I began to see things in proper perspective and to realize that all was well with the world and that the sky for me, after all, had but one dark cloud in it which, probably, would soon roll away. I felt I was in the presence of a sane, well balanced man and a man of exceptionally strong faith. In truth, never did I feel the power of faith more than that day."

A debtor, J. Golden Kimball

MISSIONARY'S HAND BOOK--1946

"Good natural cheerfulness and discreetly used humor tend to enliven the audience and breakdown barriers between the speaker and his hearers. They stimulate the nerves and raise an agreeable response in the listeners. Skillfully and carefully used, humor is a bolster to effective speech."

TEN COMMANDMENTS
FOR THE USE OF HUMOR
IN A SPEECH

1. ## HUMOR MUST BE PERTINENT TO THE MESSAGE.

    Use meaningful material; otherwise, it sounds dragged in and loses its impact. Improperly used humor can confuse the congregation. Remember that many times the only thing that the congregation will remember thirty minutes after you've finished might be the joke or humorous story you told. You have the responsibility to make sure it helps convey your message.

2. ## BE PREPARED: A FEW GOOD BITS OF HUMOR DOTH NOT A GOOD TALK MAKE.

    The use of a few laughs cannot cover up a poorly prepared speech. Good humor may well be the most difficult part of the speech to prepare. Practice punch lines many times before you try them on a congregation of sleeping skeptics. Humor is rarely effective if it is read. Please speak up with enthusiasm, don't read. Being prepared also helps ease the nervous "jitters." "...if ye are prepared ye shall not fear." D&C 38:30.

3. ## USE HUMOR SPARINGLY SO IT SPARKLES WHEN IT APPEARS.

    Humor has been likened to windows that let the sunlight into your speech or conversation. "Laughter leavens life and brings a sunny spirit." Never violate good taste in humor, lasting respect is better than an immediate laugh.

4. ## HUMOR SHOULD HAVE SOME ELEMENT OF ORIGINALITY.

    By this, we're not saying you must make up all your own jokes or stories, but they must have something of you in them. You must add some special touch or modification that will help the audience identify it with you, your style and your personality.

    In most cases the speaker is the speech. The normal listener cannot separate the content of the message from the character of the speaker. When the content of the humor does not reflect the character and personality of the speaker, the audience responds with the same emptiness which the speaker delivered. Mistrust and lack of persuasion result.

5. <u>KEEP YOUR HUMOR SIMPLE, CONCISE AND TO THE POINT.</u>

It is well to remember that a group of people who are probably hungry, and who may quite possibly be thinking of something else (like the afternoon football game) are going to try and follow you through your speech. If you permit your speech to wander through several non-related humorous stories, their minds will wander too, and you may find it impossible to get them back onto the track that carries your train of thought. It is well, therefore, to keep all humor as simple and direct as possible. Remember, "...a fool's voice is known by his multitude of words." (Eccles. 5:3)

George Burns says, "Get to your punch line fast since every joke you tell reminds your listeners of one they've heard and if you don't get there first, they'll be telling their own yarn before you've finished with yours."

6. <u>NEVER TELL A JOKE OR STORY, NO MATTER HOW HUMOROUS,</u>

<u>THAT MAKES YOU FEEL UNCOMFORTABLE OR ASHAMED.</u>

The use of improper humor reminds us of an experience we had as teenagers. Our seminary teacher taped a large piece of white paper on the wall, and then made a small black dot with his marker, right in the middle.

He then asked each of us what we saw. Each answered "A black dot." He asked the second time and we answered the same. "Tell me," he asked, "How did you all remember the tiny black dot, but no one remembered the sheet of white paper that surrounds it?"

Never forget: A little bad humor can literally destroy a good talk.

7. <u>MODIFY HUMOR TO THE AUDIENCE OR CONGREGATION.</u>

Communication can succeed only when the speaker and the listener are both satisfied that the message given results in benefits for both. You may think that it is impossible to use the same joke when speaking to the Aaronic Priesthood or giving the Relief Society Cultural Refinement lesson. This may be true, but many times by changing the situation in the joke from a football game to the kitchen table at dinner time, the same joke could be appropriately used with both groups.

Talk with and not at your audience. Take a few extra minutes in preparation to listen and pick up a few tidbits of local conversation. Generally, if worked into your speech, they immediately and dramatically bring the audience into intimate relationship with the speaker.

A small investment in time brings large dividends in attention and rapport. Try it next time; you'll find it pays.

8.   HUMOR SHOULD OFFEND NO ONE.

In your stories and jokes, don't belittle or ridicule other people, races, religions or countries. Don't lose friends in an effort to win laughs.

It's a Poor Joke:

When some woman blushes with embarrassment
When some heart carries away an ache
When something sacred is made to appear common
When a man's weakness provides the cause for laughter
When profanity is required to make it "funny"
When a little child is brought to tears
When everyone can't join in the laughter

It has been said, if you wouldn't write it and sign it, don't say it.

9.   NEVER USE HUMOR UNLESS YOU ENJOY IT YOURSELF.

One cannot expect to awake enthusiasm in the congregation without being enthusiastic himself. "Don't use a joke unless you think it's real funny," advises Jimmy Durante. "I never put one in my act unless it has first given me a healthy chuckle."

The best test for using humor is: Does the speaker think it's good? If he doesn't, then he has no right to inflict it on the audience.

10.   CONCLUDE HUMOR WITH A STRONG PUNCH LINE, THEN QUIT.

In telling humor there are several "don'ts" of which we should all be aware, or they might destroy your punch line:

☺   Don't laugh at your own jokes, but be sure to smile and let your eyes sparkle. Let the audience know you enjoyed their response.

☺   Don't try to get three or four laughs from the same line.

☺   Don't announce funny stories or jokes ahead of time. Slide into humor, easily and naturally.

☺   Don't try to explain a joke in detail. If you got little or no audience response, let it die and go on to the next point.

☺   Don't use dialects unless you are particularly suited to telling this kind of joke, or unless the dialect is absolutely necessary to express your point.

☺   Don't ramble through a joke with an explanation of every name or situation. Keep things simple.

☺   Don't forget the conclusion. Tie the humor to the purpose of the talk, but please keep it simple and brief.

WHEN SHOULD HUMOR BE USED?

We have often been asked when it is appropriate to use humor. Our answer is simple--whenever and wherever conversation and smiles are acceptable. However, nothing is more important than appropriateness in deciding whether or not to tell a joke or humorous story. We've listened and laughed at MC's, teachers and speakers in primary, sunday school, sacrament meetings, stake and general conference, roadshows, pinewood derbies, Christmas parties, funerals, etc. We have also enjoyed quiet reflective thoughts of humor long after the occasion has past.

In our complex society, we are often called upon to participate in groups of one kind or another--from cub scouts to PTA, from church socials to family reunions. Whatever the occasion, humor can be used most effectively in four ways:

1.   <u>AT THE BEGINNING OF A TALK OR SOCIAL EVENT, HUMOR IS REFERRED TO AS THE "ICEBREAKER."</u>

      The first time President Spencer W. Kimball spoke publicly after his throat operation, he started by telling the congregation that he had gone to New York and had fallen among cutthroats and thieves who had slit his throat and stolen his voice. The audience laughed heartily and both he and they relaxed.

2.   <u>AS A STORY OR INCIDENT TO BUILD YOUR THEME.</u>

      A humorous story will often be better remembered than other parts of your talk, so you can use it early in your talk and then refer back to it in your conclusion to tie both ends together.

      For example, in convincing families to spend time together, several General Authorities have used the following story:

      "It was a gorgeous October day. My husband Art and I were down at the boat landing helping our friend Don drag his skiff up on the beach. Art remarked wistfully that it would be a long time before next summer, when we could all start sailing again.

      'You folks ought to take up skiing like our family and have fun the year round.' Don said.

      'Doesn't that get pretty expensive?' I asked?

Don straightened up and smiled. 'It's funny,' he said. 'We live in an old-fashioned house---legs on the tub, that sort of thing. For years we've been saving up to have the bathroom done over. But every winter we take the money out of the bank and go on a couple of family skiing trips.

Our oldest boy is in the mission field now, and he often mentions in his letters what a great time we had on those trips. You know, I can't imagine him writing home to say: "Boy, we really have a swell bathroom, don't we, dad?"'"

3. TO ILLUSTRATE POINTS, CONCLUSIONS OR IDEAS.

An example we've used many times in our family when our children have requested extra money to attend something we didn't feel was appropriate, has been to say: "Our family follows the golden rule: Them that has the gold, sets the rules."

4. TO WRAP UP A TALK ON A BRIGHT NOTE.

Because we end our talks "in the name of Jesus Christ, Amen" we should only use what is referred to as serious humor to end a talk. A good example of this is:

During the dark days of the Civil War, an incident occurred that gave insight into Lincoln's belief that God is omnipotent. A prominent minister, hoping to cheer up the weary president, assured Lincoln that the Lord was on Lincoln's side to which President Lincoln responded:

"I am not at all concerned about that, for I know that the Lord is always on the side of right. But it is my constant anxiety and prayer that I and this nation should be on the Lord's side."

Yes, appropriate humor can be used for many reasons while speaking. A good rule of thumb is: "if you don't use humor, a good story, or a real life experience every 2 to 3 minutes, neither you nor your listeners will know what you are talking about."

Good speakers will have a good repertoire of humor, stories, and real life experiences (these do not necessarily have to be humorous). Again we recommend that you start your own personal or family file today.

PROCRASTINATION DOTH NOT A GOOD SPEAKER MAKE!

AGE

I have now reached the "Age of Metals"
--My hair has turned silver,
My teeth are partially gold,
And I've got lead in my pants.

☺☺☺

Telling a woman's age is like buying a used car.
You know the odometer has been turned back, but you can only guess
how far.

☺☺☺

My barber told me to use a new hair tonic
and my hair would come in heavy.
Only one hair grew, but it did weigh ten pounds!

☺☺☺

My hair will be gray as long as I live...
But my wife's will be black as long as she dyes.

☺☺☺

"Your age, please," asked the Census Taker.

"Well," said the woman, "Let me figure it out.
I was 12 years old when I started MIA. My father was 30.

Now, he's 60, or twice as old as he was then.

So, I must be 24!"

☺☺☺

Work hard and save your money and when you are old;
you will be able to buy the things only
the young can enjoy.

☺☺☺

Nothing ruins a class reunion like a fellow
who has managed to stay young-looking
and get rich at the same time.

☺☺☺

If you want to stay young, associate with young people;
If you want to feel your age, try to keep up with them!

Why can't life's big problems come when we are twenty and know everything?

☺☺☺

Old people like to give good advice as solace --
For no longer being able to provide bad examples.

☺☺☺

When we are young, we try to hide our poverty.
When we grow older...we brag about it.

☺☺☺

As long as I'm green I know I am growing.
It is only when I ripen that I can go rotten.

☺☺☺

The best years of a man's life are when the kids are old
enough to shovel the snow but too young to drive the car.

☺☺☺

Grandchildren are God's way of compensating us for growing old.

☺☺☺

He hadn't time to pen a note
He hadn't time to cast a vote
He hadn't time to sing a song
He hadn't time to right a wrong
He hadn't time to love or give
He hadn't time to really live
From now on he'll have time on end
He died today, my "busy" friend.

☺☺☺

My grandmother is over 80 and still doesn't need glasses.
Drinks right out of the bottle.
-Henny Youngman-

☺☺☺

Death is a congenital birth defect.

☺☺☺

On an assyrian tablet dated 2000 B.C. are the following words

"The Gods do not subtract from the allotted span of men's lives the
hours spent in fishing."

I've reached the age where the happy hour is a nap.

☺☺☺

If you're middle-aged, there are four things you should have to shovel snow: Warm clothing, high boots, a small shovel and a big teenager to use it.

☺☺☺

A message for retirement parties

And so, as he begins this well-deserved retirement,
He has only two wishes for the future:

That his bowling score will be as high as his hopes
--And his golf score as low as his pension.

☺☺☺

My face in the mirror isn't wrinkled or drawn.
My house isn't dusty. The cobwebs are gone.

My garden is lovely and so is my lawn.
I don't think I should put my glasses back on!

☺☺☺

I'm at the age where "getting it together" means bifocals.

☺☺☺

When you're 30 you want to change the world.
When you're 40 you want to change the country.
When You're 50 you want to change the neighborhood.

When you're 60 you want to change your luck.
But the big difference is when you're 70.
When you're 70 you have to rev up just to change your socks!

☺☺☺

I've always wanted to be a baby again because if I had another opportunity to sleep twelve hours a day and spend the rest of the time eating, drinking and being cuddled--you can bet that this time around I'm not gonna cry!

☺☺☺

You know you're old when you reach down to get the wrinkles out of your panty hose and you realize you aren't wearing any.

☺☺☺

By the time we have money to burn -- the fire has gone out!

The problem is: By the time you get it all together
---You're too old to lift it.

☺☺☺

You're not really successful until someone claims
he sat beside you in school.

☺☺☺

I've found that the trouble with being old is:
It's a 24 hour a day job.

☺☺☺

65 is when you finally decide what
you want to be when you grow up -- YOUNG!

☺☺☺

Traffic Officer: "Lady, as soon as I saw you coming around the
curve, I said to myself, '65 at least'."

Woman Driver: "Well, officer, you're way off. It must be this car
that makes me look so old."

☺☺☺

"I'll be one-hundred tomorrow," boasted the oldest High Priest in the ward.
"And I want you to know that I don't have an enemy in the world."

"That's a beautiful thought," said the Bishop.

"Yup," said the old man. "I've outlived every darn one of 'em."

☺☺☺

Upon accepting an award, the late Jack Benny once remarked, "I really
don't deserve this honor, but then I have arthritis and I don't deserve
that either."

☺☺☺

A patient's comment on his lab test

"My blood went out to the lab, my urine went out to the lab, my mucus
went out to the lab, but I was afraid to go out.

By mistake the lab report came to me instead of to the doctor. It
arrived in the form of dots, dashes, and holes on a plastic card.

I slipped it into my tape recorder and it played "Nearer My God, to
Thee."

When'er I pass our little Church
I linger for a visit;
So that when I'm carried in,
The Lord won't say, "Who is it?"

☺☺☺

In one of his sermons, J. Golden Kimball declared, "I would like to preach a man's funeral sermon while he is living; you can't tell the truth about him when he is dead. I have given many a man a ticket to the celestial glory that I knew wouldn't take him half way."

☺☺☺

When a man retires, we are told,
It is nice if he has a hobby that his wife can share with him.
Like if her favorite pastime is cleaning fish.

☺☺☺

Your hometown is the place where you were born,
And then grew up as a kid.
And where everyone wonders, when you return,
How you turned out as well as you did.

☺☺☺

Old age is a lousy reward for longevity.
There should be some kind of government program
Where, when you reach 70,
You're issued a new body.

☺☺☺

We all want to go to heaven,
But no one wants to die to get there!
-Billy Graham-

☺☺☺

I dreamed death came to me last night,
And Heaven's gates swung wide.
With kindly grace an angel ushered me inside.

There to my astonishment stood folks I'd known on earth.
Some I'd judged and labeled as unfit, of little worth.

Indignant words rose to my lips but never were set free.
For every face showed stunned surprise. Not one expected me!

☺☺☺

There are two kinds of fools -- One says:
"This is old, therefore, it must be good!"
The other says: "This is new, therefore, it must be better!"

The glory of young men is their strength;
And the beauty of old men is the gray head.
-Proverbs 20:29-

☺☺☺

Middle age is that time in life when your clothes no longer fit,
But it's you who need the alterations.

☺☺☺

I miss my youth--although we do keep in touch.
Only last week I sent it a postcard saying:
"Wish you were here."

☺☺☺

The future is that time when you'll wish you'd done
What you aren't doing now.

☺☺☺

Nothing is more responsible for the good old days
Than a bad memory!

☺☺☺

"You certainly are happy," said the young man to the elderly
spinster. "I always thought unmarried women were supposed to
be grouchy."

"Well," she replied, "I have a dog that growls, a fireplace
that smokes, a parrot that swears, and a cat that stays out
all night. What other joys could I possibly get from having
a man around the house?"

☺☺☺

An elderly gentleman went to the doctor to have a
blood test. The doctor looked at him. "A blood
test? Why?"

"I'm going to get married," was the answer.
"How old are you, anyway?" asked the doctor.
"I'm eighty-four" was the reply.
"And the bride?"

"Oh, she's only thirty-two."
"Thirty-two," cried the doctor. "Why that kind of
disparity could be fatal."

"Well," shrugged the old man philosophically.
"If she dies, she dies."

Friend: "How are you today?"

Old-timer: "I think I'm fine, and I'm not soliciting
a second opinion!"

☺☺☺

Isn't it amazing how many people there are who long for immortality
But can't even amuse themselves on a rainy evening?

☺☺☺

Age: In spite of the cost of living, it's still popular.

☺☺☺

In a poem, Ode to Retirement, by Len Ingebrigtsen, is this line:

"The reason I know my youth is all spent?
My get up and go has got up and went."

☺☺☺

Pushing fifty is not exercise enough.

☺☺☺

You know you're old when you're glad your mirror is fogged.

☺☺☺

Optimist: You don't go bald, you gain face.

☺☺☺

If we had known that having grandchildren would be so nice.
We would have had them first.

☺☺☺

I am now 77 and really quite a frivolous old gal.
I'm keeping company with five famous gentlemen.

First, Will Power helps me out of bed in the morning,
but immediately I leave him to go see John.

Then Charlie Horse comes along and he takes a lot
of my time and attention.

When he leaves, Arthur Ritis shows up and stays the rest
of the day, but he doesn't like to stay in one place very long,
so he takes me from joint to joint.

After such a long hard day, you can see why I'm tired
and glad to go to bed with Ben Gay.

You can stay young indefinitely if you eat wisely, get plenty of sleep, work hard, have a positive mental outlook--and lie about your age.

☺☺☺

When I was younger, I could remember anything,
Whether it had happened or not!
-Mark Twain-

☺☺☺

We are only young once.
But we can be immature indefinitely.

☺☺☺

At twenty we don't care what the world thinks of us;
At thirty we worry about what it thinks of us;
At sixty we discover that it wasn't even thinking of us.

☺☺☺

For several decades Elder LeGrand Richards brought humor, enthusiasm and a great missionary spirit to stake and general conferences. Shortly before his death a stake president asked, "Brother Richards, how are you feeling?"

The great apostle said, "Well, President, I'll tell you. My body, the house I live in, is getting old and creaky," and then he added with all of his ninety-five years of youth testifying, "but the real LeGrand Richards is still on fire."

☺☺☺

In their advanced age, President McKay and his wife Emma occupied wheelchairs. One morning after a very inspirational meeting with some young people, the car came to take them to their home in Huntsville.

As the young people bade him a quiet, respectful good-bye, President McKay leaned over and patted Emma on the hand and said, "Come on, honey. I'll race you to the parking lot!

☺☺☺

You know you're growing old
When you go hunting to please your dog.

☺☺☺

Life is a terminal disease.

☺☺☺

Advice to executives over 50

Keep an open mind and a closed refrigerator!

Nothing is more depressing than to feel bad in the morning
Without having had any fun the night before.

☺☺☺

The Bishop went to visit an old-timer in the ward who hadn't been seen in church for many years. After a cordial conversation, the Bishop said. "You know Charlie, you're not getting any younger, don't you think it is time you started to think of the here-after?"

"Oh, I do," replied the elderly gentleman, "Why several times a day I go to the closet and say to myself, 'Now what is it I'm here after?'"

☺☺☺

The good thing about growing old is that you can
whistle while you brush your teeth.

-Grandpa Forsyth-

☺☺☺

A photographer was asked to take the picture of a gentleman on his ninety-eighth birthday. Seeing the elderly gentleman was in such good health, the photographer said, "You are certainly a young acting ninety-eight year old, perhaps I'll have the privilege of taking your photograph when you're one hundred."

"I don't know why not," said the elderly gent, "you look healthy enough too me."

☺☺☺

One of the hardest decisions in life
Is when to start middle age.

☺☺☺

If you would not be forgotten, as soon as your dead and rotten,
either write things worth reading, or do things worth the writing.

-Benjamin Franklin-

☺☺☺

Our priest quorum invited one of our great old high priests who could hardly hear and barely see to visit our class one Sunday. We found out that even with his handicap this old gentleman had not missed a priesthood meeting in twenty years.

One of the priests asked, "Why in the world do you go to priesthood every Sunday, when you can't read the blackboard nor even hear the teacher? What good could you possibly get out of it?"

The old man smiled and said, "Son, I think it is important to be there to show which side I'm on!"

A man who had just been told by his doctor that he only had six months to live, went to a psychic and asked. "What can I possibly do to live longer?"

After staring into a crystal ball and reading the stars, the psychic answered, "Go out and marry the ugliest and orneriest woman you can find." "How on earth would that help?" protested the man.

"Well," replied the psychic, "it may not help you live longer, but I'll guarantee it will seem like the longest six months of your life."

☺☺☺

The old-timer returned from his missionary reunion and reported to his friends as follows: "Include me out of these missionary reunions. I found my old companions had gotten so fat and bald they scarcely recognized me."

☺☺☺

The pursuit of happiness seems to be the chase of a lifetime.
Don't take life too seriously--
You will never get out of it alive!

☺☺☺

Grandfather taught that there are two ways to climb a mighty Oak Tree.
One: "You can do it limb by limb, starting from the ground up."
Or: "You can get an acorn and sit on it for twenty years."

☺☺☺

It's sad for a girl to reach the age
Where men consider her charmless,

But it's worse for a man to attain the age
Where the girls consider him harmless!

☺☺☺

You've reached middle age
When your wife tells you to pull in your stomach
--And you already have.

☺☺☺

To be 70 years YOUNG is often better than 40 years OLD!

☺☺☺

YOU'RE GROWING OLDER WHEN...

You read the obituary column to see if you're still alive!
The little old lady you help across the street is your wife!
You sincerely hope no one remembers your birthday!
You enjoy a dull evening!

Think young.
Aging is for wine.

☺☺☺

Doctor to a man in his fifties who had just had his annual physical exam

"There's no reason why you can't live a completely normal life as long as you don't try to enjoy it."

☺☺☺

Little girl: "Mama, what happens to old cars when they stop running?"
Mother: "Someone sells them to your father."

☺☺☺

THE GOOD OLD DAYS

Adam had his troubles no doubt, in days of yore;
But no one said, when he had told a yarn--
"I've heard that one before."

☺☺☺

Thomas Edison devoted ten years and all of his money to developing the nickel-alkaline storage battery at a time when he was almost penniless. Through that period of time, his record and film production was supporting the storage battery effort. Then one night the terrifying cry of fire echoed through the film plant. Spontaneous combustion had ignited some chemicals. Within moments all of the packing compounds, celluloids for records, film and other flammable goods had gone up with a whoosh. Fire companies from eight towns arrived, but the heat was so intense and the water pressure so low that the fire hoses had no effect.

Edison was 67 years old--no age to begin anew. His daughter was frantic, wondering if he were safe, if his spirits were broken, how he would handle a crisis such as this at his age. She saw him running toward her. He spoke first. He said, "Where's your mother? Go get her. Tell her to get her friends. They'll never see another fire like this as long as they live!"

At 5:30 the next morning, with the fire barely under control, he called his employees together and announced "We're rebuilding." One man was told to lease all the machine shops in the area, another to obtain a wrecking crane from the Erie Railroad Company. Then, almost as an after-thought he added, "Oh, by the way...anybody know where we can get some money?"

Virtually everything you now recognize as a Thomas Edison contribution to your life came AFTER that disaster.

☺☺☺

Never tell a young person that something cannot be done. God may have been waiting for centuries for somebody ignorant enough of the impossible to do that very thing.

" YES SIR, I AM A MORMON. HOW COULD YOU TELL, SIR?"

ATTITUDE

A man is like a postage stamp.
He often gets licked, stuck in a corner and pressed down.
He gets sent from post to post and handled roughly,
But he will generally get where he wants if he sticks on until the end.

☺☺☺

If you're not pulling your weight,
You're probably pushing your luck!

☺☺☺

We wouldn't worry what other people think about us
If we realized how little they do!

–George Bernard Shaw–

☺☺☺

There were two identical twins. They were so identical that even their mother couldn't tell them apart. They would do all kinds of things to try to tell the twins apart...buy different clothing, etc.

As the twins grew older it became obvious that there was one difference in them. One was an optimist and one was a pessimist. The difference was so great that the mother became very worried and put them in a special Education Psychology class for observation....to see if they could work with the twins and see what had happened.

After about one month, the doctor called the parents in and said "there is nothing I can do with these twins. To let you know how bad it is, let me show you something!" So he took the one child that was a pessimist and he filled the room totally full of toys and he put the pessimist child in there and the child looked at all those good, expensive toys and sat down in the middle of the floor and cried. The mother asked what was wrong and the child said, "With all these toys, no one will like me or want to play with me or be my friend!"

Next, they took the child that was an optimist and filled the same room full of horse manure. When they showed this to the optimistic child, he asked for a shovel and spent the next several hours throwing manure all over the place, laughing and having a great time. So they stopped him and asked him why he was so happy. "Well," he said, "with all this horse manure there's got to be a pony here somewhere!!!!"

☺☺☺

A man all wrapped up in himself makes a very small package.

It may be true that there are two sides to every question,
But it is also true that there are two sides to a sheet of flypaper,
And it makes a big difference to the fly which side he chooses.

☺☺☺

My neighbor has learned how to live with his handicap. He is blind, but his humor is unmatched. The other day while on an airplane flight, he sat on a Time magazine.

The stewardess, trying to be helpful, said: "Excuse me sir, are you reading that magazine." His response was classic. "No, Ma'am, most blind people read with their fingers."

☺☺☺

"Don't be so humble....You're not that great."
–Golda Meir–

☺☺☺

"These days," says the CPA Journal,
"You have to learn to take the bad with the worst."

☺☺☺

A young man went to apply for a job. "What's your name?" asked the manager. "Ford," was the reply. "What's your first name?" "Henry," said the boy. "Henry Ford," said the manager. "That's quite a popular name around here." "Yes, sir," the boy proudly replied. "I've delivered papers in this neighborhood for the past five years."

☺☺☺

There are only two things to worry about:
Either you are well or you are sick.
If you are well, there is nothing to worry about.
If you are sick, there are two things to worry about.
Either you will get well or you will die.
If you get well, there is nothing to worry about.
If you die, there are only two things to worry about.
Either you go to Heaven or to Hell.
If you go to Heaven, there is nothing to worry about.
But if you go to Hell you will be so darn busy shaking
hands with your friends you won't have time to worry.

☺☺☺

"You remember the story of the two buckets that went down in the well; as the one came up, it said, 'This is surely a cold and dreary world. No matter how many times I come up full, I always have to go down empty.' Then the other bucket laughed and said, 'With me it is different. No matter how many times I go down empty, I always come up full.'"

–LeGrand Richards–

15

When Irvin S. Cobb was 27 years old he went to New York. With a wife and a sick child to support, he started to pound the city's pavement, going from one newspaper office to another, looking for work. For two weeks he visited and revisited them, but the managers always sent word that no help was needed.

As a last attempt, Cobb sat down and wrote a letter to each of the editors, proving that he could write effectively and had confidence in himself. The letter ended as follows:

"This positively is your last chance. I have grown weary of studying the wallpaper design in your anteroom. A modest appreciation of my own worth forbids me doing business with your head office boy any longer. Unless you grab me right away, I will go elsewhere and leave your paper flat on its back right here in the middle of a hard summer, and your whole life hereafter will be one vast, surging regret. The line forms on the right; applications considered in the order they're received. Write, wire, or call at the above address."

The next day, Cobb was offered four jobs!

☺☺☺

It is an all too common failing to expect others to inconvenience themselves on our behalf and yet become quite upset when the shoe is on the other foot, as this little story shows:

A cold wind was howling and a chilling rain was beating down when the telephone rang in the home of a doctor. The caller said that his wife needed urgent medical attention. The doctor was understanding. "I'll be glad to come, but my car is being repaired," he said. "Could you come and get me?"

There was indignation at the other end of the phone. "What," an angry voice sputtered, "in weather like this?"

☺☺☺

A good Jewish Rabbi went to heaven where St. Peter, also a good Jew, showed his faithful friend the beautiful gold streets and wonderful gardens. As they walked down the street, they heard a band playing "Onward Christian Soldiers."

"What's that?" asked the Rabbi. "The Holy Rollers," said St. Peter. "They really enjoy it here."

Later, the Rabbi heard singing and shouting. "Who's that?" he asked. "Oh, that's the Baptists. They can really enjoy themselves."

Finally, in a secluded corner they came to a high wall. The Rabbi asked, "What is behind the wall?" St. Peter said, "Shhh, that's where the Mormons live. They think they're the only ones here!"

☺☺☺

When you've got a lemon... Make lemonade!

The Priest was walking down the street one day, when he saw a little boy sprinkling some new born puppies with water. "What are you doing, son," asked the Priest. "Baptizing my new puppies, father." "What kind of puppies are they?" asked the Priest. "Catholic puppies," stated the boy. Satisfied, the Priest walked on down the street.

Several days later, the Priest noticed the same boy dunking his puppies in an irrigation ditch. "What are you doing, son," the Priest asked. "Baptizing my Mormon puppies," said the lad. "But these are the same puppies you said were Catholic puppies last week." "I know," said the boy, "but now their eyes are open!"

☺☺☺

The secret of being miserable is to have enough free time
to discuss whether you are happy or not.

☺☺☺

"Speaking of getting off to a bad start, I think I hold the record. As I was watching the Rose Bowl game on television the other day, I had a flashback of something that happened to me many years ago on a high school football field, not too far from that Rose Bowl.

It was my first year of high school football. I'd been playing second string all through the practice games, and this was the first big league game. Six thousand cheering people were in the stands. As we were breaking after our halftime pep talk, the coach suddenly said, 'Simpson, you start the second half.'

The old adrenaline came rushing, and I went charging out onto the field. This was my chance! Just about that time the coach said, 'Oh, and by the way, I want you to kick off, Simpson.'

I determined right then and there that I was going to kick that ball farther than any football had ever been kicked in history. I really wanted to make a good showing on my first chance on the first string. Well, the referee waved his arm and blew his whistle. I could hear those six thousand people. I looked at the ball and came charging down the field. I felt everything tingling in my body--the excitement was so high!

Well, you have probably already guessed it, I missed the ball. Six thousand people went wild. But that isn't the half of it. This was back in the days when the quarterback held the ball with his finger. I broke the quarterback's finger.

Now, if you think that you're off to a bad start, I just want to set your mind at ease and let you know that it could be worse. I also want you to know that I had a coach that had confidence in me....because he left me in. I don't know why, but he did...and I played the rest of the game. If I weren't so modest, I might also tell you that I made all-league that year.

-Elder Robert L. Simpson-

"WANTA BORROW A JACK?"

"A fellow from the city was speeding down a country road late at night and BANG! goes a tire. He got out and looked, and drat it! --he had no jack. Then he said to himself, 'Well, I'll just walk to the nearest farmhouse and borrow a jack.' He saw a light in the distance and said, 'Well, I'm in luck--the farmer's up. I'll just knock on the door and say I'm in trouble, would you please lend me a jack? And he'll say, 'Why certainly, help yourself--but bring it back.'

"He walked a little farther and the light in the farmhouse went out, so he said to himself, 'Now the farmer's gone to bed and he'll be annoyed because I'm bothering him--so he'll probably want some money for his jack. And I'll say, 'All right, it isn't very neighborly of you, but I'll give you a dollar.' And he'll probably say, 'You city folk just don't understand; do you think you can get me out of bed in the middle of the night and then offer me only a $1.00? Give me $5.00 or go get yourself a jack somewhere else.'

"By this time, the fellow had worked himself up into a lather. As he turned into the farmer's gate he muttered, 'All right, $5.00, but not a penny more! A poor devil has an accident in the middle of the night and all he needs is a jack. You probably won't let me have one no matter what I give you. That's the kind of fellow you are.'

"This brought him to the farmer's door where he knocked--loudly, and angrily. The innocent farmer stuck his head out of the bedroom window above and yelled down, 'Who's there? What do you want?' The fellow stopped pounding on the door and yelled up: 'You and your darn jack! You know what you can do with it,' and stomped off angrily."

How true, this little story is; most of us go through life bumping into obstructions we could easily bypass, looking for a fight and lashing out in blind rage at dreamed-up wrongs and imaginary foes. We don't even realize what we are doing until someone startles us one day with a humorous, but kind statement that hits us like a bolt of lightening on a dark night.

Take for example the other night as I was driving home from work. I was late for dinner and I hadn't phoned my wife. As I crept along in a long line of cars I became more and more frustrated and angry. "I'll tell her," I thought to myself, "that I was caught in the heavy week-end traffic," and she'll say, "Why didn't you phone me before you left work?"

Then I'll say, "What difference does it make anyway--I'm here!" And she'll say, "Yes, and I'm here too, and I've been here all day waiting to hear from you!" And I'll say, "I suppose you think I haven't anything else to do but call you up every hour on the telephone and act like a love-bird!"

By this time I had turned into the driveway and I was pretty steamed up! As I jumped out and slammed the car door, my wife flung open the upstairs window. "All right!" I shouted up to her. "Say it!"

"I will," she replied softly...."Wanta borrow a jack?"

A well-adjusted man is one who can enjoy the scenery
Even with the kids in the back seat.

☺☺☺

Life is only 10 percent what you make it
And 90 percent how you take it.

☺☺☺

According to the theory of aerodynamics, as may be readily
demonstrated through wind tunnel experiments, the bumblebee
is unable to fly. This is because the size, weight and shape of
his body in relation to the total wing spread make flying
impossible.

The bumblebee, being ignorant of these scientific truths, goes
ahead and flies anyway---and makes a little honey every day.

☺☺☺

"Tell me what you laugh at,
And I'll tell you who you are."

☺☺☺

"What a man laughs at may well be the measure of his mind,"

☺☺☺

Some time ago I noticed a friend of mine was very skilled and very
able at murmuring. In fact, I think she was the most skilled murmurer
I have ever heard. She was a professional. When she murmured
everyone listened because it was always juicy and alarming.

So I challenged this friend of mine. I said, "How would you like to try
to go two weeks without murmuring or gossiping or backbiting or
finding fault?" She ducked her head a little bit and said, "Well, if you
want, I'll try it."

After the two weeks were over she looked me up and, in response to
my question, "Did you make it?" She said, "I did. It wasn't easy but I
did make it." She said, "And I want you to know it was the dullest two
weeks of my life!"

-Marvin J. Ashton-

☺☺☺

"True humor springs not more from the head than from the heart. It is
not contempt. Its essence is love. Its issue is not in laughter, but in
still smiles which lie far deeper."

-Thomas Carlisle-

Instructions for Sunday School Teachers

A little bit of humor
    Will always make 'em smile.
A little bit of courtesy
    Will bring 'em in for miles.
A little bit of friendliness
    Will tickle 'em 'tis plain--
A little bit of Love
    Will bring 'em back again.

☺☺☺

As you ramble on through your life, brother,
    Whatever be your goal --
Learn to keep your eye upon the donut,
    And not upon the hole!

☺☺☺

Two frogs fell into a deep bowl,
One was an optimistic soul,
But the other, he took the gloomy view.
"We shall drown," cried he without more adieu.
So with a last despairing cry,
He flung up his legs and said good-bye.

Quoth the other frog with a merry grin,
"I can't get out, but I won't give in;
I'll just swim around til my strength is spent,
Then will I die the more content."

Bravely he swam till it would seem
His struggles began to churn the cream.
On top of the butter at last he stopped,
And out of the bowl he gaily hopped.

What is the moral? 'Tis easily found;
If you can't hop out, keep swimming around.

☺☺☺

He that falls in love with himself
will have no rivals.
-Benjamin Franklin-

☺☺☺

"I feel like a guy who's spilled a glass of water on his lap.
No matter what he says, nobody is going to believe him."

☺☺☺

Some men remind us of concrete
Their minds are all mixed up and permanently set.

Life is like a ten-speed bike.
Most of us have gears we never use.

☺☺☺

Definition of an "Average Comfortable Person."

If a person is standing with one foot in a bucket of ice and another foot in a fire, you could say--at least statistically --that on the average the person is comfortable.

☺☺☺

There was a Dachshund once so long,
He hadn't any notion
How long it took to notify
His tail of his emotions.

And so it happened
While his eyes were
Filled with woe and sadness,
His little tail went wagging on
Because of previous gladness.

☺☺☺

If you feel good, why not notify your face?

☺☺☺

An old lighthouse keeper had been at his post continuously for twenty years. During that entire period he had been accustomed to a gun going off, every hour, day and night. This was the method used for warning ships.

One night something happened to the gun and it failed to go off. The old fellow had been asleep and when the gun failed to fire he reared up in bed. "What was that?" he cried in alarm.

☺☺☺

When I was learning how to hang glide, I saw a boy trying to fly while his instructor yelled up from the ground, "Watch out for the parked cars. Don't hit that green car! I said don't hit that green...!!!"

Guess where the guy went? Right into the green car. My instructor said, "Let that be a lesson to you. Never look at where you don't want to go."

☺☺☺

"Pins and people don't amount to much if they lose their heads."

☺☺☺

Worry is like an old fashion rocking chair --
It gives you something to do, but gets you nowhere!

THE PARABLE OF THE POPCORN
-Wm. James Mortimer-

Behold, at the time of harvest the ears of corn did bring forth kernels which were dried and prepared for the popper's hand.

And then it was that the popper did take the kernels, all of which appeared alike unto him, and did apply the oil and the heat. And it came to pass that when the heat was on, some did explode with promise and did magnify themselves an hundred fold, and some did burst forth with whiteness which did both gladden the eye and satisfy the taste of the popper. And likewise, some others did pop, but not too much.

But lo, there were some that did just lie there and even though the popper's heat was alike unto all, they did bask in the warmth of the oil and kept everything they had for themselves.

And so it came to pass that those which had given of themselves did bring joy and delight to many munchers, but those which kept of the warmth and did not burst forth were fit only to be cast out into the pail and were thought of with hardness and disgust.

And thus we see that in the beginning all appear alike, but when the heat is on, some come forth and give their all, while others fail to pop and become as chaff to be discarded and forgotten.

☺☺☺

"When I came into the Council of the Twelve, I was so humble because of the great office that I was to hold; such a big position with such a little man. I was humbled to the dust. I appraised all my efforts as being almost nil. I compared myself with President McKay, with Brother Widtsoe and Brother Bowen and Brother Lee.

I continually kept saying, "Brother Lee (we sit together always because we are next to each other in the circle), if I could just discuss matters like you do, if I could just preach like Brother Bowen! Finally Brother Lee said to me (when he kind of got tired of listening to me) Spencer, be yourself, for goodness sake, be yourself!

And so, that's what I say to you, Be yourself, and if you are not yourself, you're nobody. You are nobody if you are not yourself."

-Elder Spencer W. Kimball-
-Uruguay, 1964-

☺☺☺

"See everything, overlook a lot, correct a little."
-Pope John XXIII-

☺☺☺

LIFE CAN BE A SMORGASBORD OF EXPERIENCES
AND YET MANY WILL STARVE TO DEATH!

THE BEST WITH WHAT YOU HAVE

There once was an oyster, whose story I'll tell,
Who found that some sand had got under his shell.
Just one little grain, but it gave him pain,
For oysters have feelings for all they're so plain.

Now did he berate the workings of fate
Which had led him to such a deplorable state?
Did he curse the government or cry for an election?
And cry that the seas should have given protection?

No! He said to himself as he lay on the shelf,
"Since I cannot remove it, I'll try to improve it."
The years rolled around as years always do.
And he came to his ultimate destiny...Oyster Stew.

And the small grain of sand that bothered him so
Was a beautiful pearl, all richly aglow.
This tale has a moral, for isn't it grand,
What an Oyster can do with a morsel of sand?

What couldn't we do, if we'd only begin,
To work on the things that get under our skin!

We are all self-made,
But only the rich will admit it.

A wife said to her husband, "Dear, we must do something about Robby. The boy is really quite lazy. He persuades little Derek next door to do all his work while he plays."

"Lazy!" exclaimed the father. "That boy's got executive talent."

YOU WIN SOME!!
YOU LOSE SOME!!
AND SOME GET RAINED OUT!!

Theodore E. Steinway, President of Steinway Pianos, noted:
"In one of our concert grand pianos, 243 taut strings exert a pull of 40,000 pounds on an iron frame. It is proof that out of great tension may come great harmony."

Don't worry too much if your dreams don't come true;
Be grateful, neither do your nightmares.

MOTIVATION

The Bishop called in an overweight young man who had been home from his mission for several years and was still single. When the Bishop asked the young man how things were going, he replied,

"Terrible, Bishop, I'm overweight and none of the young women will even give me a chance. I really want to lose weight, but I can't get excited about exercise; and I want to get married, but the good looking girls don't show any interest."

To his surprise the Bishop simply said, "I can get you into shape and introduce you to some young ladies who are interested in matrimony, if you'll agree to follow a very simple plan. Tomorrow morning at 7:00 a.m. -- you be up and ready to exercise and I'll provide the incentive."

Excited about losing weight and also finding a beautiful young lady to marry, the young man agreed.

So, the next morning at 7:00 a.m. he was up, dressed in his sweat suit and ready for exercise. There was a knock on the front door and when he opened it he saw one of the most beautiful girls he had ever seen, dressed in a beautiful sweat suit. She said, "The Bishop told me to tell you that we should exercise together with the understanding that if you catch me, I'll marry you."

Hearing that, the young man literally jumped out the front door after her, but she was quick, and started running down the road in front of him. After about a half an hour the young man realized that he couldn't catch her the first morning, but she promised that next morning at 7:00 a.m. she would be back and he could try again.

Sure enough, next morning there she was, even more beautiful than the day before. Day after day this continued. Every morning at 7:00 a.m. his door bell would ring and there stood this beautiful, healthy young lady and the promise of marriage -- if he could only catch her. After several weeks the young man was losing weight and every morning he felt he was closer to catching the beautiful young lady.

Then, one day the Bishop called to see how things were going. "Great," replied the young man, "any day now I'm going to catch her." The Bishop looked the young man over. He observed that while things were improving, he still needed to lose more weight -- to be what one could consider ideal.

Next morning when the doorbell rang, the young man was eager to begin the chase. But to his surprise, instead of the beautiful young lady, on his front step stood a homely, overweight young lady who said, "The Bishop told me that you wanted to exercise in the morning and if I could catch you, you would marry me!"

Naturally, the incentive to run continued and the young man found he even ran faster than he had previously thought possible.

We learn lessons, but we remember activities.

" I KNOW THAT I'M NOT SUPPOSED TO FISH ON SUNDAY,
BUT I AM GIVING YOU TEN PERCENT. "

BUDGET, MONEY
and TITHING

Mamma's yearning capacity is ofttimes greater
than Papa's earning capacity!

☺☺☺

Our small congregation in Toronto used to meet in a nearly condemned old schoolhouse for Sunday meetings. The bishop one day was at the pulpit asking members to donate so that we could build a new chapel. One of the brethren who was better off than most, but rather tight with his money, rose to his feet and said, "I pledge five dollars."

Just at that instant, a large piece of plaster fell from the ceiling hitting him right on his head. Stunned, he mumbled, "I-I'll raise that to five-hundred dollars." To which the bishop silently lifted his hands toward heaven and said, "Hit him again, Lord, please hit him again."

☺☺☺

Budgets are orderly systems for living beyond your means.

☺☺☺

A budget is the most orderly way of going into debt.

☺☺☺

Wife to husband: "Of course I spend more than you make...
I have great confidence in you!"

☺☺☺

Many marriages are defeated in the marketplace,
When unscheduled purchases are made.
  –Spencer W. Kimball–

☺☺☺

Two ruffians held up an unexcitable middle-aged woman on a back road. Your money or your life," they shouted.

"Then take my life," the woman answered. "I'm saving my money for my old age."

☺☺☺

Husband to Wife: "No, we're not in debt!
We can still pay our VISA with our Mastercard."

A mother was extremely upset when her little boy swallowed a quarter. "Call the doctor," she screamed to her husband.

"No, I think we should call the bishop," the father said calmly.

"The bishop?" cried the mother, "You don't think he is going to die do you?"

"Oh, no," exclaimed her husband, "but you know our bishop. He can get money out of anybody!"

☺☺☺

A counselor, whose countenance was usually bright even after a late bishopric meeting, looked very tired one night. The bishop asked him what was wrong.

"My wife," he said, "has been buying things on the lay-awake-plan."

"You mean the lay-away-plan, don't you?" asked the Bishop.

"No, I mean what I said. She buys things we can't afford, then I lay awake nights wondering how we're going to pay for them."

☺☺☺

Sometimes we don't realize how critical an audience can be

Dad criticized the sermon. Mother thought the organist played off key. Sister didn't like the way the choir sang. But they all shut up when little Billy piped up and said "I think it was a darn good show for a dime."

☺☺☺

You may have heard about the circus strong man who took an orange in his two hands and squeezed it dry. The barker then offered $500 to anyone in the crowd who could wring one more drop out of the orange.

Several muscular bystanders gave it a try without success, and then a rather small, unassuming, un-athletic individual stepped up and announced he would like to have a go at it.

They laughed when he sat down to squeeze, but derision turned to cheers when he squeezed out--not only one--but two more drops! Amazed, but not amused, the barker handed the squeezer the $500 and offered him another $500 if he could wring out another drop.

The frail fellow squeezed, and he squeezed and he squeezed, and finally out came another drop. The whole management was on the scene by this time, everybody inquiring how he was able to develop such incredible strength in squeezing out those last drops.

"Oh, it's really nothing," he replied. "I just happen to be the chairman of our church building fund."

Two men went to church to pray. One was a big-time business tycoon, the other a humble school teacher. The prominent citizen stood, and with eyes turned upward said:

"O Lord, I thank thee that I am not like some people, even as this school teacher. I help pay this teacher's salary. It is my money that built most of this chapel. I pay my tithing and subscribe to the missionary fund. I support all drives for funds in this church. It is my money that advanceth thy cause."

The school teacher bowed himself in humility and said, "O God, be merciful unto me. I was that man's teacher!"

☺☺☺

I feel sorry for the people who go to church but don't contribute.
I think their plan is to get into heaven---but on a scholarship.

☺☺☺

The good old days were when it took
A week to spend a week's wages.

☺☺☺

"Honey, can I have that fur coat?" she asked.

"Our present economic status, which has resulted from previous ostentatious displays of extravagance, precludes the possibility of such an acquisition," the college professor answered his wife.

"I don't get it," was her reply. "That's right, honey," he said with a grin, "you don't!"

☺☺☺

Next to surviving an earthquake, nothing is quite so satisfying as getting a refund on your income tax.

☺☺☺

I have almost a Siamese twin relationship with my wife.
We're joined at the wallet.

☺☺☺

My new watch does everything.
It's a calculator;
It's a slide rule;

It gives stock market quotations and weather forecasts;
It even gives you a phone number you can call if you want
the time.

Most wives feel that if they are going to have to be involved in a crash landing, they should at least help file the flight plan.

☺☺☺

A couple went to a car dealer to look at the new compact economy cars. Upon being told the price by the salesman, the husband blurted out: "But that's as much as a big car costs!"

"Well," replied the salesman, "if you want economy, you must pay for it."

☺☺☺

The most common method of balancing the family budget
Is by cutting down payments to the savings account.

☺☺☺

The only way to balance our budget is the ad hoc approach.
If you want to add something, you have to hock something else.

☺☺☺

These are the days when most of us have never had it so good
Nor have had it taken away from us so quickly.

☺☺☺

A young lady told her mother that she was going to marry an eccentric old millionaire. "But," protested the mother, "everyone thinks he's cracked."

"He may be cracked," she replied, "but he certainly isn't broke."

☺☺☺

It's nice to have the highest living standard in the world.
Too bad we can't afford it.

☺☺☺

I won't say what kind of Christmas bonus we got this year,
But sometimes I get the feeling that the boss thinks generosity
...causes CANCER.

☺☺☺

We haven't had much success in the real estate market.
I think it's because we want to sell our house complete --
With the furniture and kids.

☺☺☺

The secret of financial success
Is to spend what you have left after saving.
Instead of saving what you have left after you spend.

It is not true that banks have no sense of humor.
After all, they were the ones who coined the phrase, "easy payments."

☺☺☺

A father sought to teach his young son a moral lesson. He gave the boy a quarter and a dollar for church. "Put whichever one you want in the collection plate and keep the other for yourself," he told the boy.

After the services were over, the father asked his son which amount he had given.

"Well," said the boy, "I was going to give the dollar, but just before the collection the preacher reminded everyone that the Lord loveth a cheerful giver. I knew I'd be a lot more cheerful if I gave the quarter, so I did."

☺☺☺

If you think nobody cares if you're alive,
Try missing a couple of car payments."

☺☺☺

Contrary to what you may have heard lately, most folks are still concerned with the higher things of life--prices for example.

☺☺☺

Sign on cash register operated by a checkout girl in a supermarket

JUST MARRIED;
COUNT YOUR CHANGE TWICE!

☺☺☺

If mankind profits from its mistakes,
We have one glorious future ahead of us!

☺☺☺

A research organization was hired to poll a small town to find out how families spent their money. One elderly lady told the young researcher that she spent 30 percent for shelter, 30 percent for clothing, 40 percent for food, and 20 percent for everything else.

"But that adds up to 120 percent," the young man protested. "I know," she replied. "And it seems to get worse every year."

☺☺☺

A luxury automatically becomes a necessity --
When you find you can charge it.

Columnist Earl Wilson once said there were three classes of people

The Haves,
The Have–Nots,
And the Have–Not–Paid–for What–They–Haves.

☺☺☺

In today's society of easy credit,
Most Americans are living within 30 days of disaster.

☺☺☺

A thief met Jack Benny on the streets of New York.
"Your life or your money," said the thief.
"Just a minute, I'll have to think that one over!" said Jack.

☺☺☺

Know what happens if you don't pay your exorcist?
You get repossessed.

☺☺☺

THE FLINCH TEST

An optometrist sent his son to one of the finest optometrist schools in the East. After the boy came home the father decided to test his ability, so he watched the boy perform an eye examination and listened to him talk to the patient about lenses and interesting things of the eye. The boy's knowledge was superb....just fantastic.

After the customer left the father examined the bill and said, "I see that fine school forgot to teach you the flinch test?"

"Flinch test?" "I've never heard of the flinch test," his son replied.

"Well," said the father, "if you want to be a good optometrist you have got to learn how to administer the flinch test. It is really quite simple. Just use the following steps: When you put a nice set of frames on the customer, you say in a nice confident voice, 'That will be twenty dollars.'

Then pause for a second; if the customer doesn't flinch, you say, 'For the frames.' Pause again, and if the person doesn't flinch, you say, 'The lens will be another $10.' and if there is still no flinch, you add, 'And the case will be another $5.'"

☺☺☺

I got a great buy on a used computer...
The salesman said it was formerly owned

By a little old lady in Pasadena
Who only programmed on Sundays.

To show you how prices have changed...I went to a movie last night where they charged three dollars for the large tub of popcorn.

Three dollars, mind you! When I was a kid, if you had three dollars to spend on corn...you could have bought Kansas!

☺☺☺

SIGN ON A PRESSMAN'S MACHINE

JESUS SAVES,
But I bet He couldn't save on my salary.

☺☺☺

Sending your kids to college is sort of a do-it-yourself recession.

☺☺☺

Wife modeling a new dress to her husband: "It really didn't cost anything. It was marked down from $50 to $25, so I bought it with the $25 I saved."

☺☺☺

The college Professor drove up to his high school reunion in his worn out second-hand car. At the same time, one of his former classmates drove up in a shiny new Cadillac. The professor, knowing that his former friend had never been especially bright, said: "John, life seems unfair. I went to a prestigious university, got my Ph.D., teach at the largest university in the state and yet I can't even afford a new car. Tell me, how do you do it?"

"Well," said the friend, "as you know I never did do well in school. In fact, never got my diploma. So, I went into the junk business. I don't know how it happens, but I buy things for $1 and sell them for $4, and that 3% interest just adds up!"

☺☺☺

I heard of the salesman who sold two milking machines to a man who only had one cow, and then took the cow as a down payment.

–Matthew Cowley–

☺☺☺

"What's the average tip for a haircut?" asked the traveling businessman. "Two dollars," said the barber without batting an eye.

The businessman gave him the two extra dollars and said, "You must make quite a lot of money from tips on this job."

"Not as much as you might think," said the barber, "You're the first average tipper I've had this month."

Two farmers bought a truckload of watermelon for $2.00 each. They drove to the city and sold them for $2.00 each. When they counted their monies, they found they had made nothing. One farmer said to the other, "See, I told you we should have bought a bigger truck."

☺☺☺

"Those who understand interest collect it.
Those who don't understand interest, pay it."

-Heber J. Grant-

☺☺☺

A fellow used to go out of town every night to drink beer. One day a friend said, "Why do you drive out of town every night to drink? Are you ashamed of what you do?" "No," he said, "beer is five cents less out here."

"Gee," said the friend, "that doesn't make sense. It's 25 miles out there and 25 miles back. Even if you figure that it only costs 15 cents a mile to get there, you don't save anything."

"Oh," said the man, "I just sit and drink until I show a profit!"

☺☺☺

A small businessman from the old country kept his accounts payable in a cigar box, his accounts receivable on a spindle and his cash in the cash register. "I don't see how you can run your business this way," said his son. "How do you know what your profits are?"

"Son," replied the businessman, "when I got off the boat I had only the pants I was wearing. Today your sister is an art teacher, your brother is a doctor and you are an accountant. I have a car, a home, and a good business. Everything is paid for. So you add it all up, subtract the pants, and there's your profit!"

☺☺☺

Definition of Economic Forecasting

That's the advice given to the unknowledgeable
By the unknowing about the unknowable.

☺☺☺

An economist is a person,
Who when you forget an important telephone number,
Can estimate you a new one.

☺☺☺

If at first you don't succeed,
You'll get a lot of advice.

Once when President Franklin D. Roosevelt was preparing a speech, he needed some economic statistics to back up a point he was trying to make. His advisers said it would take six months to get accurate figures. "In that case, I'll just use these rough estimates," FDR said, and he wrote down some numbers in his text.

"They're reasonable figures and they support my point." "Besides," he added as an afterthought, "it will keep my critics busy for at least six months just to prove me wrong."

☺☺☺

I asked our accountant how we were doing and he said, "I can give you the same odds the Lord gave to Noah.

You've got forty days and nights to keep from going under."

☺☺☺

The warranty on a new color TV set had no sooner run out than the TV started having trouble. The lady of the house called the company and they sent a man to fix it. When he found that the warranty had expired, he tried to talk her into signing a contract for repair insurance.

The woman was told that, if she signed it, there would be no charge for the present call. The lady, however, didn't want to commit herself yet. She hadn't studied the plan and it's cost closely enough. She said she wanted to think it over.

"Well, madam," said the repairman resignedly, "If you want free service, don't forget, you have to pay for it."

☺☺☺

The folly of human nature is neatly summed up by the case of the middle–aged school teacher who invested her life savings in a business enterprise which had been elaborately explained to her by a swindler.

When her investment disappeared and the wonderful dream was shattered, she went to the office of the Better Business Bureau.

"Why on earth," they asked, "didn't you come to us first? Didn't you know about the Better Business Bureau?"

"Oh, yes," said the lady sadly, "I've always known about you. But I didn't come because I was afraid you'd tell me not to do it."

☺☺☺

We have only two things to worry about

One is that things will never get back to normal.
The second is that they already have.

34

A member of our High Priest group is a mail man. One day he picked up an envelope addressed to "God" in care of "Heaven". Curious about what it might say, he opened the letter and found the following tale of misery:

"Dear God,
      I have been out of work for several months and I just can't seem to make ends meet. My family is young and we don't have enough to buy groceries. I visited the Parish Priest who said he couldn't help, but that I should ask you. Well, you know God, that I have never been one to bother you much in the past. But if you could spare $100, it would sure help."

The mail man was touched by the sincerity of the letter, so he brought it to church on Sunday and asked if we would be willing to help. The hat was passed around and $90 was collected, which we put in one of the church envelopes.

On Monday, our friend the mail man delivered the envelope personally to the man. At first a big grin came across his worried face. He counted the money, not once, but three times. Then he asked the mail man to wait a second and ran back into his house.

After a short time the man returned with another envelope addressed to "God" in care of "Heaven". As soon as he was out of sight of the house, the mail man opened the envelope and found the following letter.

"Dear God,
      Thanks very much for the $90; however, next time please send it through the Parish Priest, those darn Mormon's kept their ten percent."

☺☺☺

Last October, I invited a minister friend to the BYU -- University of Utah football game. The crowd was over 65,000 people. They began the game as usual with a prayer. After the prayer, I asked my friend if he would like to pray before such a large congregation.

"Not really," he said, "but I would sure like to pass the plate."

☺☺☺

Husband to close friend: "My wife lost her Visa and Mastercards
      about eight months ago."
Friend: "Did you report them stolen?"
Husband: "No, I consider it a blessing. Whoever found them has
      been spending far less than she did."

☺☺☺

Every time a family gets a little bit ahead --
It discovers something it hadn't previously needed.

☺☺☺

One way to stop all those traffic jams...
Is to allow on the streets only those automobiles that are paid for!
-Will Rogers-

35

Three clergymen, were discussing how to determine what percentage of the collection at the church was to be used for the Lord in charitable service, and what should be kept for salaries and daily expenses.

The first said, "It's simple. I just take all the collections in the plate, draw a circle on the floor, and throw the money in the air. I figure all that lands in the circle belongs to Lord and I can keep the rest."

The second said, "I do about the same except, I figure that all the money that lands in the circle belongs to me and all that lands outside belongs to the Lord."

The third said, "Well, in my opinion, you've both got it wrong. I throw the money in the air and assume that all that God wants he will keep and all that hits the floor belongs to me."

☺☺☺

"You'll be lucky if you pull through," said the doctor to his patient, "you're a pretty sick man."

"Please, doctor," begged the patient, "do everything you can for me. And if I get better, I'll donate $100,000 to your new hospital fund."

The patient survived. Many months later the doctor met his former patient on the street.

"How are you?" he asked.

"Thanks to you I'm feeling marvelous!" replied the man.

"I assume then," said the doctor, "that you intend on making good your promise to donate a large sum of money to the new hospital fund."

"What are you talking about?"

"You promised if you got well," the doctor reminded him, "that you would contribute $100,000 to the new hospital."

"I said that?" the former patient exclaimed. "Now you know how sick I was!"

☺☺☺

A famous philanthropist was once asked: "How are you able to give so much, and still have so much?"

"Well," replied the generous man, "as I shovel out, He shovels in; and the Lord has a bigger shovel than I have."

–Christian Science Monitor–

☺☺☺

Ron: A man with six children is more satisfied than a man with $6 million.
John: How can that be?
Ron: The man with $6 million wants more!

CAREERS
and
PROFESSIONS

Three men were arguing the merits of their respective professions, a doctor, an architect, and a politician. "Mine is the most venerable of professions," boasted the doctor. "It's obviously the oldest. Remember, in the Bible it says that Eve was created from the rib of Adam. Undoubtedly, the world began first with a surgical operation."

"Oh, that's nothing," retorted the architect. "Long before that, the book of Genesis, says that 'order was brought out of chaos.' An architectural feat, of course."

The politician merely smiled and inquired blandly, "But gentlemen, who do you think was responsible for the chaos?"

☺☺☺

The boss is someone who isn't afraid to confront a dirty job head on
--and order his secretary to do it.

☺☺☺

A law professor's advice to his students:
When you're fighting a case, if you have the facts on your side, hammer them into the jury; and if you have the law on your side, hammer it into the judge. But if you have neither the facts nor the law on your side, then hammer the table.

☺☺☺

I don't know about the others, but we got the mushroom treatment.
Right after the acquisition we were kept in the dark.
Then they covered us with manure.
Then they cultivated us.
After that they let us stew awhile.
And finally they canned us.
-Isadore Barmash-

☺☺☺

Definition of an Auditor: He's the guy who comes in after the war's over and kills all of the wounded.

☺☺☺

Good executives never put off until tomorrow
What they can get someone else to do today.

Consultant: Do you have any trouble making decisions?

Businessman: Well, yes and no.

☺☺☺

Comment from goalie of New York Rangers:

"How would you like to have the kind of job where every time you make a mistake a light goes on and 18,000 people know it immediately?"

☺☺☺

And the Lord said unto Noah: "Where is the ark which I have commanded thee to build?" And Noah said unto the Lord: "Verily I have had three carpenters off ill. The gopher-wood supplier hath let me down---yea, even though the gopher-wood hath been on order for nigh upon 12 months. What can I do, O Lord?" And God said unto Noah: "I want that ark finished after seven days and seven nights." And Noah said: "It will be so."

And it was not so. And the Lord said unto Noah: "What seemeth to be the trouble this time?" And Noah said unto the Lord: "Mine subcontractor hath gone bankrupt. The pitch which Thou commandest me to put on the outside and the inside of the ark hath not arrived. The plumbers have gone on strike. Shem, my son who helpeth me on the ark side of the business hath formed a pop group with his brothers, Ham and Japath. Lord, I am undone."

And the Lord grew angry and said: "And what about the animals, the male and female of every sort that I ordered to come unto thee to keep their seed alive upon the face of the earth?" And Noah said: "They have been delivered unto the wrong address, but should arrive on Friday." And the Lord said: "How about the unicorns, and the fowls of the air by seven?" And Noah wrung his hands and and wept, saying: "Lord, unicorns are a discontinued line; thou canst not get them for love nor money. And the fowls of the air are sold only in half-dozens. Lord, Lord, Thou knowest how it is."

And the Lord in his wisdom said: "Noah, my son, I know. Why else thinkest thou that I shall cause a flood to descend upon the earth?"

☺☺☺

An atheist is a person who has no invisible means of support.

☺☺☺

There are ways to pump someone up and make them go faster, longer and stronger. In sports it's called steroids. In our office, it's called fear.

☺☺☺

My doctor only gave me six months to live,
But when I didn't pay his bill....he gave me another six months.

After many years of service, the gardener of a wealthy family was dismissed for dishonesty. When the man asked the family for a letter of reference, the following letter was written:

To whom it may concern:

I hereby certify that the bearer of this note has been my gardener for many years, and during that time I can truthfully say that he has gotten more out of my garden than any man I have ever employed.

OFFICE HOURS:

-- We open most days about 9 or 10, occasionally as early as 7, but somedays as late as 12 or 1.

-- We close about 5:30 or 6, occasionally about 4 or 5, but sometimes as late as 11 or 12.

-- Somedays or afternoons, we aren't here at all, and lately I've been here just about all the time, except when I'm someplace else, but I should be here then, too!

The difference between a general practitioner and a specialist is that one treats what you have, the other thinks you have what he treats.

Most people wish to serve God --
But in an advisory capacity only.

A young man, tired of working for others, went into business for himself. Later a friend asked him how it was to be his own boss.

"I don't know," he replied. "The police won't let me park in front of my own place of business. Tax collectors tell me how to keep books. My banker tells me how much balance I must maintain. Freight agents tell me how to pack my goods. Customers tell me how my goods must be made. Federal, state, county and local agencies tell me how to keep records. The union tells me who I can work and how and when. On top of that, I just got married!"

I once asked a farmer if there was any real money in farming.
He said, "Does Cadillac make combines?"

Bosses are contagious. You catch <u>Heck</u> from them.

Garry Moore once devised an answer to take care of crank letters. "The enclosed letter," he would write, "arrived on my desk a few days ago.

I am sending it to you in the belief that, as a responsible citizen, you should know that some idiot is sending out letters over your signature."

☺☺☺

During World War I, Will Rogers had a suggestion for getting rid of the German submarines. "All we have to do," said Rogers, "is heat up the Atlantic Ocean to 212° Farenheit. Then the subs will have to surface and we can pick them off one by one.

Now somebody's going to want to know how to warm up the ocean. Well, I'm not going to worry about that. That is a matter of detail, and I'm a policymaker."

☺☺☺

The president of a highly-rated company was asked the secret of his success. "It's really very simple," he said. "I always apply the Rule of the 3 D's:

DO IT, DELEGATE IT OR DESTROY IT."

☺☺☺

A businessman at a party was bragging that he accomplished more than most men because he occasionally worked around the clock. "Take last Wednesday, for example," he said, "I worked all night to get out an important job."

His wife, who happened to overhear the remark, brought the man back to reality by adding, "Which probably explains why he stayed in bed all day Thursday and Friday."

☺☺☺

An authority is a person who can tell you more about something
than you really care to know.

☺☺☺

Three executives were sitting around trying to put a definition on the word "fame." One said: "Fame is being invited to the White House for a talk with the President."

The second executive said: "No, fame is being invited to the White House for the talk with the President--and when the Hot Line interrupts the conversation, he doesn't answer it."

The third executive said, "You're both wrong. Fame is being invited to the White House for a talk with the President and when the Hot Line rings, he answers it, listens a moment, and then says...'Here, it's for you.'"

As nearly everyone knows, an executive has practically nothing to do, except to decide what is to be done; to tell somebody to do it; to listen to reasons why it should not be done, why it should be done by someone else, or why it should be done in a different way; to follow up to see if the thing has been done; to discover that it has been done incorrectly; to point out how it should have been done; to conclude that as long as it has been done, it may as well be left where it is; to wonder if it is not time to get rid of a person who cannot do a thing right; to reflect that he probably has a wife and a large family, and that certainly any successor would be just as bad, and maybe worse; to consider how much simpler and better the thing would have been done if one had done it oneself in the first place; to reflect sadly that one could have done it in twenty minutes, and as things turned out, one has to spend two days to find out why it has taken three weeks for someone else to do it wrong.

-Attributed to John L. McCaffrey-
CEO of International Harvester

☺☺☺

The famous painter, Picasso, wanted a special piece of furniture made for a large room. He went to a cabinetmaker, and to make his wishes clear, sketched on a piece of scrap paper exactly what he wanted. When he finished, he asked what the price would be. "No charge," said the craftsman, "just sign the sketch."

☺☺☺

An architect is said to be a man who knows a very little about a great deal and keeps knowing less and less about more and more until he knows practically nothing about everything, whereas on the other hand, an engineer is a man who knows a great deal about very little and who goes-along knowing more and more about less and less until finally he knows practically everything about nothing. A contractor starts out knowing practically everything about everything, but ends up by knowing nothing about anything, due to his association with architects and engineers!

☺☺☺

An executive was complaining about his job. "My mistake," he told a friend glumly, "was buying stock in the company. Now I worry about the lousy work I'm turning out."

☺☺☺

Our competition offers the St. Francis of Assisi Guarantee

If their product fails to perform as advertised, this guarantee asks the good Lord to grant you the wisdom to accept that which you cannot change.

☺☺☺

A typical thirty year career goes like this:

You start off by being the youngest person on the staff---
And you wind up by working for the youngest person on the staff.

A businessman's success had gone to his head. His constant bragging was beginning to grate on his wife's nerves. After one such session, during which the husband had compared himself favorably with everyone from J. Paul Getty to John D. Rockefeller, he turned to her and asked, "Do you know how many really outstanding business leaders there are in the world today?"

"No," replied the wife quietly, "but I know there is one less than you think."

Once there was a man who made millions and millions of dollars by perpetrating fraud. He would steal money from every little old lady and everyone else he could steal from. There were three people who helped him in this business: His accountant, who helped him with his taxes, his lawyer, who helped him stay out of jail, and his minister, who accepted his weekly confession and forgave him of his sins.

The man became very ill and on his death bed he called his three friends together and said "The whole world knows you can't take it with you when you die....but I'm going to prove them all wrong. I am going to give each of you $50,000 and when you file past my coffin, just stick it in the frame so that when I get on the other side I'll have $150,000 to start me off right." So, the minister, the lawyer and the accountant each took the money and promised they would do as he had asked.

The man passed away. Several weeks later the minister got feeling a little guilty because he hadn't put all the money in the coffin, so he called the other two together and confessed that he hadn't put the full $50,000 in the coffin, but had put in $25,000 in $100 bills and had kept $25,000 for the poor.

The lawyer was moved by the minister's honesty and admitted that he, too, hadn't put in the full $50,000. He had put in $10,000, given $15,000 to the Cancer Society and had bought himself a $25,000 boat.

At this point the accountant became totally "unglued." He said "I can't believe such dishonesty! You promised him on his death bed that you would each put $50,000 in his coffin. How could you cheat him like that?! I hope he comes back to haunt you! I want you to know that I wrote him a check for the entire $50,000!!"

One night a private saw another soldier passing and called out, "Hey buddy, give me a light!" The other soldier stopped and held out a lighted match. Raising his eyes to speak his thanks for the favor, the first soldier saw the star of a Brigadier General and at once apologized.

"I beg your pardon, sir. I didn't mean any disrespect. I didn't notice you were a General." That's all right," replied the General, "but you should thank God I wasn't a Second Lieutenant."

Freedom is doing what you like.
Happiness is liking what you do!

"SALESMANSHIP BEGINS WHEN THE CUSTOMER SAYS -- NO!"

☺☺☺

An Airline executive, tired of constant problems with people, longed for perfect employees. His hopes seemed fulfilled when the company engineers suggested that they were now smart enough to replace people with automatic planes. They explained that computers would replace pilots and even stewardesses. The executive was delighted. At last, he thought, no more emotional difficulties, no more people problems.

A demonstration flight was quickly arranged for the Board of Directors. Everything went perfectly; the plane took off, reached cruising altitude, and leveled off. A very pleasant voice announced they could loosen their seat belts and relax. They were all smiles.

Just as they were congratulating the executive, a voice came over the speaker system: "This is your computer pilot speaking. Welcome to the completely automated airplane. Cocktails will now be served. Merely press the button at your seat and they will arrive automatically." The president pushed the button and sure enough just like the voice said, he had his favorite cocktail made just the way he liked it best. Then the voice added, "During cocktails, may I suggest that you sit back and enjoy the flight. I am in complete control of the aircraft. Nothing can go wrong...Nothing can go wrong...Nothing can go wrong..."

☺☺☺

An expert is -- A DRIP UNDER PRESSURE!

☺☺☺

When Robert Kennedy was Attorney General he was reported to greet new young lawyers entering the department with the following message: "This may appear to be a large organization, but when you do something well, I will hear about it and it will go on your record. I want you to recall that I was recently a lowly worker in the Justice Department myself, but that I now serve as Attorney General of the United States of America, due to perseverance, long hours, hard work, and the fact that my brother became President of the United States....not necessarily in that order."

☺☺☺

Employee to boss: "For twenty years I've been doing three people's work for one paycheck. It's time you gave me a raise."

Boss to employee: "Sorry, I can't give you a raise, but if you tell me who the other two people are, I'll fire them."

☺☺☺

Crime is everywhere. I went into surgery last month--
And some guy in a mask pulled a knife on me.

John Eisenhower was an aid on his father's staff during World War II. On one occasion the general gave him a message to deliver to a colonel in the front lines.

The young lieutenant found the colonel and told him, "My dad says to watch your right flank." "Really?" said the puzzled officer. "And what does your mommy say?"

☺☺☺

When I was a youngster working in a pharmacy, I remember an old fellow who came in one day and asked if he could use the telephone. Because I knew him I told him, "Sure, go right ahead Charlie." To my surprise, Charlie put a hanky over the mouthpiece of the telephone and said to the person on the other end "I'm calling to see if that job you advertized is still open." (and he described the job).

Evidently the man on the other end said, "No, it's not open." Charlie said, "I'm a very capable worker. Is the man doing a good job?" "Yes he is," said the voice on the other end. Charlie asked "Are you sure there isn't someone that could do a better job?" The man assured him that there was not. Charlie said, "Then, if you're sure you don't have an opening, I'll have to look somewhere else."

I asked Charlie what on earth he was doing! He had a good job why on earth did he want to change? He said, "No, I don't want a different job. I was just calling my place of business to check on how I was doing."

☺☺☺

The good news is when you're finally assigned your own parking place.
The bad news is when it's at the employment center.

☺☺☺

An old-fashioned, autocratic boss reprimanded the secretary who attempted to improve the grammar in a letter he'd dictated. "But I thought...," she offered. "We're not paying you to think," the manager roared. "Write what I tell you."
Her next letter for his signature went as follows:
Today's date.
To John--Hey, George, how in the devil does John spell his last name? S-m-y-t-h-e?
John Smythe.
Look his address up.
Dear John:
I am writing to give you the final estimate on the piping for the project.
Harry---how much was the Smythe estimate? 3 thou? OK, we'll make it 3200 for the idiot way he spells his name.
We have enjoyed the chance to work with you on this project.
Then blah, blah, blah, you know the typical garbage.
Close it and
Sign it.

An EXPERT is any person with an ordinary knowledge of a subject who carries an attache case and is more than 50 miles from home.

☺☺☺

DEVELOPMENT CYCLE FOR NEW PRODUCTS:

First: An American firm announces an invention.
Second: The Russians claim they made the same discovery 20 years ago.
Third: The Japanese start exporting it.

☺☺☺

The story is told of a judge who explained to a case-hardened criminal: "Because of the gravity of this case, I am going to give you three lawyers."

"Never mind the three lawyers," replied the experienced defendant, "Just get me one good witness."

☺☺☺

SIX PHASES OF A PROJECT:

I   ENTHUSIASM
II DISILLUSIONMENT
III PANIC
IV SEARCH FOR THE GUILTY
V   PUNISHMENT OF THE INNOCENT
VI PRAISE AND HONORS FOR THE NONPARTICIPANTS

☺☺☺

Two balloonists became lost in the fog. They started to descend, hoping they wouldn't hit something in their effort to get their bearings. As they neared the ground they spied a man standing in a field. "Where are we?" one of the balloonists called. "Up in the air in a balloon," came the reply.

"Obviously he is a lawyer," one of the balloonists said to the other. "His answer is entirely accurate and totally worthless."

☺☺☺

The businessman walked into the Internal Revenue Office, sat down and smiled at everyone. After a short time a guard approached him and asked, "What can we do for you?"

"Oh, nothing at all," replied the businessman. "I just wanted to meet the people I'm working for."

☺☺☺

PRINCIPLES OF MANAGEMENT:

Rule 1: The Boss is always right.
Rule 2: If the Boss is wrong, go back to Rule 1

OPTIONS: A GAME TWO CAN PLAY

A farmer shopped around for a new car and became thoroughly disgusted with the pricing system. Every item he wanted was listed as optional equipment and cost extra. But eventually he made his purchase and paid the bill.

A few days later, the dealer who sold him the car arrived at the farm to buy a cow for his small country place. The farmer sized up the situation and quickly scribbled the following itemized bill:

Basic Cow	$200
Two-tone exterior	45
Extra stomach	75
Production storage compartment	60
Dispensing device (4 spigots $10 each)	40
Genuine cowhide upholstery	125
Automatic fly swatter	35
Dual horns	15
Total (exclusive of tax & delivery)	$595

An employee of a major corporation grew so nervous and insecure in his job that he consulted a psychiatrist. "Doc," the fellow moaned, "I'm miserable. I'm not a worker; I can't run a machine. I'm not a salesman; I can't sell. I'm not a creative man; I can't create new products. If it comes right down to it, I can't really do anything. What should I do?"

"Why don't you quit?"
"Doc, I can't do that. I'm the boss!"

A dentist called a repairman to fix his leaky faucet. After doing only fifteen minutes work, the repairman asked for $40.

The dentist was so surprised he almost dropped his dentures and said, "Man, you're expensive. I don't even charge that much for oral surgery."

Uncompromising, the repairman simply replied, "I know. I didn't charge that much when I was a dentist either."

Dr. Harold C. Urey, Nobel prize winner in Chemistry, was walking along a sidewalk one day when he ran into another professor. They chatted for a few minutes then, as they parted, Dr. Urey asked the other:

"John, which way was I going when I met you?"
"That way," said the other, pointing the direction.
"Oh, good, that means I've already had my lunch," muttered the professor as he walked away.

A young insurance salesman walked into a factory and asked to see the sales manager. When the manager finally greeted him in his office, the man nervously said, "You don't want to buy any life insurance, do you?"

"No," curtly replied the sales manager.
"I didn't think you would," said the young man as he got up and headed for the door.

"Wait a minute!" said the sales manager. "Come back here."
"Yes, sir," said the young man, obviously nervous and frightened.

"You are without a doubt the worst salesman I've ever seen."
The young man looked down...."Yeah, I know...."

"Man, you've got to have enthusiasm when you sell--you have to be positive, not negative. You have to believe in yourself. Now, look, I'm a busy man, but I'll show you how." And for the next thirty minutes the salesman gave the young man all the benefits of his experience and wisdom.

"I don't know how to thank you," said the young man.
"That's all right, son," said the sales manager. "Now, because you're obviously new at this, I'll buy a small policy from you."

The young man quickly dug out a policy. The sales manager signed it, then said, "Remember, don't go in cold, not knowing what you're going to say. Work out a planned and organized sales pitch." The young salesman smiled. "Oh, I have. What you've just seen is my organized approach to sales managers."

Bosses are large people
Who frequently declare
That other secretaries
Always sit straight in their chair.

Other secretaries are polite
According to my boss
They're never curt, they're never sharp
And they're surely never cross.

Other secretaries, my boss says
Do the things they're told to do
They always know what's expected of them
The way I'm supposed to do.

I'm so sorry for my boss,
Just as sorry as can be
He knows so many lovely secretaries
And gets stuck with one like me.

Many a live wire, would be a dead one,
If he didn't have the right connections!

A widow went to a spiritualist to see if she could contact her deceased husband. The spiritualist went into a trance and soon a voice was heard: "Mary," it said, "are you there?"

The woman was overjoyed. "Elwood--is it really you? Are you all right?" "I'm fine, I'm fine." "Is it nice there, dear?"

"Beautiful. Absolutely beautiful. Blue sky, pure air, green grass. And the cows, Mary. You've never seen such beautiful cows!" "Elwood---cows in heaven?" "Who's talking about heaven? I'm a bull in Texas!"

☺☺☺

Now there's a new group called The First Church of the Trial Balance. It was started by accountants who believe that God created heaven and earth and all the living creatures upon it in six days--and would have gone further only He was over budget.

☺☺☺

When Joe Wilson finished college and joined his father in a small family-owned business, Mr. Wilson was overjoyed. "It will be good to have some aggressive young management around the place," he said.

"Your first duty as my new partner is to replace that sign out front with one of those father-and-son signs--you know the kind."

"Yes, I know just what we need," Joe said. Later he invited his father out to inspect the new sign. Mr. Wilson was speechless for a moment...then he said, "Now that's what I call real aggressive young management."

The sign read: Joe C. Wilson & Father.

☺☺☺

Hell is the responsibility --
Without the authority to do it

☺☺☺

A direct-mail ad for Alka-Seltzer Plus Cold Medicine carried a photo of and testimonial from one Harold "Butch" Brooks, a truck driver, who was quoted as saying:

"When I'm out on the road, bad weather, bad cold, my load's still gotta go...so I rely on Alka-Seltzer Plus."

The same ad carried a warning in fine print at the bottom: "Product may cause drowsiness -- use with caution if operating heavy machinery or driving a vehicle." Kind of makes you hope Butch's load is going somewhere else.

☺☺☺

Minds are very much like parachutes --
They don't function unless their open!

A fellow got a job at the highway department to paint the yellow line down the middle of the road. The first two days everything went great, but after three days the guy seemed to be tired and so the foreman called him in to complain:

"The first day you did great, you were able to paint that yellow line for three miles. The second day was pretty good, you painted the line for two miles. But today you have only painted one mile of line, so I guess I'm going to have to fire you!"

As he left the office, the guy looked back with a tear in his eye and said: "It's not my fault. Each day I got farther away from the paint bucket."

☺☺☺

"Then said the king to the servants, Bind him hand and foot, and take him away, and cast him into outer darkness; there shall be weeping and gnashing of teeth." (See Matt. 22:2-13)

I used to be a little puzzled about that last part, but now I think I know why we have so many Latter-day Saint dentists.

-Paul H. Dunn-

☺☺☺

Accounting is an exact science.
They do exactly what they want too.

☺☺☺

So much of what we call management consists
in making it difficult for people to work.

☺☺☺

Motto of the Year:

Watch your desk, watch your phone:
The job you lose may be your own!

☺☺☺

A business executive trying to impress a wealthy client who was in his office, pushed the intercom button and barked at his secretary:

"Miss Jones, get my broker on the line!"
"Yes Sir, Stock or Pawn?"

☺☺☺

"Is that sign in the window that says, 'We Aim To Please', yours?" asked the irritated customer.
"Yes," replied the manager, "that's our motto."
"Well," said the customer, "may I suggest that your employees need a little time off for target practice."

"YES, BUT I BELIEVE YOU TO BE THE PARENT AS FAR AS YOU ARE TRANSLATED CORRECTLY."

CHILDREN
and
FAMILIES

"Where did I come from Mommy?" asked our six year old.

Thinking this was a good moment to explain the facts of life, my wife gave her a thirty minute discourse on the birds and the bees, and everything else that seemed to be important for a six year old to know.

After she finished, she asked, "Now Sweetheart, do you understand where you came from?"

"I--I--I guess," replied our six year old. "I just wondered, because Jenny said she came from Texas."

Of dubious authenticity is the story about John D. Rockefeller, Sr., registering at the Willard Hotel in Washington D.C. and asking for the cheapest room without bath.

The hotel clerk was dumbfounded. "But, Mr. Rockefeller," he protested, "whenever your son stops here he always occupies the finest suite we have!"

"My son has a rich father," replied Mr. Rockefeller sternly. "I am not so fortunate."

Jack's mother ran into the bedroom when she heard him screaming as if he were being attacked by a monster. There she found Jack with his head pulled back and his two-year-old sister, pulling his hair with both hands and a big smile on her face.

She gently released the little girl's grip and said comfortingly to Jack, "There, there, she didn't mean it. She's still too young to know that it hurts to pull hair."

She was barely out the bedroom when Jack's little sister began to scream. Rushing back into the room, she said, "What happened?"

"She knows now," Jack explained.

Dandelions are the children's flower.
It is the only one they can pick without being yelled at.

Three year-old: I can put the bread in the toaster, but I can't flush it.

☺☺☺

More children are punished for mimicking their parents
Than for disobedience.

☺☺☺

A first grader had an explanation for the fire at his school.

"I knew it was going to happen," he told his parents, "because we've
been practicing for it all year."

☺☺☺

What should not be heard by little ears,
Should not be said by big mouths!

☺☺☺

A priest was walking along a residential street lined with fine old Victorian
homes. It was a bitter cold day, the sky overcast, the wide spacious lawns
covered with snow. Suddenly he spotted a small boy on the front porch of one
house. The doorbell was one of those old-fashioned manual types set high in
the door. The boy was too short to ring it, but was trying his hardest to
jump-up and reach it. Every now and then the boy would stop and warm his
hands by breathing on them.

"The poor little devil will never get in," thought the priest, so he altered his
direction, and walked up to the boy on the porch.

As he patted the boy protectively on the shoulder, he rang the bell vigorously
with his other hand. "And now what do you say, my little man?" the priest
asked as he smiled down at the boy.

"Mr.," said the boy breathlessly, "now, we both better run like crazy!"

☺☺☺

Machines are becoming more human all the time.
Now they have a TV set that lies on the floor and watches the kids.

☺☺☺

A mother with her young boy, ready for bed, interrupted a family gathering in
the living room. "Excuse me for a minute, I'm going up with Tommy to say his
prayers. Anybody want anything?"

☺☺☺

Protective is when you pin a kid's mittens to his coat.
Over-protective is when you pin them to
his bathing suit.

Danny was asked to draw a picture in Primary. He drew a line dividing the page in half and stopped to think. The teacher asked:

"Danny, what are you going to draw today?"

"A picture of Heaven and Hell," he explained.

"That's a tough picture to draw," the teacher replied, "I don't think anyone knows for sure what heaven and hell look like!"

Undisturbed by the teacher's apparent lack of faith, Danny responded confidently, "They will when I'm finished!"

My brother-in-law became one of the first male teachers in our primary. After a few weeks one of the mothers asked her son how he liked the new teacher.

"I don't know, Mom," he said. "She keeps sending her husband."

Grandpa was sitting in his big easy chair reading the paper, when his grandson came running in and asked: "Grandpa, why are lions so mean?"

Grandpa, half asleep and without looking up from his newspaper, responded: "I don't know."

A little later the grandson came running in again and asked, "Grandpa, why are giraffes so tall?" Grandpa, with no emotion and without looking up replied, "I don't know."

A third time the boy came running in very excited and asked: "Grandpa, grandpa, why are elephants so big?" Grandpa, again without looking up responded, "I don't know."

Finally, the boy asked, "Grandpa, am I bothering you?" Grandpa finally looked up and said, "Oh heaven sakes, No! You won't learn anything if you don't ask questions."

A little boy and his mother stopped in front of an abstract painting in a gallery exhibition.
"What is that?" asked the boy.

"It's supposed to be a child and his dog," she replied.
"Well," demanded the boy. "Why isn't it?"

Children have license to do what their Parents do...
And expand upon it.

Danny: "Who scribbled in this Book of Mormon?"
Lori: "Daddy."

Danny: "Why would Daddy scribble in the Book of Mormon?"
Lori: "He always scribbles out the parts he doesn't like!"

☺☺☺

Don't tell me that kids aren't influenced by television. I asked my son where he would like to spend his next vacation and he said, "FANTASY ISLAND."

I asked him how would we get there, and he said, "THE LOVE BOAT."

So, I asked him how we could pay for it and he said, "FATHER KNOWS BEST."

☺☺☺

When I was younger one of my greatest desires was to grow. You see, I was small. My brothers were all bigger than me, and oh, how I wanted to grow.

One of my friends, who I considered older and wiser said, "If you really want to grow, you have to put oil all over your body. It cuts down on the friction and then you can grow."

Well, I tried it for a week, but it didn't work. So I asked my wise friend what had happened? He said, "Explain to me what you did?"

So I told him how I had spread oil all over me from head to foot, faithfully for a whole week. "What kind of oil did you use?" he asked.

"Crisco," I told him. "Oh, no wonder nothing happened," he responded wisely, "Crisco is shortening."

☺☺☺

Children have finally grown up --
When they start asking questions that have answers.

☺☺☺

Little Danny, sitting upon his grandfather's knee asked, "Grandpa, were you on Noah's ark?"

"No," laughed his Grandfather.

"Then why didn't you drown?" he asked.

☺☺☺

People who tell you to not let little things bother you.
Have never tried sleeping in a room with a mosquito.

No matter what the critics say,
It's hard to believe that a television program
Which keeps four children quiet for an hour
Can be all bad!

Two rough and tough little boys (about age 8) kept running up and down the hall of the church, disrupting class, etc. The Primary President had told them to go into their class and be quiet several times. Finally, the bishop took the two by the arm and marched them down the hall to his office.

One little boy whispered to his friend..."I'll go in and talk to him first. If what we have done is really bad, I'll jump-up and run out of his office. When you see me coming, you run too, then we can meet behind the church and talk it over. If it's not too serious, I'll smile and wink at you when I come out, then you'll know it's okay."

So the bishop took the first boy into his office and asked, "Why do you act the way you do?" "I don't know," was the answer. "Why do you make so much noise in the church?" "I don't know," again was the reply.

"Do you know where your Heavenly Father is?" asked the bishop. Startled the little boy said, "No!"

"Come on," the bishop questioned, "Surely, you know where Heavenly Father is?" Again the little ruffian promised the bishop, "No, honest, I don't know!"

The bishop, wanting to teach a lesson added, "You know it is embarrassing to your teachers and your mom and dad when you act like this. Are you sure you don't know where your Heavenly Father is?"

At this the boy jumped up and ran out of the office, grabbing his little friend as he left. They didn't stop running until they were safely hidden in some tall grass behind the church. "What happened?" asked the friend.

"Jimmy," said the lad, "this is serious. Heavenly Father is missing and they think we did it."

The loaded station wagon pulled into the only remaining campsite. Four youngsters leaped from the vehicle and began feverishly unloading gear and setting up a tent. The boys then rushed off to gather firewood, while the girls and their mother set up the camp stove and cooking utensils.

A nearby camper marveled to the youngsters' father: "That, sir, is some display of teamwork."

"I have a system," the father replied. "No one goes to the bathroom until the camp is set up."

Banks have a new checking account for children.
It's a combination checkbook–coloring book.

To induce the children to write,
The checks are made of wallpaper!

☺☺☺

On Stake Conference Sunday, a member of the Stake Presidency was asked to go in and give a short talk to the children in Primary.

Addressing a rather large group of young children, he asked if there was anyone who could tell him something about the Apostle Peter. A little girl raised her hand and waved it excitedly.

Encouraged to see someone so enthusiastic, he said, "Come up here, sweetheart. I'm glad to see that your mother and father have taught you lessons from the Bible. Now, would you please tell all the other boys and girls what you know about the Apostle Peter?"

The little girl stepped up to the microphone and began, "Peter, Peter, Pumpkin eater, had a wife and couldn't keep her. So he put her..."

☺☺☺

President Eisenhower's mother was a deeply religious woman, but she was anything but fatalistic. When Ike was a boy she would say to him:

"The Lord deals the cards,
But the way you play them -- that's up to you."

☺☺☺

To say you're sorry does a funny thing.
It warms the heart and cools the sting.

☺☺☺

For Family Home Evening, the family decided to look through some old family photo albums. When they came to a handsome young man with a mustache, the teenage daughter asked: "Who's that?"

"Why, that's your father," said the mother proudly.

"Yeah?" said the daughter skeptically. "Then who's that baldheaded man that lives with us?"

☺☺☺

The good news is when your son and daughter-in-law
present you with a grandchild.

The bad news is when it's for the entire summer.

In Primary our son Jeff once drew a picture of the family of Jesus. When the teacher asked him who the fourth person in the picture was, his response was a classic:

"This one is Jesus, here is Mary, and this is Joseph; the other one is the baby-sitter for when Mary and Joseph want to go out."

☺☺☺

A Primary teacher teaching about the promised land asked, "Jason, what do you think a land flowing with milk and honey would look like?"

Jason's response: "Sticky!"

☺☺☺

"I'm afraid I'll never see you in heaven, Tommy," the Primary teacher said to her most mischievous child.

"Why," questioned Tommy, "What have you been doing wrong?"

☺☺☺

Greg arrived home with both eyes black. "Have you been fighting again?" asked his mother. "Didn't I tell you when you lose your temper to count to one hundred before you do anything!"

"Yes," replied Greg, "but Mark's mother only told him to count to fifty."

☺☺☺

"What did you learn in Primary today," asked the 9 year old's mother.

"Oh, we learned how Moses led the Israeli amphibious battalion into the Red Sea against a much larger Egyptian Army and by superior military strategy completely destroyed the Pharoah's Air Force, Navy, and Marines in one afternoon."

"Are you sure that's what the teacher said."

"Well, not exactly mom, but you would never believe it the way the teacher told it."

☺☺☺

If you don't want your children to hear what you are saying...
Pretend you are talking to them.

☺☺☺

They get along like brothers --
Cain and Abel!

"Greg, What's new at your house."
"Who knows; they spell everything!"

Primary Teacher: "Johnny, what's that a picture of?"
Johnny: "That's a cow eating grass."

Primary Teacher: "Where's the grass?"
Johnny: "The cow's eaten it!"

Primary Teacher: "Where's the cow?"
Johnny: "You don't suppose the cow would be dumb enough to stay around after she's eaten all the grass do you?"

Trying to get acquainted with a new teary-eyed nursery student, the Primary teacher began to ask her some questions about her grandparents. "Where is you grandfather, dear?"

"He's in heaven," came the shy reply. "And your grandmother? Is she still on earth?" "No," the child responded, "She's in Utah."

On Halloween, we placed a phonograph near the front porch to greet the trick-or-treaters with the sounds of frightened cats, howling wolves and eerie organ music.

During the evening we opened the door to three youngsters dressed as monsters -- a very small child, flanked by two slightly older ones.

Pointing to the little child in the middle, one of the older children shyly asked, "Would you mind turning off your record player? It's scaring Dracula."

Nathan was an only child who wanted badly to have a brother to play with. So in his prayers he always asked for a little brother. After many months with nothing happening, Nathan finally gave up. Soon after that, his mother became pregnant, and eventually went to the hospital where she had twin boys.

"My heavens!" Nathan exclaimed when he heard the news. "It's a good thing I stopped praying when I did."

There are too many kids in the tub.
There are too many elbows to scrub.
I just washed a behind,
That I'm sure wasn't mine!
There are too many kids in this tub!
-Shel Silverstein-

Yesterday should be regarded as experience, Tommorrow as hope!
Today is simply the art of getting from one to the other as best we can!

☺☺☺

One evening, during a violent thunderstorm, my wife was tucking our frightened young son into bed.

As she turned the light off, he asked with a quiver of fear in his voice, "Please mommy, won't you sleep with me tonight?"

Understanding his fear, she returned and gave him a big reassuring hug. "Be brave son," she explained. "I can't sleep in your room, I have to sleep in daddy's room!"

The silence was broken at last by a shakey little voice saying, "Hmmm, the big sissy!"

☺☺☺

Man's capability to tell ONLY ONE LIE is directly proportional
To man's ability to eat ONLY ONE POTATO CHIP!

☺☺☺

It was the usual muddy day in the country. Our first grade teacher, Miss Brown, had just finished putting on the 36th boot on the 18th pair of little feet and quickly prepared to finish the last pair so she could go to lunch.

The last pair of boots was for little Johnny Smith, a quiet boy. Miss Brown had a very difficult time getting his boots on as they were a bit too small for his growing feet, but finally the battle was won

To her dismay, little Johnny looked blandly up into her face and announced: "Teacher, these boots aren't mine." In a hurry, but wanting to be kind, Miss Brown groaned, but with grim gentleness removed the boots and straightened her aching back.

Whereupon Johnny continued: "They're my little brother's, but Mommy said I could wear them to school today."

☺☺☺

Visitor: "Why does your dog sit and watch me eat?"

Young Host: "I don't know, unless he's angry because you have the
plate he usually eats on."

☺☺☺

Every summer I relearn the theory of relativity...namely,
If you've got a swimming pool, you're gonna
See a lot of relatives.

Little Jimmy: "I'm going to be the first astronaut to go to the sun."

Uncle Bill: "You can't go to the sun. It's too hot!"

Little Jimmy: "That's alright, I'll go at night".

☺☺☺

"Thank you very much," said the Missionary. "I'll call this afternoon and thank your mother for those eight beautiful apples."

"Please, Elder," said little Tommy. "When you call, would you mind thanking her for twelve apples."

☺☺☺

Older sister to younger brother: "Johnny, where are your manners? If I choose first, I always take the smaller piece of cake."

Younger brother: "Why are you complaining? That's exactly what you got!"

☺☺☺

When his oldest son came home from school with his report card, his father almost had a heart attack-- "3 F's and 1 D."

"How in the world can you get 3 F's."

"Gee, Dad, I don't know. I guess I concentrated too hard on one subject!"

☺☺☺

One day as my eighteen year old daughter, Jenny, and I walked through the mall she saw a beautiful bracelet in the jewelry store window. Suddenly with that dazzling smile and a twinkle in her eyes, she asked me in her sweetest voice:

"My dearest dad, won't you please buy me that gorgeous bracelet?"

"My dearest daughter," I replied, "I would be delighted to comply with your exorbitant solicitation, but extenuating pecuniary circumstances preclude the acquisition of such an extravagant bauble."

"I don't get it, dad!" she responded.

"That is exactly what I said," I explained. "You don't get it!"

☺☺☺

Things were different when I was a boy. My son's room has a color TV, a video player, a stereo, and his own telephone. Now when I want to punish him, I have to send him to my room.

"Are you troubled by the fact that your children occasionally tell lies?" asked one distraught mother to a friend.

"Not nearly as much," said the friend, "as when they tell the truth at inappropriate times."

☺☺☺

My son came home from kindergarten one day with the following comment:

"Teacher made me say five hundred times today, 'I'm a bad boy.' But I got even with her. When I returned to my chair, I said to myself five hundred times, 'No I ain't.'"

☺☺☺

One day in Primary the teacher was reviewing the pictures drawn by the five year olds. Johnny had drawn a very nice picture of an airplane. In the cockpit he had drawn two people.

"That is a very nice picture, Johnny," said the teacher, "Who is that in the airplane?"

"Oh, that's Jesus!" was his reply.

"How nice," responded the teacher, "and who is the other person with him?"

With all of the sincerity he could express, Johnny replied, "Oh that's Pontius the Pilot."

☺☺☺

The bristles on my daddy's chin
Sometimes are stiff as anything,
And scratchy, too, like kitten claws.

But if he rubs them on my face
I never even cry--because
Even if they hurt my skin,

I guess the other ends inside
Are sticking into him.

☺☺☺

Our family follows the golden rule:

"Them that has the gold, sets the rules."

☺☺☺

Our house is right out of Genesis!
It's full of every creeping thing!

Before I was married I had 6 ideas for raising children.

Now I'm married I have 6 children and no ideas.

☺☺☺

A father wearily dropped into a sleeping bag after a strenuous day which included, among other things, a game of softball, three-legged relays and making a climb up the mountain to view the sunset.

As he contemplated a burned finger from cooking over a campfire, a young voice from the corner of the tent said happily, "This has been so much fun. I'll bet it was a mother that thought up fathers and sons outings."

☺☺☺

Older brother to younger brother: "Don't say anything to daddy about his short haircut. Remember, it's important to him to look like his peers."

☺☺☺

Shortly after our first child was born, we moved. My wife thought it would be simpler to buy two kinds of baby formula: one could be used straight from the can, the other had to be mixed with water.

One night we were in a motel in an unfamiliar city, when inadvertently she put the concentrated formula in the baby's bottle without mixing it with water. Our baby finished the entire 6 ounce bottle before my wife realized the error.

Alarmed, she called the emergency room of a nearby hospital. The doctor on duty showed his sense of humor when he said, "No problem, lady, just give the baby 6 ounces of water and then shake him good before putting him to bed."

☺☺☺

Kids are the salt of the earth
And as everyone knows, salt gives you high blood pressure.

☺☺☺

Our friend Marilyn agreed one Saturday morning to take all the children to their soccer game. She piled all the kids in the car (12 or so). And wouldn't you know it she missed a stop sign, right in front of a police officer.

After he stopped her, the officer stuck his head in the car window and said, "Lady, don't you know when to stop?"

Embarrassed with all of the children in the car she said, "Oh sir, you're mistaken, all of these children aren't mine!"

A deaf husband and a blind wife --
Almost always make a happy couple.

☺☺☺

Three new fathers-to-be were nervously pacing the waiting room floor when the nurse came in and said to one, "Congratulations, you're the father of twins." "Terrific," said the new father, "what a coincidence, I'm a player for the Minnesota Twins baseball team."

A little later the nurse came in again and announced to the second father, "Congratulations, you're the father of triplets." "What a coincidence," shouted the new father, "I work for the 3-M Company."

At this moment of jubilation, the third father-to-be promptly fainted. When the nurse finally revived the poor fellow, she asked. "What's the matter?" The soon to be father's reply was, "Quick get me out of here, I work for 7-up."

☺☺☺

The little boy greeted his grandmother with a hug and said, "I'm so happy to see you grandma. Now maybe daddy will do the trick he has been promising us." The grandmother was curious. "What trick is that my dear," she asked. The little boy replied, "I heard daddy tell mommy that he would climb the walls if you came to visit us again."

☺☺☺

I remember the story of one of our children who spent all day bugging his mother. But true to the lesson she had learned in Relief Society, my wife decided she would just ignore his little temper tantrums and see if he would calm down. Finally, he settled on the sofa and exclaimed, "I wish Daddy would come home and make me behave."

☺☺☺

HOUSE RULES

IF YOU SLEEP ON IT	MAKE IT UP
IF YOU WEAR IT	HANG IT UP
IF YOU EAT OUT OF IT	PUT IT IN THE SINK
IF YOU STEP ON IT	WIPE IT OFF
IF YOU OPEN IT	CLOSE IT
IF YOU EMPTY IT	FILL IT UP
IF IT RINGS	ANSWER IT
IF IT HOWLS	FEED IT
IF IT CRIES	LOVE IT

☺☺☺

Youth is a time of rapid changes.
Between the ages of twelve and seventeen
A parent can age thirty years.

Family units are like banks.
If you take out more than you put in,
They go broke.

☺☺☺

When our children were small, we thought they were brilliant.
Now they're adolescents, and they think we're retarded.

☺☺☺

To have children in their teens is to know that you are living,
Just as having a headache is proof that you have a head.

☺☺☺

The simplest toy, one which even the youngest child can operate,
Is called a grandparent.

☺☺☺

We had a large family, six boys and five girls.
I was the scorekeeper.

☺☺☺

OUR FAMILY'S NATIONAL ANTHEM

"BUT! THAT'S NOT MY JOB!"

☺☺☺

Both my wife and I have dark hair, yet our firstborn was a real "toehead " blond. Everyone we met asked, "How did the two of you have a blond–headed baby?"

"The same way you would have a redhead," was my wife's innocent reply.

☺☺☺

I was so surprised at my birth,
I couldn't speak for a year and a half.

☺☺☺

One lady robin flew up to another and asked if she could help build her nest. The other robin asked, "Oh, have you finished yours already?" "Yes, why don't you come and see it." So they both flew off to see the nest.

After looking at the beautiful nest, the one robin said, "My, that is a beautiful nest, but why the hole in the bottom?"

"Oh, said the other, I love to knit, but I can't be bothered with children."

"My husband and I never argue in front of the children," said the mother training teacher. "If a difference comes up we just send the children out of doors while we settle it."

"Now I understand," whispered a sister to her friend. "Just the other day I asked her why her children looked so healthy, and she replied that it's because they spend so much time out of doors."

A large family, with seven children, moved to a new city. They were having a difficult time finding an apartment to live in. Many apartments were large enough, but the landlords objected to the large family. After several days of searching, the father asked the mother to take the four younger children to visit the cemetery one morning while he took the older three to find an apartment.

After they had looked most of the morning they found a place that was just right. Then the landlord asked the usual question: "How many children do you have?" The father answered with a deep sigh, "Seven....but four are with their dear mother in the cemetery." The truth it was, but he still got the apartment!

Primary teacher: "Would you rather have a brother or a sister?"
Little boy: "I'd rather have a pony."

Teacher: "If you had six apples and I asked you for three, how many
                would you have left?"
Jeffrey: "Six."

One dad to another: "I'm no model father. All I'm trying to do is behave so that when people tell my son that he reminds them of me, he'll stick out his chest instead of his tongue."

☺☺☺

Fathers should not get too discouraged if their sons reject their advice. It will not be wasted. Years later the sons will offer it to their own children.

☺☺☺

Raising a family is like shaving.
No matter how good of a job you do today, you must do it again tomorrow.

☺☺☺

"I've had everything...wife, house, children, the FULL catastrophe!"
-Zorba the Greek-

A pedestrian is a man with a son in high school,
And only one car in the the family.

As a young Frenchman pushed his son's carriage down the street, the youngster howled with rage. "Please, Bernard, control yourself," the father said quietly. "Easy there, Bernard, keep calm!"

"Congratulations, monsieur," said a woman who had been watching. "You know just how to speak to infants--calmly and gently." Then she said, "So the little fellow's named Bernard?" "No, madame," corrected the father. "He's Pierre. I'm Bernard."

A research organization, making a study of juvenile delinquency, telephoned fifty homes between 9:30 and 10:30 at night to ask parents if they knew where their children were. Over half of the calls were answered by children who had no idea where their parents were.

A young mother, wishing to tell her friend in a distant city of the birth of her first child, telegraphed the following passage: "Isaiah 9:6." This passage begins, "For unto us a child is born, unto us a son is given."

The friend who was not familiar with the scriptures read the telex several times to her husband, and then said, "Evidently Elizabeth had a boy who weighs nine pounds and six ounces, but I can't imagine for the world why she would name him Isaiah."

Several years ago when our son was eleven, my wife said, "Things can't continue to go on like this." Sure enough she was right. Now he's a teenager and things have gotten worse.

Family Home Evening may be the only fight
that starts and ends with prayer.

The primary teacher described how Lot's wife looked back at Sodom and was turned into a pillar of salt.

Suddenly Jimmy interrupted. "My mother looked back once while she was driving," he announced triumphantly. "and she turned into a telephone pole!"

Nothing in the world is friendlier than a wet dog.

"Now Robby," said his mother, "don't be selfish. Let your little brother have the sled half the time."

"I do," replied Robby. "I have it going downhill and he has it coming up."

☺☺☺

Little Danny ran to his mother sobbing as though his heart would break. "What's the matter, Danny?" she asked. "Daddy was hanging up a picture and it dropped on his toe."

"Why, that's nothing to cry about," laughed his mother. "You should laugh at that." "I did!" sobbed Danny.

☺☺☺

Mother: "Tell me, what did you learn in Sunday School today, Billy?"
Billy: "Oh, the teacher told us some story about Jonah and the whale."

Mother: "That's good. What's the moral of the story?"
Billy: "Beats me. The only thing I can figure out is that you can't keep a good man down."

☺☺☺

"What'll you do," the Beehive teacher asked, "when you are as big as your mother?"

"Diet," replied the young girl.

☺☺☺

Ten year old to her mother: "It isn't fair. At night you tell me I'm too little to stay up. In the morning you say I'm too big to stay in bed."

☺☺☺

A father was trying to read the Sunday paper. His son wanted to play with his father. To keep the boy busy, dad pulled a fullpage map of the world out of the current events section of the newspaper, sliced it up into jigsaw patterns, scattered them on the floor, and told the youngster:

"See if you can put these back together as a map of the world. Just follow the colors and shapes."

The father had barely begun to read his paper when he felt the kid tugging at his sleeve. In about three minutes he had reassembled the map correctly.

"How did you do that?" asked the father.

"I got the clue." said the youngster. "On the other side of the page was a big picture of a man. All you have to do is put the man together right and then the whole world comes out right."

A lady wrote to a resort hotel to ask if her dog would be allowed to stay with her. She received the following response:

Dear Madam: We have been in the hotel business for over thirty years. We have never yet had to call in the police to eject a dog for disorderly conduct in the wee hours of the morning. No dog has ever passed off a bad check. Never has a dog started a fire by smoking in bed. We have never found a hotel towel or blanket in a dog's suitcase. Your dog is certainly welcome at our hotel.

P.S. If he will vouch for you, you can come too.

Every dog is entitled to a few fleas.
-David O. McKay-

Husband: "My dear, I really don't think you can ever teach that dog to obey you."

Wife: "Nonsense darling, remember how obstinate you were when we were first married?"

Mrs. Thorpe had recently acquired a new dog and was explaining his good points to a neighbor. "He's not what you would call a pedigree dog," she said, "but no thief or robber can come near the house without his letting us know about it."

"Why?" asked the friend. "Does he bark loudly?" "No," responded Mrs. Thorpe, "he crawls under the sofa."

The ad in the local newspaper read: "Purebred Police Dog $25." Thinking that to be a great bargain, Mrs. Freeman ordered the dog to be delivered. The next day a van pulled up and left her the mangiest-looking mongrel she had ever seen.

In a rage, she telephoned the man who had placed the ad..."What do you mean by calling that mangy-mut a purebred police dog?" "Don't be deceived by his looks, Ma'am," he replied. "He's in the Secret Service."

A young child listened intently to the preacher say, "Dust thou art, and unto dust thou shall return!" After church he hurried home and looked under his bed at the balls of dust that had accumulated there. After looking at them for a few pensive moments, he when into the kitchen and very seriously asked his mother:

"Mommy, somebody is under my bed! How do I know if they are coming or going?"

An independent eight-year-old, announced to his mother and father at the dinner table, "I'm going to run away from home tomorrow. Who is going to drive me?"

☺☺☺

Leaning on your family tree will never get you out of the woods.

☺☺☺

A rarely seen relative from back east dropped in to visit us one day. He was met at the door by our youngest son. Not really knowing who he was, the boy escourted him into the living room and asked, "Are you really related to us?"

"Yes," replied the visitor, "I'm a cousin on your father's side of the family."

The boy replied, "Guess, you don't know it, Mister, but in this house, you're on the wrong side."

☺☺☺

HOME

"Home ain't a place that gold can buy or
  get up in a minute;

Afore it's home there's gotta be a heap o'
  livin in it;

You've got t' sing and dance fer years
  you've got to romp an' play

And learn t' love the things ye have by
  usin' 'em each day;

You've got to love each brick an' stone
  from cellar up t' dome --

It takes a heap o' livin' to make a house a Home."

-Edgar A. Guest-

☺☺☺

Father: "Son, I'm what is referred to as a 'Self-made Man'."

Son: "That's what I admire about you dad. You're always willing to accept the blame for things."

☺☺☺

Perhaps any of us could get along with perfect people.
But our task is to get along with imperfect people.

-Richard L. Evans-

"Yeah, I know what you mean, I'm a deacon myself."

CHURCH LEADERS

The Lord one day had a job for me,
    But I had so much to do;
So I said, "Please, Lord, get somebody else,
    Or wait 'till I get through!"
I don't know how the Lord came out,
    But he seemed to get along;
But I felt a kind of sneaking like,
    And knowed I'd done him wrong.

One day I needed the Lord myself,
    Needed Him right away;
But He never answered me at all--
    But yet I could hear Him say,
Away down in my accusing heart,
    "I've got so much to do--
You get somebody else this time,
    Or wait 'till I get through."

Now when the Lord has a job for me,
    I never try to shirk;
I drop whatever I have on hand,
    And do the good Lord's work.
And my affairs can run along,
    Or wait 'till I get through;
For nobody else can do the job
    That the Lord has marked out for you!
        -Paul L. Dunbar-

☺☺☺

Bishop to the ward custodian. "Brother Jones, I understand you have been trying to go over my head regarding your employment."

Ward custodian: "I'm sorry bishop I haven't said anything to anyone as far as I know."

"Now Brother Jones," laughed the bishop. "Isn't it true that you have been praying for a raise?"

☺☺☺

THE BEST EXECUTIVE
IS THE ONE WHO HAS SENSE ENOUGH
TO PICK GOOD MEN
TO DO WHAT HE WANTS DONE,
AND SELF-RESTRAINT ENOUGH
TO KEEP FROM MEDDLING WITH THEM
WHILE THEY DO IT!
    -Theodore Roosevelt-

I shall never forget my first priesthood blessing. I had just been ordained an elder and was called upon to go to the hospital to bless a lady that was having a gall bladder operation.

As I was trying to pronounce the blessing, the only thing I could think of was to bless her that everything would come out all right.

To my dying day, I think that lady will laugh every time she sees me.

The Sunday before New Years Day, our new young Bishop told the congregation that when he had been made Bishop he had set a goal of visiting every family in the ward before year end.

Apologizing that he had not met this goal, he asked anyone he had missed who really needed a visit before year's end to raise their hand.

Only one person raised her hand....the Bishop's wife.

"There ought to be a special place in heaven for Bishop's wives, commented the spinster." "Perhaps you're right," responded the Bishop's wife, "but I would much rather go with my husband."

Priesthood Leader's Lament
-Karl Mitchell-

If I hadn't let the bishop in
When he came to call that night;
If I hadn't made the promise
That I'd strive with all my might
To inspire those home teachers
To get their teaching done,
To urge, incite and stimulate
And encourage everyone;

If I hadn't made this statement:
"My reports will not be late."
That "I'll surely have them handed in
On the appointed date."
If I did not have the knowledge
That on judgment day I'd find
That the other guys had gone ahead
And left me far behind,

Then tonight I'd just relax a bit,
And from all worry cease,
Turn on TV, then settle back
And go to Hell in peace!!

One Sunday evening my wife was surprised to have our fourteen year old son put his arm around her shoulders, give her a resounding kiss on the cheek and say, "Mother, I love you."

She didn't have long to bask in motherly glory, however. His seventeen year old sister sarcastically commented, "Handed out a new priesthood assignment I see."

A bishop met a member of his congregation who had been inactive for years. After their brief conversation, the bishop said, "Just what do you have against coming to Church?"

"Plenty," snarled the inactive member. "The first time I went they threw me in the water. The second time, they tied me to a woman I have had to support ever since."

"I see," said the bishop quietly. "And the next time they will probably throw dirt on you."

In our Stake Presidency, President Walker is known as the rich one, President Grider is known as the famous one, and I'm simply called "the other one."

A young lady from Salt Lake was visiting a friend in a very small congregation in Vermont. "You certainly have a small congregation in this branch," said the girl from Salt Lake to her friend.

"Yes," agreed her friend, "So small sometimes that when the branch president says 'dearly beloved,' you feel you've received a proposal."

A bishop, who was noted for his energy and his strong feelings against laziness, also operated a small welfare farm. One day he observed one ward member sitting idly by the plow as the horses took a needed rest. This rather shocked the good man's sense of economy. After all, when you are on the Lord's errand, you should put in a good day's work.

So he said gently, but reproachfully, "Ted, wouldn't it be a good plan for you to have a pair of clippers and be trimming the bushes while the horses rest?"

Somewhat disgruntled, Ted replied, "I would be more than happy to follow your request, Bishop, if you would promise me that you'll take a bushel of potatoes to the pulpit with you next Sunday and peel them during the opening hymn."

God so loved the world --
That He didn't send a committee to organize it.

Several bishops were flying to general conference in Salt Lake City when one of the plane's engines conked out. The pretty stewardess bustled about, reassuring the passengers that everything would be all right. One of the bishops felt that she needed a little reassurance herself. "Nothing can happen to this plane," he reassured her. "There are eight bishops aboard."

The stewardess forced a smile and said she would relay the comforting news to the pilot. In a few moments she was back, looking a little uncertain.

"I told the captain that there were eight bishops aboard, but he said, no offense intended, but he'd rather have four good engines."

A brash new pastor, upset by being assigned to a rural church, dropped into a Sunday school class and began quizzing the students to test the effectiveness of their teacher. "Who knocked down the walls of Jericho?" he demanded of one boy. "It sure weren't me, Reverend," the boy said.

Turning to the teacher, the pastor exclaimed, "I suppose that's a sample of the kind of instruction you give in this class?" "Now, Reverend," said the embarrassed teacher, "Timmy is a good boy and doesn't tell lies. If he said he didn't do it, I believe him."

Thoroughly appalled by the teacher's lack of knowledge, the pastor took the matter to the church's board of deacons. After due consideration, the board sent the following message to the upset pastor: "We see no point in making an issue of this incident. The board will pay for the damages to the wall and charge it off to vandalism."

Two old friends, a Priest and a Rabbi, meet regularly to discuss theology. "Now that we Catholics have become progressive enough to eat meat on Fridays," the Priest asked, "when will you Jews start eating pork?" The Rabbi paused a moment, then answered, "At your wedding."

The Church has just announced a new policy:

They are going to ordain all babies High Priests
So they will sleep in Church.

If you think you're confused, consider poor Columbus. He didn't know where he was going. When he got there, he didn't know where he was. And when he got back, he didn't know where he'd been.

The man who feels he is indispensable should stick his fist in a pale of water, and see what a big hole it leaves when he pulls it out.

A Priest, and a Minister invited a Mormon Bishop to go golfing. They teed off on a difficult hole that had a water trap midway down the fairway. The Priest teed off first. His ball fell squarely in the middle of the small pond. He walked out to the middle of the pond --on the surface of the water--rolled up his sleeve and fished out the ball.

The Bishop couldn't believe his eyes, the Priest hadn't even got his pants wet; but he said nothing. Then the Minister hit his ball, it also dropped squarely into the water trap. He too walked out on the water, hardly getting his shoes wet, rolled up his sleeves, stuck his arm down into the water and retrieved his ball.

Amazed but saying nothing, the Bishop teed off. And sure enough his ball dropped squarely in the center of the pond. He hesitated for a moment, but decided if the other two could walk on water so could he, and he then strode off onto the pond. To his embarrassment, he sunk up to his waist in the water.

After enjoying a friendly chuckle, the Priest turned to the Minister and asked, "Do you think we should tell the Bishop where the rocks are?"

To err is human.
To blame it on the other guy
Is even more human.

The preacher's car broke down just after the evening service. So on Monday he drove into the local garage to have it repaired. "I hope you will go a little easy on the price," he said to the mechanic. "After all, I am just a poor preacher."

"I know," he answered, "I heard you preach in church last night."

How many people does it take to hold a Mormon meeting?
Two to have the meeting and four to bring refreshments.

Someone once described a football team this way:

"A center, two guards, two tackles, two ends, two halfbacks,
one fullback and 50,000 quarterbacks in the grandstands."
(That is also true for Bishops)

America has become so tense and nervous
It has been years since I've seen anyone asleep in church
...And that is a sad situation.

–Norman Vincent Peale–

Brigham Young interviewed a young farmer to see if he was ready to live the United Order: "If you had two farms, would you be willing to give one of them to the church?"

"Certainly," said the young man. "If you had two houses, would you be willing to give one to the church?" "Oh, without a doubt," he replied.

"If you had two cows, would you be willing to give one to the church?" The young man thought for a moment and then said, "I guess I'm not ready for the United Order." "Why?" asked Brigham, "You were willing to give up a farm, and a house, why would you hesitate with giving up a cow?"

"I have two cows," said the young farmer.

☺☺☺

A bishop is said to be a man who knows a very little about a great deal and keeps knowing less and less about more and more until he knows practically nothing about everything.

Whereas on the other hand, a stake president is a man who knows a great deal about very little and who goes along knowing more and more about less and less until finally he knows practically everything about nothing.

A Regional Representative starts out knowing practically everything about everything, but ends up by knowing nothing about anything, due to his association with bishops and stake presidents!

☺☺☺

The chapel was full to overflowing. Shortly after the meeting started the bishop noticed the stake presidency had made a surprise visit and were standing by the back door. Since there were no empty seats on the stand, he leaned forward and whispered to one of the deacons on the front row: "Jimmy, please get me three chairs."

Jimmy, an athletic little lad who was willing to do almost anything for his friend the bishop, couldn't quite hear what the bishop had said. So he replied, "What?", in a rather loud whisper. The bishop, not wanting the entire congregation to hear, whispered back, "Get me three chairs."

Jimmy, a bit puzzled looked at the bishop and said, "What?" Again the bishop said, "Get me three chairs." Jimmy smiled and leaned back and winked at the bishop. The bishop, a bit puzzled, looked at Jimmy and said, "Did you understand?" Jimmy smiled, winked again, and nodded his head. Then the bishop said, "Well, then do it now!"

Jimmy looked at the bishop and said, "Now?" The bishop nodded. So Jimmy shrugged his shoulders, jumped to his feet and yelled, "Rah, Rah, Rah, Bishop!"

☺☺☺

Many a man who can't even paddle his own canoe,
Wants to be captain of the ship!

I heard that one morning in the High Priests Quorum someone died and they called the paramedics. They carried out five brethren before they found the right one!

☺☺☺

A bishop, a stake president and an IRS agent died the same day. When they got to heaven, Saint Peter greeted them at the gate. After listening to them explain what they had done in life, he turned to the IRS agent and said, "We've been waiting for you. Please come right this way."

He then turned to the bishop and stake president and said, "I'll need more supportive evidence before you fellows can come in." Shocked, they asked why an IRS agent would be able to go right in and they would have to wait and provide more evidence.

To this Saint Peter solemnly answered, "My records show that that single IRS agent scared the Devil out of more people than you two put together."

☺☺☺

The bishop had just started sacrament meeting when there was thunder, lightening and rain....which poured down in torrents.

"Isn't the Lord wonderful," he said to the congregation. "While all of us sit here dry and comfortable, He's washing our cars."

☺☺☺

"Bishop, I'd like to join your church. I enjoy the choir and the fellowship immensely."

"That's very kind of you to say," replied the bishop, "but you realize that if you join our church you must be willing to pay tithing and to work in the church as well."

"Oh, no, that's not really my intention. I'd just like to attend church and enjoy it."

"Oh," replied the bishop, "Then I would recommend that you look into joining the church just down the street."

"Why? What's the name of the church down the street?" asked the investigator.

With a twinkle in his eye the bishop smiled and said, "The Church of Heavenly Rest."

☺☺☺

The heights by great men reached and kept
Were not attained by sudden flight,
But they, while their companions slept,
Were toiling upward in the night.
　　　－Henry Wadsworth Longfellow－

"Just think," said the priest advisor. "In Africa there are six million square miles where they have no Sunday School. Now what should we all strive to save our money for?"

"To go to Africa," enthusiastically shouted the priest quorum.

☺☺☺

Sign in a well-stocked but cluttered ward library:

"The question is not: To have or not to have;
But to find or not to find?"

☺☺☺

I was lying in the hospital waiting for an operation. I had been there six days in preparation and in nervous anticipation of the event. The operation was serious. The doctor said I needed "considerable fixing." Later, I learned that over twenty inches of incision was required, most of it in the bone.

The day before the dreadful ordeal, a mutual friend brought Brother J. Golden Kimball to administer to me. First, he talked and visited a considerable time and then blessed me. There was nothing frivolous about his talk, and yet he soon had me smiling. Later, the smiles were interspersed with laughter. I began to see things in proper perspective and to realize that all was well with the world and that the sky for me, after all, had but one dark cloud in it which, probably, would soon roll away. I felt I was in the presence of a sane, well-balanced man and a man of exceptionally strong faith. In truth, never did I feel the power of faith more than that day.

-A debtor to J. Golden Kimball-

☺☺☺

Comments from a Bishop on date of his release:

"I guess today is the day they revoke my 'hugging' license."

"I've just gone from Who's Who to Who's He, with the raise of hands!

☺☺☺

President J. Reuben Clark's advice to church leaders:

As a leader in the Church it is most important that you realize that around here we must obey the eleventh commandment!

Now I suppose that there are some who are not familiar with the eleventh commandment.

It simply states: "THOU SHALT NOT TAKE THYSELF TOO SERIOUSLY!"

President N. Eldon Tanner's advice to me when he called me to be a counselor in a Stake Presidency:

"Brother Briggs, it is our intent through this call, to work 'Hell' right out of you!" The advice was appreciated and I sincerely pray that it was successful.

WHO IS THIS STRANGER, MOTHER DEAR

Who is this stranger, mother dear?
Ain't he funny, ain't he queer?
Hush my child, don't ramble so.
He's your father, don't you know?

He's my father? No such thing...
Father passed away last spring.
No, he did not die, dear chick,
Your father joined the bishopric.

Now he meets and meets and meets.
He has no time for sleep or eat.
He at funerals must preside,
He must kiss the pretty bride.

There are meetings every day,
Welfare, Priesthood and MIA,
Sunday School and picture show.
Or what have you, he must go.

Kiss him darling----he won't bite.
Let us treat this stranger right...

A convincing leader is one who can tell you to go to Hell in such a way that you'll enjoy the trip!

The bishop, after preaching a beautiful sermon on the fact that Salvation is free as a gift of Jesus Christ, reminded the congregation about tithing settlement and asked that each family specifically remember to look at their personal situation to help the ward budget.

One of the ward members protested saying, "Bishop, you have just told us that salvation was free -- free as the water we drink."

"Salvation is free, brother," replied the bishop. "It's free and the water is free, but when we pipe it to you, you have to pay for the piping."

Speakers should finish before the congregation does!!

The eye's a better student and more willing than the ear.
Fine counsel is confusing, but example's always clear,
And the best of all the preachers are the men who live their creeds,
For to see the good in action is what everybody needs.

I can soon learn how you do it if you'll let me see it done.
I can watch your hands in action, but your tongue too fast may run;
And the lectures you deliver may be very wise and true,
But I'd rather get my lesson by observing what you do.

For I may not understand you and the high advice you give;
But there's no misunderstanding how you act and how you live.

-Edgar A. Guest-

When in charge -- PONDER.
When in trouble -- DELEGATE.
When in doubt -- MUMBLE. -- Then refer it to a committee for review.

Don't be an AVERAGE leader, for an AVERAGE leader is only
the WORST of the BEST, and the BEST of the WORST!

'Twas a sheep, not a lamb, that strayed away
In the parable that Jesus told;
A grown-up sheep had gone astray
From the ninety and nine in the fold.
Out on the hillside, out in the cold,
'Twas a sheep the Good Shepherd sought.

And why for the sheep should we earnestly long
And so earnestly hope and pray?
Because there is danger, if they go wrong;
They will lead the lambs astray.
For the lambs will follow the sheep, you know,
Wherever the sheep may stray.

When the sheep go wrong it will not be long
'Til the lambs are as wrong as they.
And so, with the sheep, we earnestly plead
For the sake of the lambs today;
If the lambs are lost, what a terrible cost
Some sheep will have to pay.

A leaders formula for failure:

TRY TO PLEASE EVERYBODY!

Do you know why a little puppy has so many friends?
It's because he has learned to wag his tail not his tongue.

☺☺☺

The most valuable lessons I ever learned in life
Were ON or ACROSS my mother's knee.

☺☺☺

A young man brought his friend to church. The Bishop announced the first speaker would be Brother Johnson. The friend asked, "What does that mean?"

The young man replied, "Oh, that means Mr. Johnson is going to preach the sermon today."

Brother Johnson stood up at the pulpit, looked at the congregation and opened his Bible.

"What does that mean?" asked the friend.

"That means he is going to preach from the Bible."

Then Brother Johnson, took off his watch and carefully placed it on the pulpit.

"What does that mean," asked the friend.

"Nothing!" responded the young man.

☺☺☺

Men are like spaghetti:

If you get in front and pull, they will follow along behind;
But if you get in back and push, they will all wad up.

–President N. Eldon Tanner–

☺☺☺

The secret of success is putting your best foot forward,
Without stepping on someone else's toes.

☺☺☺

If we want to leave footsteps in the sands of time
Lets put on our work shoes.
We can't leave any footprints sitting down.

☺☺☺

"Don't fret that you can't do exceptional things;
Just strive to do basic things exceptionally well!"

"WELL, I WAITED FOR YOUR SON FOR TWO YEARS. AND NOW HE TELLS ME HE'S CHANGED AND THAT CHANGES EVERYTHING. YOU'LL FIND HIM LOCKED IN YOUR TRUNK."

COMMUNICATION

Blessed are they who have nothing to say
And cannot be persuaded to say it.

–James Russell Lowell–

☺☺☺

A gossip is one who talks to you about other people.
A bore is one who talks to you about himself.
A brilliant conversationalist is one who talks
to you about yourself.

–Dr. William King–

☺☺☺

Don't knock the weather; nine tenths of the people couldn't start a
conversation if it didn't change once in a while.

☺☺☺

It's a good idea to keep your words soft and sweet to the taste.
You may have to eat them.

☺☺☺

A farmer asked his neighbor if he might borrow a rope. "Sorry," said the
neighbor, "I'm using my rope to tie up my milk."

"Rope can't tie up milk!" said the farmer.

"I know," replied the neighbor, "but when a man doesn't want to do something,
one reason is as good as another."

☺☺☺

The story is told of a man who refused to sign up for the company's new group
insurance policy which required 100% participation.

After he had given a flat "no" to his supervisor, plant manager and personnel
director, he was led into the office of the president of the company.

"Do you like working here?" the president asked. "Yes, sir," the man
answered. "Then sign this application!"

"Yes, sir," was the quick reply.

When asked by his supervisor why he had changed his mind so quickly, the man
replied: "Nobody ever explained it to me quite as clearly as the president did!"

"What's sex?" our eight year old asked as he tried to fill out his soccer form.

My wife, thinking this was just the right moment to explain the facts of life, gave him a twenty minute discourse on the facts of life. After she finished she asked the child if he had any questions,

"Yeh," he replied. "How can you get all that in this little box?"

☺☺☺

If you are to understand others,
And have them understand you,
Know the BIG words but use the SMALL ones.

☺☺☺

Someone once asked Perle Mesta, the greatest Washington Hostess since Dolly Madison, the secret of her success in getting so many rich and famous people to attend her parties.

"It's all in the greetings and good-byes," she claimed. As each guest arrived she met him or her with "At last you're here!" As each left she expressed her regrets with: "I'm sorry you have to leave so soon!"

☺☺☺

TO ALL HIGH COUNCILORS:

The Presidency of this Stake, after due and careful consideration of certain regrettable practices which have recently come to our attention, is desirous of again reminding you of the fact--which has of course, been pointed out on several previous occasions, but which nevertheless has apparently been overlooked or ignored by an all-too-preponderant proportion of our present high council--that all members of this council should make an earnest, sincere, continuous and persistent effort to eschew and avoid all excessive wordiness, repetitive phraseology, unnecessarily complicated sentence structure, and lengthy, involved or obscure paragraphs in their internal communications of any nature whatsoever to one or more fellow bishoprics and wards.

THE PRESIDENCY

P.S. In other words--make it brief!

☺☺☺

"...let not the inhabitants of the earth slumber,
because of thy speech."
-D.& C. 112:5-

☺☺☺

The difference between a conviction and a prejudice is that you can explain a conviction without getting angry.

One definition of "positive"
Is being mistaken at the top of your voice.

☺☺☺

The weaker the argument, the stronger the words.

☺☺☺

I have always loved the story of the little country church that was given a large gift of money. They had a meeting of the members to see how the money should be spent. One lady stood and timidly proposed that they purchase a new chandelier for their chapel.

At this suggestion, an old gentleman got quickly to his feet, his face red with emotion, and blurted out, "This church don't need no chan-de-leer. In the first place I doubt that anyone here can even spell chan-de-leer.

In the second place, even if we had a new chan-de-leer I doubt that anyone here could play it. And in the last place, what we really need in our chapel is a new light!"

☺☺☺

Our company has always had a problem with interoffice communications. For instance, last week the Personnel Department sent around a memo on sexual harassment. Three people initialed it and six people signed up for it.

☺☺☺

A man went into the doctor's office for his appointment. To his surprise the nurse told him to step into the next room and remove his clothes. "But-but, Nurse," he said in a hoarse whisper, "It's my throat." "Do as I tell you," snapped the Nurse, "or I shall be forced to cancel your appointment."

So, shrugging his shoulders, the man went into the room. There sat a young fellow looking very uncomfortable and quite naked except for a large parcel he held across his lap. "Doesn't that beat everything," said the man, removing his coat. "I came in here with a sore throat and I have to take my clothes off." "Don't complain," was the reply, "I just came in here to deliver this package!"

☺☺☺

Television is a MEDIUM.
They call it that because a lot of the stuff you see on it
is neither RARE, nor WELL DONE.

☺☺☺

Mrs. Ricks: "Here take these flowers home to your mother."
Little boy: "I can't do that she'll think I've done something wrong!"

Mrs. Ricks: "She already knows you've done something wrong son, now take these flowers home to your mother."

A lot of people don't have much to say, and that's fine. The trouble with some of them is that you have to listen a long time to find it out.

☺☺☺

Who so tooteth his own horn, tooteth not --
It ain't braggin' if it's true!

☺☺☺

The millennium is here, but no one knows it yet...
Because it hasn't cleared Church Correlation.

☺☺☺

Walking into a noisy classroom, the teacher slapped her hand on the desk and ordered sharply: "I demand pandemonium!"

The class quieted down immediately. "It isn't what you demand," she explained, "but the way you demand it."

☺☺☺

A tourist spending the night in a small Vermont town joined a group of men sitting on the porch of the general store. After several vain attempts to start a conversation, he finally asked, "Is there a law against talking in this town?"

"Nope, no law agin it," replied one crusty old Vermonter. "We just like to make sure it's an improvement on silence."

☺☺☺

A personnel director for a large company once delivered a complicated speech on his company's new quality control program before an audience of production workers.

He spoke of "zero defects," "primary, secondary and tertiary inspections," and "incentives." "Are there any questions?" he asked. There were none.

"So, I've explained it so well that everyone understands," he said after a short pause.

"That ain't it," an old country boy said. "You've done muddied up the water so bad we don't even know what to ask!"

☺☺☺

Laughter is the shortest distance between two people.

–Victor Borge–

☺☺☺

He who fails to thump his own drum,
Shall in the end not be heard.

We are all manufacturers of sorts:
Either making good, making fun or making excuses.

☺☺☺

Some people are never at peace unless they're fighting.

☺☺☺

One reason the Ten Commandments are so short and clear
is that Moses didn't have to send them through
the Church Curriculum Committee.

☺☺☺

There isn't much to talk about at most parties
Until one or two couples have left.

☺☺☺

Every man needs a wife, because many things go wrong that he can't blame on the government.

☺☺☺

Donald Ogden Stewart, the writer, had a son away at prep school. When the boy reached the age of fourteen, Stewart wrote him the following letter:

"Dear son, now that you have reached the magic age of fourteen, the time has come to tell you about the bees and flowers. There is a male and a female bee, although I haven't the slightest idea which is which. As for the flowers--we get ours from the Plaza Florist, Inc. Well, that takes care of that.

Write soon, Affectionately,
Father."

☺☺☺

In the conference room of a large corporation was the framed motto of the President:

"Intelligence is no substitute for information;
Enthusiasm is no substitute for experience;
Willingness is no substitute for action."

The motto is no longer there because one morning, after a series of long meetings, someone added:

"A meeting is no substitute for progress."

☺☺☺

DON'T CURSE THE DARKNESS -- LIGHT A CANDLE!

"McCracken, Batchelder, Smith and Robertson...Good morning."
"May I speak with Mr. Robertson?"
"Certainly Sir. Who may I say is calling?"
"Mr. Potter--of Meyer, Graham, Potter and Butler."
"Just one moment, I'll connect you with Mr. Robertson's office."

"Hello, Mr. Robertson's office."
"May I speak with Mr. Robertson, please?"
"I'll see if he's in. Who's calling please?"
"Mr. Potter."
"Are you with a company, Mr. Potter?"
"Yes, Meyer, Graham, Potter and Butler."
"Thank you!"

"Mr. Robertson, a Mr. Potter of Meyer, Graham, Potter and Butler is on line two."
"O.K., put him on."

"Just one moment, Mr. Robertson... Mr. Potter, here's Mr. Robertson. Go ahead please."

"Hi, Bill. How about lunch?"
"Great. Usual time and place?"
"Right. See you there!"

A plumber wrote the U.S. Bureau of Standards about using hydrochloric acid to clean drain pipes. Several days later he received this reply:

"The efficacy of hydrochloric acid is indisputable, but the corrosive residue is incompatible with metallic permanence."

Confused, he sent a second letter asking simply if the acid was 'Okay to use or not?'

The Bureau's second letter advised him, "We cannot assume responsibility for the production of toxic and noxious residue and suggest that you consider an alternative procedure."

Still uncertain, he wrote: "Please just tell me if it is okay to use hydrochloric acid to clean metal pipes?"

The final letter resolved the problem: "Don't use hydrochloric acid. It eats the heck out of pipes."

Be careful of the words you say,
Make them soft and sweet.

You never know from day to day.
Which ones you'll have to eat.

A man was sent to prison. As he observed the prison life he noticed that different prisoners were calling numbers out and the inmates would roar with laughter. "34," "19."

The new inmate inquired what was going on and his cellmate said, "Well, we aren't close enough to tell each other jokes, so we have numbered each joke. When someone gets in the mood to tell a joke he just shouts out a number."

The new inmate wanted to be one of the gang, so he yelled out "28!" No response. He then yelled out "15!" No response. Finally he asked his cellmate what was going on.

"Well," said the cellmate, "some can tell 'em and some can't."

Praise does wonders for the sense of hearing.

Most of us can't stand people who keep talking
When we are interrupting.

A fellow was crossing a cemetery one dark night and fell into an open grave. With a badly injured leg, it was impossible for him to get out without help, so he yelled with all his might for help.

Finally a passing drunk heard his cries for help and came over to the grave. "What's the matter," he asked. "What happened." The man in the grave said, "I'm cold."

The drunk looking down at him cocked his head to one side and said, "Well, you ought to be. You had no business kicking all that dirt off in the first place!" With that he turned and went on his way.

A traveling evangelist in a small Western city stopped a newsboy and inquired the way to the post office. He received an intelligent answer, thanked the boy, and then said: "You're a bright lad. Do you know who I am?"

"No sir," was the reply.

"Well, I'm the preacher who is holding revival meetings in the church up yonder. If you come to my services tonight, I'll show you the way to heaven."

"I won't be there, sir," said the newsboy, quickly. "How can you show me the way to heaven, when you don't even know the way to the post office?"

A preacher got a new assignment to a small little town in Southern Utah. He cleaned the chapel and prepared an excellent one-hour sermon.

Sunday morning only one old farmer came in to church. The preacher was upset but decided since he had a well prepared sermon that one soul was better than none. So he started his eloquent discourse. Halfway through the talk, the farmer went to sleep. When the preacher finished he went down to meet the farmer.

He said, "I had prepared an excellent sermon and was disappointed when you were the only person to show up, and then you didn't have the courtesy to hear but half of what I had to say. What do you have to say for yourself?"

"Well," said the farmer, "if I had a whole load of hay to feed my sheep and only one showed up, I wouldn't dump the whole load on him!"

A distinguished international columnist was assigned to interview some of the world's leading men. As he went around the world he noticed that several world leaders had a strange, multi-colored phone in their office.

During his interview with the Pope he said, "I've noticed several of the world's leaders have a similar multi-colored phone in their office. Would you mind telling me what it is for?" "Certainly," replied the Pope. "It is a direct line to God. I don't use it very often, though, because it costs about $500 for a 20 minute call."

Some days later as the columnist visited the President of the U.S., he noticed the same multi-color phone. To his surprise, however, he was informed that a 20 minute call cost only $100.

Finally, he visited the Prophet in Salt Lake City, where again he noticed the same multi-colored phone. So he said, "How wonderful that the Mormons, too, can have a direct line to God. Do you mind if I ask approximately how much a 20 minute call would cost?" To his astonishment the Prophet said, "Only 25 cents." "That is very strange," the columnist commented. "The Vatican had a similar phone, but a call cost $500. The White House has to pay $100. Why would it cost you only 25 cents?"

"Well, you see," came the answer, "from Salt Lake City, it's only a local call."

☺☺☺

Manager to Secretary: Mrs. Smith, I have a message of great importance for all employees......Please connect me with the grapevine.

☺☺☺

A Diplomat is a gent who can think twice before he says nothing.

☺☺☺

Eye-level sign for children in toy shop.
"If You See Something You Want, Tell Grandma!"

A guy goes to Las Vegas and loses all of his money except the $20 he had been smart enough to leave in his car to buy gasoline for the trip home. As he is driving out of Las Vegas, all of a sudden, out of the air, he hears a voice say: "Go back, go back."

He figures this is a good omen, so he drives back, walks into a casino and hears the voice say, "Go to the roulette table and put $20 on red." So remembering his sunday school lesson about obeying still, small voices, he puts his last $20 on red, watches the table spin, and wouldn't you know it, he loses his last $20.

As he turns to leave the casino in disgust he hears the voice say, "I'll be darned! How about that?"

(We must learn to listen to the right voice)

Many are probably aware that thoroughbred horse racing has become a very popular sport in the Caribbean. The influx of older tourists from the east has made for big purses on the gambling circuit and everyone is trying to get in on the big money.

One day a poor Jamacan trainer was out walking a beautiful big thoroughbred, when a black limosine stopped and an eastern dude got out and examined his horse. He felt the horses big beautiful muscles and checked his teeth.

Then he said to the Jamacan trainer, "I want to buy your horse!"

"Sorry, mista, Dis hoose, him no looka too good!"

"What do you mean," said the easterner, "he's a beautiful animal. I'll give you two thousand for the horse."

"No thanx, mista, dis here hoose him no looka so good."

"All right," said the buyer. "You strike a hard bargain, here's five thousand for the horse." Well, the old trainer didn't look like he wanted to part with the horse, but the five thousand was too much. So he let the man have the horse and walked away with the five thousand in cash.

Next day the black limosine came screeching up to the barn, the easterner jumped out, grabbed the man by the collar and demanded: "You crook, that horse can't see. You sold me a blind horse."

"Sho nuff, mista, but I warned ya! I said, that hoose him no looka so good!"

Bad news doesn't get any better
When you let it age for a while!

Boats and People both toot the loudest when they are in a fog!

ON UNDERSTANDING LOCAL CONDITIONS

Two men, on a stroll, in the midst of a field
Ascended a knoll, there to face
A cantankerous bull, who snorted and pawed,
And then lowered his head for the chase!

One man found a tree, that provided escape.
He leaped to secure a safe limb.
The other poor fellow, who ran for a cave,
Found the bull's full attention on him!

He ducked in the hole with the bull at his heels;
And imagine his colleague's surprise,
When he darted back out from the safety he'd found,
Again looking the bull in the eyes!

He was in, then back out; then back in, and back out.
An incongruous way to behave.
"Stay in there, you dummy!" the treed colleague yelled.
Then he heard, from the mouth of the cave:

"You don't understand, from your perch there on high,
All the local conditions, I swear!
I know it seems folly to keep running out;
But I'm sharing this cave with a bear!!!"

Ted Hindmarsh

Sign on a fence in the Indiana countryside:

If you cross this field, you had better do it in 9.8 seconds.
The bull can do it in 10!

NO TRESPASSING!

It doesn't take a very brave dog to bark at the bones of a lion.

Salesman: "Do you find that advertising brings quick results?"

Store Owner: "I should say it does. Why, only the other day we advertised for a night watchman, and that night the store was robbed."

An ounce of communication is worth
A pound of preaching.

The Lord's prayer contains 66 words.
Lincoln's Gettysburg Address has 266 words.
The Ten Commandments are presented in just 297 words and
The Declaration of Independence has only 300 words.

An Agriculture Department order setting
The price of cabbage has 26,911 words.

As William Freund has said,
"If the government had given the Ten Commandments,
Moses would have come down,
Not with two tablets,
But with a double hernia."

-From the National Program Letter-

☺☺☺

With some people you can spend an evening --
With others, you invest it.

☺☺☺

"I have a hard time remembering people's names when we're introduced," said the Bishop to the Stake President. "So do I", replied the President, "but I found a clever way to get around the awkwardness of asking them to repeat their name later. I just ask, 'Do you spell your name with an i or an e?' It usually works splendidly." The Bishop thought that sounded great and promised the Stake President to give it a try.

Several weeks later the Stake President was visiting with the Bishop and asked, "How did the new system for learning people's names work?"

"Well, it worked great several times," replied the Bishop, "but then one family I asked if they spelled their name with an i or an e, and they got quite upset and I doubt they will come back soon."

"What was their name."

"Hill"

☺☺☺

I can easier teach twenty what is good to be done;
Than to be one of the twenty to follow mine own teaching.

☺☺☺

True communication has been achieved when
Silence between two people is comfortable.

☺☺☺

Some people are like blisters...
They don't show up until the work is done!

COURTSHIP
and
MARRIAGE

James Hart and the late J. Golden Kimball fell in love with the same girl. Golden Kimball was concerned and took up the matter with one of the Church leaders. It was suggested that he fast and pray.

Months later, Golden met the leader who had advised him, and the latter asked about his affairs. Golden replied, "While I was fasting and praying, James Hart married the girl."

The leader said, "That just proves to us all, that faith without works is dead."

☺☺☺

"I've been asked to marry a thousand times," said the ward young adult representative.
"Oh, who asked you?" said the Bishop.
"My mother and father," she replied.

☺☺☺

Returned Missionary: "You must marry me. I love you. I know there can be no other."
Young Lady: "But I don't love you. You will find some other girl, a beautiful girl."
Returned Missionary: "But can't you understand, I don't want a beautiful girl....I want you!"

☺☺☺

Guest to Best man in a wedding reception line: "Are you the groom?"
Best Man: "No, ma'am. I was eliminated in the semi-finals."

☺☺☺

Sign in the Army Recruiting Office
Marry a veteran, girls.
He can cook, make beds, sew, is in perfect health;
And is already used to taking orders.

☺☺☺

The father cried as the twin daughters selected costly wedding gowns. His wife said, "Honey, don't be sad."

The husband replied, "Darling, I don't mind giving them away in marriage, but must they be so expensively gift-wrapped?"

"I really don't think I'm being too picky," said the pretty young girl to her mother. "All I want is a nice man that loves me and understands me. Is that too much to expect from a millionaire?"

☺☺☺

Sandra: "I hear Roy has finally proposed to you. Did he happen to mention that he proposed to me first?"

Cheryl: "Not specifically. He did say, however, that he had done a lot of foolish things before he met me."

☺☺☺

Young man at a basketball game: "Take a good look at that fellow out there playing center...he'll be our best man before the season's over."

Young coed: "Oh darling, what a wonderful way to propose."

☺☺☺

Love at first sight is easy to understand.
It's when two people have been looking at each other for years
that it becomes a miracle.

☺☺☺

Man can climb the highest mountain,
Swim the widest ocean, fight the strongest tiger,
But once he's married...He mostly takes out the garbage.

☺☺☺

Teenage Daughter: "The man I marry must shine in company, be musical, tell jokes, sing, dance, and stay home at night."

Mother: "You don't want a husband. You want a T.V. set!"

☺☺☺

The movie was sad and the coed sat there with tears streaming down her cheeks. "I'll kiss those tears away," said her date. He did the best he knew how, but the tears still flowed on.

Finally he asked, "Will nothing stop them?" "No," she murmured, "It's hayfever, but please go on with the treatment."

☺☺☺

Grandmother: "Karen, I know you date a lot, but why don't you marry?"

Karen: "I suffer from Bible-itis. Men with their lips draw near unto me, but their hearts are far from me."

A smart girl is one who can hold a man at arm's length
And not lose her grip on him.

☺☺☺

Many years ago, my wife and I were dorm parents at BYU for 120 freshmen co-eds. One day as I walked across the campus, I found a textbook on marriage laying on the sidewalk. Thinking that someone had dropped it while running between classes, I picked it up and opened the cover to see if there was a name. The instructions inside were written in beautiful handwriting:

"If found by person, return in mail;
If found by male, return in person."

Realizing the book hadn't been put there for me, I quietly placed the book back on the sidewalk and walked away.

About five months later I received a wedding invitation from a young couple in our ward. Enclosed in the invitation was a short thank you note, which said:

"Dear Brother Briggs, thanks for putting the book back on the sidewalk, we will be eternally grateful."

☺☺☺

Never kiss behind the gate.
Love is blind but neighbors ain't.

☺☺☺

Lord Halifax, a former foreign secretary of Great Britain, once shared a railway compartment with two prim-looking spinsters. A few moments before reaching his destination, the train passed through a tunnel.

In the utter darkness, Halifax kissed the back of his hand noisily several times. When the train drew into the station, he rose, lifted his hat, and in a gentlemanly way said: "May I thank whichever one of you two ladies I am indebted to for the charming incident in the tunnel."

He then beat a hasty retreat, leaving the two ladies glaring at each other.

☺☺☺

I heard that one of our young people went out on a date the other night. He said to his girlfriend, "If I try to kiss you, will you yell for help? And she said, "Only if you think you need help."

☺☺☺

In the beauty shop on the morning of my wedding I began to fret about the darkening sky and official predictions of rain that afternoon.

The young woman setting my hair exclaimed, "Oh, don't worry. Rain on your wedding day is a sign of good luck. It rained on both of mine."

During the course of his remarks to a group of young people, J. Golden Kimball said "I'm reminded that this is the month of June and that it's mating time. I suppose some of you young folks will be getting hitched up to each other.

I just want to warn you not to expect too darn much of each other, and then maybe you won't be disappointed. Now, when I got married, I thought I was marrying an angel, and many are the times since I wish I had."

☺☺☺

Some select a girl because she has pretty eyes; some because she has pretty hair. I knew a man who chose a girl because she could sing.

He married her, and the next morning, when he saw her without any paint or powder on, and saw a part of her hair on he dresser, he looked at her and said, "Sing, for heavens sake, sing!"

–J. Golden Kimball–

☺☺☺

Juan & Juanita

Juan was a bright young Mexican who was on his way to market. On the trail he met the beautiful Juanita. Now Juanita, who was fond of Juan, was a very fast thinker. Quickly she said, "Juan this is not good that we should meet like this on such a remote trail." When Juan asked why, she quickly said, "Well you might find me attractive and try to steal a kiss."

Now Juan, who was very smart, responded: "I do find you to be very attractive, but don't worry Senorita, I couldn't possibly kiss you because I have a large sack in my one hand, a box of eggs under my arm, two chickens in my other hand and a watermelon under my other arm. I could never kiss you without breaking some of my merchandise and perhaps losing my chickens."

But Juanita, who was also very smart, added: "Oh, you clever fellow. You could put the sack on the ground, place the eggs gently on the sack and hold the watermelon; then, she added, if I held the chickens you could kiss me if you tried."

☺☺☺

A young man went to his Bishop and declared, "I'm never going to marry." When the Bishop inquired as to why, the fellow stated, "The woman I love has just rejected my proposal of marriage."

Now, now, don't let that get you down," said the Bishop, trying to cheer him up. "Many times a woman's 'no' really means 'yes!'" "But Bishop, she didn't say no," stated the young man sadly. "She yelled, 'Phooey.'"

☺☺☺

Alimony is like paying for your car after it has been totaled.

Einstein's Theory of Relativity: When a young man sits on a hot stove, a minute seems like an hour.

But when a beautiful girl sits on that same young man's lap, an hour seems like a minute.

☺☺☺

Daughter to Mother before date: "What is a good word that sounds like 'yes,' but more or less means 'no.'"

☺☺☺

Jolynn: "You shouldn't be discouraged. In this world there's a man for every girl and a girl for every man. You can't improve on an arrangement like that."

Marge: "I don't want to improve on it. I just want to get in on it!"

☺☺☺

Son: "How much does a marriage license cost?"

Father: "Five dollars down and your income for the rest of your life."

☺☺☺

A wedding ring may not be as tight as a tourniquet,
But is should do an equally good job of stopping circulation.

☺☺☺

"If you'll make the toast and pour the juice, sweetheart," said the newlywed bride, "breakfast will be ready."

"Good, what are we having for breakfast," asked the new husband.

"Toast and juice," she replied.

☺☺☺

Marriage is a union of heart, might, mind and soul,
But many a marriage fails when they realize the price of the union dues.

☺☺☺

To prove his love for her, he swam the deepest river,
Crossed the widest desert and climbed the highest mountain.
She divorced him. He was never home.

☺☺☺

The honeymoon is really over when he telephones to say he'll be home late for dinner, and she's already left a note on the table saying it's in the refrigerator.

One night we were working on family photo albums and genealogy. In the box full of old photos we found a picture of a terrible looking ape, swinging from a tree. I ask one of the children to go ask their mother if it was one of her relatives. When the child returned I asked, "What did she say?"

"Yes," the child replied, "she said it was, through marriage."

☺☺☺

"I know my cooking is no good" said the young bride. "I don't like it anymore than you do, but you don't hear me complaining about it, do you?"

☺☺☺

I'm reminded of a young bride who said to her mother on her wedding day, "I'm the happiest girl in all the world because I have come to the end of all my troubles."

The wise mother answered, "Yes dear, you just don't know which end!"
                                    –Hugh B. Brown–

☺☺☺

"Many subjects suggested themselves, but I finally decided to speak upon marriage. Young men, think about it; and young girls, give it at least an occasional thought!"
                                    –David O. McKay–

☺☺☺

A middle–aged couple on the farm had a violent quarrel at breakfast time. Later in the day they started for town in the buggy, with a fine team of horses. As the horses trotted along, Mary said, "John, why can't we travel together like these horses do? They don't quarrel and fight." John said, "Mary, we could if there was only one tongue between us."
                                    –Hugh B. Brown–

☺☺☺

Try this recipe. It's guaranteed to cook up a happy marriage:

1 Cup of Love	5 Spoons of Hope
2 Cups of Loyalty	2 Spoons of Tenderness
3 Cups of Forgiveness	4 Quarts of Faith
1 Cup of Friendship	1 Barrel of Laughter

Take Love and Loyalty, and mix them thoroughly with Faith.
Blend it with Tenderness, Kindness and Understanding.
Add Friendship and Hope. Sprinkle abundantly with Laughter.
Bake it with Sunshine. And serve generous helpings daily.

☺☺☺

LOVE IS A FEELING YOU FEEL WHEN YOU FEEL A FEELING
YOU HAVE NEVER FELT BEFORE!

At our parents' Golden Wedding Anniversary, my father said, "Your mother is just as beautiful today as she was when I married her fifty years ago."

Then with a smile he added, "Naturally, it takes her a little longer than it used to."

George Jean Nathan once said: "The man and woman who can laugh at their love, who can kiss with smiles, and embrace with chuckles, will outlast in mutual affection all the throat-lumpy, cow-eyed couples of their acquaintance. Nothing lives on so fresh and ever-green as the love with a funny bone."

The Bride, white of hair, is stooped over her cane.
Her footsteps, uncertain, need guiding.
While down the Church aisle with a wan, toothless smile,
The groom in a wheelchair comes riding.

And who is this elderly couple thus wed?
You'll find when you've closely explored it.
That here is that rare, most conservative pair,
Who waited 'till they could afford it.

A large crowd of friends and relatives had been called together to celebrate my wife's parents fiftieth wedding anniversary. At the close of the program, a special surprise speaker was called upon to say a few final words.

The surprise speaker was Charlie, the hired man who had worked for the family for forty years and probably knew the couple better than anyone else in the crowd. There were a few snickers and a smattering of light applause as the embarrassed Charlie cleared his throat.

"Well," he said, "all I can say is that you two have kept the faith, fought the good fight, and endured to the end."

The businessman phoned his home and asked, "Hello, honey, would it be all right if I brought home a couple of fellows for dinner tonight?"

"Why, certainly dear," was the reply, "I'd love to have them."

"I'm sorry," the businessman said apologetically after a brief pause, "I must have the wrong number."

Behind every successful man stands a surprised father-in-law.

My wife was washing our car in the driveway one day when a car slowly cruised past. Minutes later the same car drove slowly down our street. Later the car came by again, this time it stopped, she looked up wondering if the driver needed directions.

"Are you married, ma'am?" Asked the driver.
"Why, yes, I am," she replied.
"Too, bad," he exclaimed, shaking his head. "I've always wanted a wife who would wash a car."

☺☺☺

How do you tell a Mormon wedding?
The bride isn't pregnant, but the mother is.

☺☺☺

Wife: Are you going to stay with me when my hair is silver?
Husband: Why not? I've been with you through all of the other colors.

☺☺☺

A young, BYU student buying an engagement ring: "Will you please engrave it, 'To my dearest Claire, from Henry."
Jeweler: "Take my advice, son, just say 'From Henry.'"

☺☺☺

A friend of mine married his secretary. Several months later I met him on the street and asked how things were going.

"Well," he said, "before we were married she was my secretary, now she thinks she is my controller."

☺☺☺

Getting a divorce after 20 years of marriage is like opening
the barn door after the horse is too tired to get out.

☺☺☺

Marriage is like taking a hot bath.
After you've been in it for a while....it isn't so hot.

☺☺☺

Alimony is the billing without the cooing

☺☺☺

Is Chivalry Dead?
Today when a fellow opens the door of a car for his wife,
You can either assume that the car is new
Or the wife is new!

Kissing is a means of getting two people so close together
That they can't see anything wrong with each other.

☺☺☺

Woman to friend: "I got a set of golf clubs for my husband."

Friend: "Gee, I wonder how much I could get for my husband?"

☺☺☺

A judge was interviewing a woman regarding her pending divorce, and asked: "What are the grounds for your divorce?" "About four acres with a nice little home in the middle of the property with a stream running by."

"No," he said, "I mean what is the foundation of this case?"
"It is made of concrete, brick and mortar," she responded.

"I mean," he continued, "What are your relations like?"
"I have an aunt and uncle living here in town, and so do my husband's parents."

He said, "Do you have a real grudge?"
"No," she replied, "we have a two-car carport and have never really needed one."

"Please," he tried again, "is there any infidelity in your marriage?"
"Yes, both my son and daughter have stereo sets. We don't necessarily like the music, but the answer to your question is yes."

"Ma'am, does your husband ever beat you up?"
"Yes," she responded, "about twice a week he gets up earlier than I do."

Finally in frustration, the judge asked, "Lady, why do you want a divorce?"
"Oh, I don't want a divorce." she replied. "I've never wanted a divorce. My husband does. He says that he can't communicate with me."

☺☺☺

"A wholesome sense of humor will be a safety valve that will enable you to apply the lighter touch to heavy problems and to learn some lessons in problem-solving that 'sweat and tears' often fail to dissolve."

–Hugh B. Brown–

☺☺☺

One day at the family reunion, my grandparents were reminiscing. My grandfather remarked, "I wonder what ever happened to the old-fashioned girls who fainted when a man kissed them."

Grandmother gave him a withering look, "What I'd like to know," she said, "is what happened to the old-fashioned men who made them faint!"

Our son Robby loves sports, but isn't to excited about homework. One night as I came home from work Robby was sitting on the couch watching a ballgame. When I asked if he had written his paper for History, he said, "No!".

So I promptly turned the T.V. off and told him he couldn't watch the game until his paper was completed. Several minutes later, I noticed that he had returned to the couch and was watching T.V. Irritated, I turned the T.V. off, which brought from him a major protest. He said, "I've finished my history paper, why can't I watch T.V.?"

Not believing him, I demanded to see the history paper. He gave me a small sheet of paper on which he had written the following masterpiece:

"Benjamin Franklin"

"Benjamin Franklin was born in Boston, but he soon got tired of that and moved to Philadelphia. When he got to Philadelphia he was hungry, so he bought a loaf of bread. He put the bread under his arm.

He walked up the street, and he passed a woman. The woman smiled at him. He married the woman and discovered electricity."

☺☺☺

There is a Russian proverb that says that before going to war, pray once; before going to sea, pray twice; before getting married, pray three times.

☺☺☺

The principle charge made against the Elders was that of inducing young women to go to Utah for polygamous purposes. The only "evidence" adduced in support of this charge was a quotation from one of our Articles of Faith—an adaptation of the well known words of St. Paul: "If there is anything virtuous, lovely, or of good report or praiseworthy, we seek after these things."
                                          –Orson F. Whitney–

☺☺☺

"Oh," said one girl to another, speaking of her two boyfriends, "they're such wonderful boys. If I could only combine their respective qualities, I'd be the happiest girl in the world.

George is strong, handsome, and rich. He's also very witty, and he gets good grades. But it's David who really wants to marry me."

☺☺☺

The most shocked women in the world
Are those who get married because they get tired of working.

☺☺☺

There is one advantage to being a married man.
You can't make a fool of yourself without knowing it.

In an interview, General Mark Clark was asked: "General, what is the best advice you have ever received?"

After pondering the question for a minute, the general replied: "The best advice I've ever had was to marry that wonderful girl that has been my wife and sweetheart for nearly 50 years."

Impressed, the interviewer asked, "If you wouldn't mind sharing it with us General, who gave you that great advice?"
Without hesitation the great general replied, "Oh, she did."

☺☺☺

Our daughter, Jennifer, was concerned about how much money her boyfriend was spending on her each time he took her out.

"Mother," she said, "how can I stop Jerry from spending so much money on me when he takes me out?"

"Marry him!" was my wife's reply.

☺☺☺

My daughter isn't talking to me this week. When I asked her why her boyfriend was majoring in Philosophy, she said it was because he was trying to find himself.

I simply said, "Tell him to look near the refrigerator."

☺☺☺

A young man went out on a date with a young lady and parked his car on a hillside. "May I kiss you?" he asked. And she said, "It's kind of stuffy here in the car. If you could lower the top on your car, then you could kiss me."

He was telling one of his friends about this, and he said, "It took me five whole minutes to get the top down on that car." The friend said "Well, I can take the top down on my car faster than that." To which the young man replied, "Yes, but you have a convertible."

☺☺☺

From a classified ad in the personal section of the Rexburg Journal:

> Farmer looking for wife.
> Have farm. Looking for lady with tractor.
> Please send picture of tractor!

☺☺☺

Before a man gets married, he lies awake in bed all night thinking about what his beloved said.

After they are married, he falls asleep before she has finished saying it.

In a little town in Idaho, a woman went to court seeking a divorce. The judge was shocked to see her. "Why, Hazel, I can't believe it. You and old Harold have always seemed to be such a happily married couple. After 40 years of being together, what in the world makes you want to separate now?"

"Well, Your Honor," came her sad response, "the trouble with Harold is that for the last several years he's been acting more like a husband and less and less like a friend."

☺☺☺

Love may not make the world go round,
But it sure makes the trip worthwhile.

☺☺☺

"Many a man who is a 5-ton truck at the office,
Is nothing but a trailer at home."

☺☺☺

"A man doesn't have to know much about music to learn that he can produce harmony in the home by playing a second fiddle."

☺☺☺

GRATITUDE

She took my hand in sheltered nooks
She took my candy and my books;
She took my lustrous wrap of fur
She took those gloves I bought for her.

She took my words of love and care
She took my flowers; rich and rare.
She took my ring with a tender smile,
She took my time for quite a while.

She took my ardor, maid so shy,
She took I must confess my eye;
And took whatever I could buy --
And then she took another guy.

☺☺☺

Before you flare up at anyone else's faults,
Take time to count to ten -- ten of your own.

☺☺☺

SYMPATHY: Is a plan that enables two hearts to tug at one load.

-C.H. Parkhurst-

"Well ma'am," said the traffic cop to the homely but vivacious Single Adult's representative, "I suppose you know why I stopped you?"

"Don't tell me," she replied with a twinkle in her eye, "Let me guess."

"Ah yes, I know, I bet you're lonely!"

A young man was invited to see his future mother-in-law for the first time. He hesitated briefly when she asked him to try and guess her age. "Surely, you must have some idea?" said his future mother-in-law.

"Oh, I have several ideas," said the young man with a smile, "the only trouble is I hesitate whether to make you ten years younger on account of your good looks, or ten years older on account of your intelligence."

After marraige you soon learn that:
One good turn will generally get you the whole blanket.

Some girls are like bathtubs...
They acquire one ring after another.

We have been married twenty-five years...seems like yesterday.
And you know what a lousy day yesterday was!

In spite of all the talk about marriage becoming extinct with the modern generation, we really have very little to fear.

At the present time there is no other situation in which man and woman can be certain that some one can <u>worry about them</u>, <u>wish them well</u>, and <u>be mad at them at the same time.</u>

Marriage is the first union to successfully defy management!

You've heard that the Church has outlawed waterbeds.
There are too many families drifting apart!

Marriage is the only game -- Where two can play and both can win.

" QUIT TORTURING YOURSELF ELDER. THERE'S NOT
A McDONALDS WITHIN FIVE THOUSAND MILES OF THIS PLACE. "

DIETS, FOODS
and FASHIONS

Time, obviously, is relative. Two weeks on vacation
is not the same as two weeks on a diet!

☺☺☺

One day, a friend of ours who was significantly overweight announced to our group that she was on a new diet. "Oh," I asked, "what kind of a diet is it?"

"A seafood diet," she replied. "I eat all the food I see."

☺☺☺

My wife was having a hard time following her diet until I explained to her that there were at least twenty pounds of her that I wasn't married to.

☺☺☺

Younger brother: "To look at you, a person would think there is a famine in the land."

Older sister: "Yes, and one look at you and they'd think you were the cause of it."

☺☺☺

I decided to go on a diet when my little boy patted my tummy and said, "Dad, is this what the Bishop means by a year's supply?"

☺☺☺

Mom puts it on my plate and says,
"You'll like it, Son, its very good."

And I'm supposed to eat it up--
As if it tasted good.

But if you'd really like to know--
I wish that spinach didn't grow!

☺☺☺

Waiter: "Is your steak tough today, sir?"

Customer: "I don't know. I'm still trying to cut
through the gravy ."

The trouble with bucket seats is that
not everyone has the same size bucket!

☺☺☺

I just joined a new organization of overweight people. They could care less about fancy diets and counting calories. Their motto is:

"A WAIST IS A TERRIBLE THING TO MIND"

☺☺☺

Doctor to patient: "With this diet you can eat anything you like.
Now here is a list of what you are going to like!"

☺☺☺

My wife was asked by an envious friend how she managed to keep her weight down. "I eat very slowly," she replied.

"How does that help?" the friend wanted to know.

"I have two teenage boys," was the answer. "By the time I'm ready for seconds there aren't any!"

☺☺☺

Some Mormons are eating their way to the
Cholesterol Degree of Glory

☺☺☺

Though George Bernard Shaw was a vegetarian, he once turned down an invitation to a vegetarian luncheon with this reply:

"The thought of 2,000 people munching celery at the same time horrifies me."

☺☺☺

Mealtime is the period of the day when the kids sit down
to continue eating.

☺☺☺

Fear less, hope more; eat less, chew more;
whine less, breathe more; talk less, say more;
hate less, love more; and all good things are yours.
–Swedish Proverb–

☺☺☺

The Lord's Advice regarding Diets
"LET YOUR SOUL DELIGHT IN FATNESS."
–2 Nephi 9:51–

There's a new diet that is all the rage.
You can eat all you want of everything you don't like.

☺☺☺

Father-in-law to prospective son-in-law: "You can tell when dinner
is ready; that's when the smoke alarm goes off."

☺☺☺

<u>Sign in Mother's Kitchen</u>
BLESSED ARE THOSE WHO CLEAN-UP!

☺☺☺

An unusually overweight lady was trying to enter the bus. A passenger who
was waiting to get on began to laugh at her efforts.

"If you were half a man, you'd help me get on this bus," snapped the lady.

To which the younger man retorted, "Madam, if you were half a lady, you
wouldn't need any help."

☺☺☺

No man can be wise on an empty stomach.
-George Elliot-

☺☺☺

A resident in a seaside hotel breakfast room called over the headwaiter one
morning and said, "I want two boiled eggs, one of them so undercooked it's
runny, and the other so overcooked, it's about as easy to eat as rubber; also
grilled bacon that has been left on the plate to get cold; burnt toast that
crumbles away as soon as you touch it with a knife; butter straight from the
deep-freeze so that it is impossible to spread; and a pot of very weak coffee,
lukewarm."

"That's a complicated order, sir," said the bewildered headwaiter. "It might be
a bit difficult." "Oh!" replied the guest. "I'm sure you will do your best, that's
exactly what you gave me yesterday."

☺☺☺

The menu of a cannibal restaurant featured: Broiled Missionary, $1.00;
Sauteed Rebel, $2.00; Fried Hippie, $5.00.

When a customer ask why the fried hippie cost so much, the waiter answered,
"Do you realize what it takes to clean one of those up?"

☺☺☺

Life is like a mirror
You can't get more out of it than you put into it!

One year, in the spirit of the original Thanksgiving, we invited two Indians to our Thanksgiving dinner, and I think they enjoyed it. I say "think," because halfway through, one of the Indians looked over the table loaded with a turkey that had been fattened by hormones, vegetables that had been fertilized by chemicals, white bread, refined sugar and cider that had been artificially flavored and processed to retard spoilage.

One Indian looked over all this, turned to the other Indian and whispered, "No wonder they look so pale!"

Welfare is a program where the recipient eats steak and potatoes --
While the donors eat pork and beans.

This being self-sufficient is all right for some folks, but not me. I tried to raise chickens once, had absolutely no luck. Perhaps I planted 'em too deep.

Happiness is like a good homemade jelly.
You can't spread even a little without getting some on yourself.

A man went into the Greasy Spoon to have breakfast and asked for cocoa and toast. The waitress said, "Sorry, we don't have toast." The man said, "That's funny. You have as the special a toasted bacon and tomato sandwich."

She said, "Yeh, but we don't have toast." He said, "O.K., I'll take one bacon and tomato sandwich, but hold the bacon, tomato, lettuce and mayonnaise."

☺☺☺

The forbidden fruit is responsible for many bad jams.

☺☺☺

The indignant young soldier, barely into his basic training, wrote a furious letter to his congressman, detailing all the various indignities and evils to which he was being subjected:

"And the food, sir, I can describe only as slop. I wouldn't feed it to the pigs for fear they would get sick to their stomachs and die of it. It would be rejected by an decent garbage man. And to make matters still worse, they serve such small portions."

☺☺☺

A small boy was refusing to eat. The father, whose temper had grown short, yelled, "Twenty years from now you'll be telling some girl what a great cook your mother was. Now eat your dinner!"

An American Protestant's company moved him to Northern Ireland. He was somewhat concerned when he found the company house was in an all Catholic neighborhood. So he decided, for his safety, he had better change religions. The Friday after his baptism he was barbecuing steak in his back yard. Some of his neighbors looked over the fence to remind him that good Catholics only eat fish on Fridays. Unashamed, the man said, "This is fish."

"Come-on there, me friend," said his neighbor, "I know the difference between steak and fish, and that is steak." "No," said the recently baptized man, "I brought home some holy water from the church, sprinkled it on the steak and said, 'I pronounce you fish.' If a little water converted me from Protestant to Catholic, it will surely make steak into fish!"

☺☺☺

A student, eating in the cafeteria, found that he could not possibly cut his steak, no matter how he tried to jab it. Finally he took it back to the cook and said, "You'll have to take this steak back and get me another piece; I can't even cut it."

After examining the steak closely the chef replied: "Sorry sir, I can't take this back now, you've bent it."

☺☺☺

"It looks like a bad storm coming up," said the hostess to the visiting neighbor. "You had better stay for dinner." "No, thanks," the neighbor said absently. "I don't think it will be that bad."

☺☺☺

There is no sure-fire, guaranteed way to lose weight;
Although living on Social Security comes close.

☺☺☺

Nutritionists have definitely proven that obesity is catching;
You can get it from your knife, fork and spoon.

☺☺☺

Swallow your pride occasionally, it's non-fattening.

☺☺☺

I still have the first two loaves of whole wheat bread my wife ever baked.
I use them for book ends.

☺☺☺

Waiter: "How did you find your steak, sir?"

Young man: "Quite accidentally, I assure you. I moved that piece of lettuce and there it was."

The new primary teacher was carefully explaining the story of Elijah the Prophet and the false prophets of Baal. She explained how Elijah built the altar, put wood upon it, cut the steer in pieces and laid it upon the altar. And then Elijah commanded the people of God to fill four barrels of water and pour it over the altar. He had them do this four times.

"Now," said the primary teacher, "can anyone in the class tell me why the Lord would have Elijah pour water over the steer on the altar?"

A little girl in the back of the room raised her hand with great enthusiasm. "To make the gravy," came her enthusiastic reply.

One day a lady was asked to prepare a ham for the ward picnic. She did a beautiful job. The bishop's wife called her the next morning to get the recipe. The lady explained how she took so much time to fix the pineapple and various condiments to make it very pleasant tasting. "But," she said, "then the most important thing is you must cut one end off."

The bishop's wife asked, "What benefit do you get from cutting the end off?" "I don't know," she replied, "but I do know it is very important. My mother always cut one end off."

Wondering why it was so important to cut one end off, the lady decided to call her mother and ask her. The mother said, "I'm not sure, but I know there was some real benefit in cutting it off because my mother always did it. Your grandmother would enjoy very much a call and I'm sure she would know the answer...so why don't you give her a buzz?" So the lady called her grandmother and asked her why cutting one end of the ham off was so important.

Grandmother just kind of chuckled and said, "I don't know if it has any benefit for the taste, but when I was raising my young family I had to cut the end of the ham off because I never had a pan big enough to hold the whole thing!"

Madison Avenue is where they spend massive amounts of money trying to sell products that "taste homemade" to a generation that doesn't even remember what "homemade" tastes like.

One mother to another: We used to have a year's supply --
Until John came off his mission last week and ate it!

I asked the cook at the Waldorf Astoria once how he made apple pie. "Perfectly," was the reply. "How do <u>you</u> think I do?"

Beauty is only skin deep...but uglyness goes clear to the bone.

Son: "Wow, I must be getting stronger."
Mother: "Why, what makes you think that?"

Son: "A few years ago I couldn't carry $10 worth of groceries, and now it's easy."

☺☺☺

Two women were discussing what they would wear to the Elder's Quorum social. "We're supposed to wear something to match our husband's hair, so I am going to wear something black," said Mrs. Brown.

"What are you going to wear?"

"Goodness," gasped her friend, "if I have to wear something to match my husbands hair, I don't think I'd better go!"

☺☺☺

One year the Elder's Quorum decided to have a Mexican dinner. We invited some non-member friends who had never eaten Mexican food. The evening was delightful with hot chili, tacos, green peppers and other typical Mexican dishes. Our friends seemed to enjoy the party, although the husband didn't eat much.

On the way home I asked: "Well, how did you enjoy the evening?" to which he replied, "You know, I have attended many churches in my day that preached Hellfire and Damnation....but yours is the first church I have ever seen that served it!"

☺☺☺

Today the law requires food packages to describe the content with words like 'Monosodium glutamate, sodium phosphate, sodium citrate, etc."

These are all preservatives. The doctors are not sure about all this stuff, but they say if it kills you, you will be surprised at how long you'll keep.

☺☺☺

I refuse to eat canned vegetables...I eat only fresh garden ones.
At least that way I know what I'm eating: <u>DDT</u>!

☺☺☺

The six-year-old trotted obediently after his grandpa, picking up potatoes. Finally tiring of the whole project he asked, "Grandpa, why did you bury these things anyway?"

☺☺☺

The cafeteria gets its knives sharpened four to five times a week. When the knife sharpener asked why they had their knives sharpened so often, the cafeteria manager whispered, "It's cheaper than buying tender meat."

ACTIVITIES TO BURN CALORIES

Activity	Calories Per Hour
Beating Around the Bush	75
Jumping to Conclusions	100
Swallowing Pride	50
Grasping at Straws	75
Throwing your Weight Around	300
Wading Through Paperwork	300
Running in Circles	350
Dragging Your Heels	100
Making Mountains Out of Molehills	175
Climbing the Ladder of Success	750
Wrapping Up at a Days End	12
Jogging the Memory	125
Climbing the Walls	150
Passing the Buck	25
Beating Your Own Drum	100
Turning the Other Cheek	75
Bending Over Backwards	75
Eating Crow	225
Pushing Your Luck	250
Flying Off the Handle	225
Adding Fuel to the Fire	400
Patting Yourself on the Back	400

–From the REALTOR July 1984–

The sign in a small truck stop read: "We serve all appetites, if we can't serve you the meal of your choice, we'll serve your second choice free!"

Charlie, a faithful customer, tried daily to get a free meal, but every time the owner served his unusual request without hesitation. One day Charlie entered the small diner and with a smile asked for "Elephant trunk on rye."

Thinking he had finally found something the owner didn't have, Charlie laughed out loud. The owner, however, without any hesitation quietly went into the back room. Charlie saw him look frantically in the storage room, then under the counter, in the display and through all the cupboards.

Finally, the owner returned to Charlie's table and said, "Well, Charlie, I hate to admit it, but this time you've finally got me...I'm completely out of rye bread."

The world is full of two kinds of people -- GETTERS AND FRETTERS!

GETTERS build airplanes.
FRETTERS make parachutes.

Salesclerk: "You would be irresistible in this new polka-dot bikini."

Woman: "Well, it is lovely, but I had in mind something with about 30 more dots."

☺☺☺

His wife was in a terrible mood all day and Gordon couldn't think of anything he had said to upset her, so he asked: "What's wrong, sweetheart?" "Oh, that terrible Marilyn Jones next door has a new dress exactly like mine," she sobbed.

"I suppose that means you want me to buy you a new one?" "Well," she grinned slyly, "It's cheaper than moving."

☺☺☺

Once when a girl went out to swim
She was dressed like Mother Hubbard.

Now, she is not so prim;
She's dressed more like her cupboard.

☺☺☺

"That perfume costs $50 an ounce. Here, have a smell of it," said the sales clerk.

"That's lovely," said the lady, "I'll take fifty cents worth."

"Lady," said the clerk, "You've just had fifty cents worth."

☺☺☺

Poise is the quality that enables you to buy a new pair of shoes
While ignoring the hole in your sock.

☺☺☺

A man was stranded in the desert without water. As he crawled across the burning sands, he met a salesman who attempted to sell him a necktie. "You must be crazy," the man rasped. "I'm dying of thirst, and you want to sell me a necktie?"

The salesman shrugged his shoulders and continued on his way. Late in the afternoon, the parched traveler looked up and could hardly believe his eyes. There in the middle of the barren waste was a modern lounge, neon lights and a parking lot filled with cars.

He crawled to the door. "Please, I've got to have something to drink," he said, near collapse. "Sorry," said the doorman. "No one's admitted without a tie."

☺☺☺

People don't wear out... They give up!

A woman who lived in our neighborhood began to have a serious problem with her weight. It seems that every time she opened the refrigerator she simply could not resist eating a snack or drinking another pop. So she went to her doctor for advice.

The doctor suggested that perhaps she needed a role model, someone with a beautiful figure that she could think about whenever she was tempted. So our friend decided to paste inside her refrigerator door, where none of the neighbors would ever see it, a fairly risque picture of a lovely, slender, perfectly built, but scantly clad young woman. This she reasoned would become the constant reminder of the ideal figure to which she would aspire through dieting.

The picture worked like a charm. Every time she opened the refrigerator she looked at the beautiful picture and was able to close the door without taking that extra snack. In one month she lost fifteen pounds. Unfortunately, however, for some unknown reason, her husband gained twenty.

☺☺☺

Money still talks, but it has to catch its breath more often.

☺☺☺

Obesity is a condition which proves that
The Lord does not help those -- who help themselves
and help themselves and help themselves
AND HELP THEMSELVES!

☺☺☺

If you fed your body like you feed your spirit,
Would you be overweight or anorexic?

☺☺☺

Three younger men were looking for another golfer to complete their four-some, when an old man staggered up and ask if he might join them. They were hoping to find some one younger who might be a little more competitive, but not wanting to be rude, they let the older man join them. After the first couple of holes, they realized that although the man was older he could play an excellent game of golf. In fact after the game was over he had the lowest score.

The younger men were amazed and asked the older gentleman, what he felt the main factors were for his fantastic ability to play the game of golf. The older man answered, "I don't really know unless it is the two packs of cigarettes I smoke every day or the two six packs of beer I drink every morning for breakfast."

The younger golfers were stunned. Here appeared to be a living example of proof that the Word of Wisdom wasn't true. "How old are you anyway," asked one of the group. "Oh, I'll be twenty-seven next month," he answered. "Why, do you ask?"

DECISIONS

Boy, I've looked back on my week and what a disaster,
I wish I'd learn how to make a decision faster.

I went to bed Sunday night saying, "No I won't, yes I will,"
But when the alarm went off Monday, I was tired still;
So instead of getting to aerobics for the exercise I need,
I laid there in bed being very lazy indeed.

Tuesday I went to pick up a prescription--
Passed the candy counter with much temptation;
I hummed and I hawed at whether or not to indulge
Knowing full well it would not help my bulge;
But since I couldn't decide which one I liked best
I bought two candy bars, eating them both with great zest.

Wednesday, I had so much ironing to do,
I also needed to clean out a closet or two;
My yard needed attention and my house was a mess;
Deciding what to do first, just put me in distress.
Soon the day was over and nothing was done;
Wish I'd made a decision to do at least one!

Thursday I went shopping, had so many gifts to buy,
But didn't come home with anything and do you know why?
I couldn't decide on how much money to spend
For a birthday gift I needed to send.
I found several things, but they cost fifty cents or more
Than what I bought last week to send Aunt Lenore.

Friday was here and Kay said, "Let's go out to dinner."
Now, what place, I thought, would be a real winner.
Do I want Chinese food, pizza, seafood or steak;
And of course, I wanted some place that had good cheese cake.

Well, it took an hour to decide and we couldn't agree
So we stayed home and had soup and sandwiches you see.

Well, by Saturday I wasn't in too good a mood,
And to my family and friends I was really quite rude.
Unfortunately it hadn't been a week of precision
Simply because I couldn't seem to make a decision.

"Alot of what passes for depression these days is nothing more than
the body saying that it needs work.
-Geoffrey Worman-

"Your imagination is your preview of life's coming attractions."
-Albert Einstein-

"DEAR JOURNAL... MY FIRST DAY IN SCHOOL. MY ROOMMATE .APPEARS TO BE A TRAVEL BROCHURE FOR SODOM & GOMORRAH.."

EDUCATION

I'm your new PTA president.
It was a hard fought campaign, but I lost anyway.

☺☺☺

The Board of Education has determined how to keep pornography out of the hands of teenagers: "Put it in the textbooks--They'll never find it there!"

☺☺☺

Many college students look at college as
little more than a four year LOAF made out of daddy's DOUGH.

☺☺☺

I have always promised my children $5 for every "A" grade they get on their report cards. Last year my teenage daughter smiled at me when she came home with her report card and said: "Dad, I've got great news for you." Hoping for the best, I smiled and asked "What is it?"

"Remember you promised me $5.00 for every "A" I got in school this year?" I nodded. "Well, dad," she smiled, "I'm not going to cost you a cent this year."

☺☺☺

Question on History quiz: "What is a minuteman?"

Answer: "A minuteman is anybody who can get to the bathroom and back during a commercial."

☺☺☺

On what do you BIAS your opinion?

☺☺☺

The absent-minded professor told the class he was going to show them how to properly dissect a frog. So he reached in his pocket, but to his surprise pulled out a sandwich. "That's funny," he said, "I know I ate my lunch."

☺☺☺

My son WILL go to college! I want him to start
out in life with the same handicap the other boys have.

☺☺☺

Education is what remains when we have forgotten
All that we have been taught.

In high school I could never seem to please my English teacher. She normally would return a paper with more written in red than what I had written. The most humiliating one, however, was the one which she returned with these simple words written in bold letters along the top: "I'm returning this paper--someone wrote on it."

Friend: "What's your son going to be when he finally gets out of college?"
Father: "An old man."

A mother mouse was out for a walk with her five babies when a big cat suddenly jumped up right in front of them. The little ones hid behind their mother who stood her ground and began to bark loudly: "Arf! Arf!"

This frightened the cat, who suspecting a dog nearby, turned and fled. Turning to her offspring, the mother mouse said: "Now children, that should teach you the value of knowing a second language."

This is the time of year when college graduates move
into that in-between stage of life:
Too old to go to summer camp and too young to retire.

The trouble with some people today is that they are educated beyond their intelligence.

Giving an apple to a teacher is a good thing for three people. For the grocer, it's business. For the student, it's goodwill. And for the teacher, it's dinner.

College becomes the only vacation a guy gets between
his mother and his wife.

A woman went into her son's bedroom and said, "Come on now. It's time to get up. It's time to go to school." Her son pulled the covers over his head and groaned, "I won't...I won't go...I hate school!"

Mother said: "You have to go. It's important." He stuck his head out from under the covers and said, "Yeah? Just give me two important reasons for going to school."

His mother's reply was: "First, you're forty-two years old. Second, you're the principal."

While teaching college, a professor friend of mine found himself with quite a bit of free time, since he only taught four classes a week. To fill his spare minutes, he became involved with golf, little league soccer and other community activities.

When his time for a sabbatical came, he decided to work a year in industry to gain some practical experience. After his first week or so on the job, he stopped in to see me. When I asked how he enjoyed his job, he simply shrugged his shoulders and said: "Well, I'll tell you, working sure puts a dent in your day."

☺☺☺

A good education has its drawbacks. In grade school, I was told if I wanted a good job I had to graduate from high school. In high school, they told me that the good jobs went to those who graduated from college. When I was about to graduate, I found that everyone had a simple bachelors degree. The really good jobs were reserved for those with a masters degree. So I got my masters.

Then my advisor assured me that a masters degree would be limited, the real top positions were reserved for those with a Ph D. So I got my doctorate and went out to look for that ultimate of all jobs...only to be told that they were looking for younger men.

☺☺☺

Nowadays, when a boy is accepted by a college,
He can't tell whether they liked his test scores
Or his father's credit rating.

☺☺☺

A hunter went out one day looking for a bear, so he could make him a new fur coat. He finally found a huge old hungry bear and took aim to shoot. Now, this bear was no ordinary backwoods bear; when he saw his predicament, he quickly held up his paw and said: "Let's reason this out together. All you want is a nice fur coat, and all I want is something to eat. If we sat down for a moment, I'm sure both of us could meet our goals."

Well, the hunter, who had been trained how to set goals in the Masters of Business program at BYU, said, "That sounds reasonable; what's your plan?" "Well, said the bear, "let's sit here together for a moment and discuss the alternatives." So the hunter put his gun down against the tree; and sure enough, within minutes both had met their goals: The hunter had a new fur coat and the bear had a full stomach.

☺☺☺

Early to bed, early to rise,
Until you've learned and earned enough to do otherwise.

☺☺☺

University professor to friend: "I view my son as a child of the universe -- so far, no signs of intelligent life."

Sumerset Maugham, the English writer, once wrote a story about a janitor at St. Peter's Church in London. One day a young vicar discovered that the janitor was illiterate. Not wanting an illiterate employee on the staff, he fired him.

Jobless, the man invested his meager savings in a tiny tobacco shop, where he prospered, bought another, expanded, and ended up with the chain of tobacco stores worth several hundred thousand dollars.

One day the man's banker said, "You've done well for an illiterate, but where would you be if you could read and write?" "Well," replied the man, "I guess, I'd still be the janitor of St. Peter's Church in Neville Square."

☺☺☺

A high school teacher displayed the following notice on the bulletin board:
FREE...Every Monday through Friday: KNOWLEDGE
--please bring your own containers.

☺☺☺

We sympathize with the teacher who wrote a note to her pupil's parents that read like this:

"If you won't believe everything your child says happened at school,
I won't believe everything your child says happened at home."

☺☺☺

Father: Well, dear, how are your marks this year in college?
Daughter: Under water.
Father: What do you mean "under water?"
Daughter; They are all below "C" level.

☺☺☺

As any parent with a kid in college already knows:
A little learning is an expensive thing.

☺☺☺

One day a recruiter from Exxon visited the BYU campus. He looked at the new construction of at least a half dozen buildings. He inspected the labs in the engineering and chemistry departments. He watched a class in the modern study rooms. He walked across the miles of neatly trimmed lawns and athletic fields with the Dean of the College of Business. He was impressed. "My," he said, "How many students do you have here?"

"Let me see," the Dean of Business, answered thoughtfully. "I'd say about one in every hundred."

☺☺☺

Professor: "This exam will be conducted on the Honor System.
Please seat yourselves three desks apart and in alternating rows."

A college student called home late at night. When his father answered the phone, the boy said: "Hi, Dad. Did I wake you up?" "No," replied the father. "Why? Do you want to call back later?"

☺☺☺

The one thing most of us do better than anyone else is
read our own writing.

☺☺☺

In the computer room of one large corporation, a glass case is mounted on the wall next to the company's enormous new computer. Inside the case is an abacus, an ancient form of calculator. On the case is a sign that reads:

"IN CASE OF EMERGENCY, BREAK GLASS."

☺☺☺

A man attending his twentieth class reunion stopped in to see one of his old professors. While chatting about old times, he idly picked up an exam on the professor's desk and examined it.

"This is surprising," he said. "Many of the questions on this paper are the same ones I had in my final examination twenty years ago. I would have thought they'd be different by now." "No," said the professor, "the questions change very little over the years. It's the answers that change."

☺☺☺

A man bought a new gadget--unassembled, of course, and after reading and rereading the instructions he still couldn't figure out how it went together. Finally, he sought the help of an old handyman who was working in the back yard. The old fellow picked up the pieces, studied them, then began assembling the gadget. In a short time he had it all put together.

"That's amazing," said the man, "and you did it without even looking at the instructions." "Fact is," said the old man, "I can't read, and when a fellow can't read, he's got to think."

☺☺☺

Landlord: You didn't pay the rent last month.
Student: No. Well, I suppose you'll hold me to your agreement.
Landlord: Agreement, what agreement?
Student: Why, when I rented from you, you said I must pay in advance
　　　　　or not at all.

☺☺☺

A photographer had been hired to take a picture of a man and his college age son. The photographer suggested that the boy stand with his hand on his father's shoulder. It would be more appropriate said the long-suffering parent, if he stood with his hands in my pocket.

126

The clerk in the campus bookstore told the incoming freshman student, "This book will do half of your work for you."

"That's great," said the freshman. "I'll take two of them."

☺☺☺

Two first graders were standing outside their school one morning. "Do you think," said one, "that rocket ships will ever pierce the speed of light barrier?" "No," said the second, "the stratosphere is so dense that they would burn." Just then the bell rang.

"There goes the bell," the first one replied. "Now we've got to go in and stack alphabet blocks."

☺☺☺

The story is told of a number of good spirits who requested admission to the Celestial kingdom. St. Peter inquired of the first, "Who's there?" "It's me, Albert Jones," the voice replied. And St. Peter bade him enter.

Another knock, again the same question. "Who's there?" Another answer, "It's me, Charlie Jones." And St. Peter bade him enter. Finally there came a sharp rap. "Who's there," demanded St. Peter.

"It is I, Verla Chapman," a voice replied. "Oh, boy," whispered St. Peter. "Another one of those English teachers."

☺☺☺

The world's smartest man found himself with the President of the United States, a preacher and a hippie on a plane doomed to crash. On board were only three parachutes.

The President took one, saying it was his responsibility to the American people to survive. The world's smartest man stepped up, claiming he was an irreplaceable asset to humanity and jumped.

The preacher stepped up and said, "I have lived a good life and now it is in God's hands. Then he turned to the hippie and offered, "Son, you take the last parachute, you've still got a long life to live." "No problem," said the hippie. "We've both got chutes. The world's smartest man just jumped out with my knapsack."

☺☺☺

When our oldest son came home from his first day in school, his mother asked him if he had learned very much that day, to which Jeff replied, "Nah, I got to go back again tomorrow."

☺☺☺

In our new dormitory you can hang a picture and ask the neighbor to flatten out the nail when it comes through.

There's one young man who didn't go to college this fall. Last spring he asked his parents to give him the money it would cost to send him. They did, and he retired on it.

☺☺☺

Two college students were trying to be fair about how they spent their time one evening. So they decided to flip a coin.

"If it's heads we'll go to the movies; if it's tails we'll go see if there are any new girls in the dorms; and if it stands on edge, we'll study."

☺☺☺

"Permit me to congratulate you on the miracles you have performed at the university," remarked an educator. "Since you became President, BYU has become a storehouse of knowledge."

"That's true," laughed the President, "but I scarcely deserve the credit for that. It's simply that the freshmen bring so much knowledge in, and the seniors take so little out."

☺☺☺

Don't fail to get a good education while you're young. It will come in handy when you have to help with your children's home work.

☺☺☺

The more we study, the more we know.
The more we know, the more we forget.

The more we forget, the less we know.
The less we know, the less we forget.

The less we forget, the more we know.
So why study?

☺☺☺

In an exam just prior to the Christmas break, one of the questions was: "What causes depression?"

One of the students in a hurry to get home wrote: "God knows! I don't. Merry Christmas!"

The test paper came back with the following notation from the professor: "God gets 100. You get Zero. Happy New Year!"

☺☺☺

Sign under classroom clock
Time will pass. . .
Will you?

The new family in the neighborhood overslept and the six year old daughter missed her school bus. The father, though late for work, agreed to drive her if she'd direct him to the school.

They rode several blocks before she told him to turn the first time, several more before she indicated another turn. This went on for 20 minutes--yet when they finally reached the school, it proved to be only a short distance from their home.

Asked why she'd led the father over such a circuitous route, the child explained, "That's the way the school bus goes, and it's the only way I know."

☺☺☺

A college English professor wrote the words "Woman without her man is a savage" on the blackboard and directed his students to punctuate it correctly.

The males wrote: "Woman, without her man, is a savage."

The females wrote: "Woman! Without her, man is a savage."

☺☺☺

George Bernard Shaw had a great deal of dislike for the English language. He once stated that anyone with any knowledge of English would know the word "fish" should obviously be spelled "G-H-O-T-I" -- "Ghoti."

In "enough" the "F" sound is spelled with "GH";
"O" becomes "I" in "women;"
and the "SH" blend is spelled "TI" in the word "nation."

☺☺☺

The trouble with Man is twofold

He cannot learn truths which are too complicated;
And he forgets truths which are too simple.

☺☺☺

Harvey, a balding dairy farmer who always wore bib overalls and rubber boots, decided to go to a big Salt Lake City bank for a loan to expand his dairy business. He was sitting outside the loan officer's office when an elegantly dressed young man sat down and asked if Harvey was a dairy farmer.

"Yes, how did you know?" Harvey asked.

"You have manure on your boots," the man answered.

So Harvey asked the man if he had attended Harvard. The man smiled smartly and said, "Yes, how did you know?"

"Oh," Harvey replied, "I saw your nice ring when you picked your nose."

"I had rather have a fool make me merry
Than experience make me sad."

-William Shakespeare-

☺☺☺

A former President of Yale University some years ago gave the following advice to the new President of BYU.

"Be kind to your A and B students. Someday one of them will return to your campus as a good professor. But most of all remember to be good to your C students. Someday, one of them will return and build you a ten-million-dollar science laboratory."

☺☺☺

At a certain college the trustees decided to hire the wives of faculty members, as these women often were well qualified and available at minimum salaries.

The plan worked very well for a while. Then they began having trouble with pregnancies. The expectant wives all wanted to teach right up to the date of delivery. This made faculty planning most difficult.

So the board of trustees passed a rule. All wives were required to stand facing a wall with their toes touching the baseboard. If they could stand erect without their tummies touching the wall, the could go on teaching.

The wives accepted the rule, but insisted that it must apply to male faculty members as well.

Their point was well taken, for when the trustees put the men to the test, they lost five professors and three department heads!

☺☺☺

The boss handed the new employee a broom. "Sweep up that mess on the floor," he commanded.

"But sir," objected the employee, "I'm a college graduate."

"Oh," replied the employer, "in that case; I guess I'll have to show you how to do it."

☺☺☺

A graduate from the state agricultural college looked over the farmer's field and criticized his methods of farming.

"Why, I'll be surprised if you get ten tons of beets from this field this season," commented the young graduate.

"So would I," responded the irate farmer, "That's a potato field!"

ALL I EVER REALLY NEEDED TO KNOW
I LEARNED IN KINDERGARTEN

Most of what I really need to know about how to live and what to do, and how to be, I learned in kindergarten. Wisdom was not at the top of the graduate school mountain, but there in the sandbox at nursery school. These are the things I learned: Share everything. Play fair. Don't hit people. Put things back where you found them. Clean up your own mess. Don't take things that aren't yours. Say you're sorry when you hurt somebody. Wash your hands before you eat. Flush. Warm cookies and cold milk are good for you. Live a balanced life. Learn some and think some and draw and paint and sing and dance and play and work every day some.

Take a nap every afternoon. When you go out into the world, watch for traffic, hold hands and stick together. Be aware of wonder. Remember the little seed in the plastic cup. The roots go down and the plant goes up and nobody really knows how or why, but we are all like that. Goldfish and hamsters and white mice and even the little seed in the plastic cup--they all die. So do we.

And then remember the book about Dick and Jane and the first word you learned, the biggest word of all: LOOK. Everything you need to know is in there somewhere. The Golden Rule and love and basic sanitation. Ecology and politics and sane living.

Think of what a better world it would be if we all--the whole world--had cookies and milk about 3 o'clock every afternoon and then lay down with our blankets for a nap. Or if we had a basic policy in our nation and other nations to always put things back where we found them and cleaned up our own messes. And it is still true, no matter how old you are, when you go out into the world, it is best to hold hands and stick together.
                                                          -Robert Fulghum-

FAILURE IS NEVER FATAL AND SUCCESS IS NEVER FINAL!

PABLO PICASSO (1881-1973) Spanish Painter
Picasso could barely read or write at age 10 and he was considered a "hopeless pupil" because he refused to learn mathematics.

SIR WINSTON CHURCHILL (1874-1965) British Statesman
Churchill's father considered his son so "dull" that he doubted whether he could ever earn a living. He failed entrance exams to Sandhurst twice.

THOMAS EDISON (1847-1931) U.S. Inventor
Edison's teachers described him as "addled," his father thought he was a "dunce," and his headmasters warned that Edison "would never make a success of anything."

ALBERT EINSTEIN (1879-1955) German Physicist
Einstein spoke haltingly until he was nine and after that responded to questions only after much deliberation. His poor performance in all classes except math prompted a teacher to ask him to drop out of school, telling him he'd never amount to anything. He failed his first college entrance exams.

OH, MY ACHING BACCALAUREATE

The month of June approaches,
    And soon across the land
The graduation speakers
    Will tell us where we stand.

We stand at Armageddon,
    In the vanguard of the press;
We're standing at the crossroads,
    At the gateway to success.

We stand upon the threshold
    Of careers all brightly lit.
In the midst of all this standing,
    We sit and sit and sit.

             –Laurence Eisenlohr–

☺☺☺

Your graduation represents many years of hardwork, frustration, and agony.
Thank goodness your teachers have lived through it!

☺☺☺

It is not half as important to burn the midnight oil,
    As it is to be awake in the daytime!

☺☺☺

There is just one discouraging thing about the rules of success..
    They don't work unless we do!

☺☺☺

One generation plants the trees
    Another gets the shade.

☺☺☺

If the right side of the brain controls the left side of the body, and the left
side of the brain controls the right side of the body, does that mean then that
those of us who are left handed are the only ones in our right mind?

☺☺☺

Do you get the feeling that kids today are getting a Teflon Education?
    Nothing Sticks!!!

☺☺☺

If you consider education to be expensive,
    Try ignorance!

"YEAH, MY FOUR GENERATIONS CHART LOOKS JUST LIKE THAT ONE. BUT IT'S NOT CLUTTERED UP WITH ALL THOSE WORDS AND NUMBERS."

GENEALOGY

He who said "The past cannot be changed," had not yet written his personal history.

☺☺☺

One seldom worries about heredity before marriage...they wait until they need someone to blame for their teenager's actions.

☺☺☺

It is amazing how the teenage boy who was not good enough to marry your daughter, can become the father of the most wonderful grandchildren in the whole world.

☺☺☺

The courtroom drama was at the height of excitement. The accused murderer's life hung on the testimony of the last witness. The beautiful young lady squirmed uncomfortably under the cross-examination of the lawyer.

"Listen closely, Miss," the lawyer shouted. "For the fourth and last time, Where were you on the night of February 14, 1985?"
"Oh, I-I cannot tell you," she sobbed.
"But, Miss," the judge said, "you must tell us!"
"All right. I-I was home doing my genealogy."

After a pause, the lawyer asked, "Why were you ashamed of that?"
"Oh, it's terrible," she sobbed. "A young girl like me, wasting Valentine's night at home alone, doing my genealogy."

☺☺☺

"I don't mind you helping me look up my family tree," she said.
"Just don't get any wise ideas about starting any new branches."

☺☺☺

"I understand you Mormons are very proud of your ancestry," said Arthur Haley to the clerk at the entrance of the Genealogical Library. "Oh yes," said the clerk happily. "We can trace our ancestors back to...to, well, I don't know exactly who, but we've been descending for centuries."

☺☺☺

I understand that the wives of Brigham Young were quite financially astute. At least history records that one evening they met in the Lion House to discuss a "Prophet Sharing Plan."

"Oh, what a terrible thing," remarked the genealogist. "The Smith family employed me to look up their family tree, and now I've gotten to the point where one of the relatives was actually a criminal. After spending many years on death row he was finally electrocuted."

"Oh, don't worry about that," said one of the older gentlemen who had been doing genealogy for people for many years. "Just write that the relative in question had occupied a chair of applied electronics at one of our states finest public institutions."

☺☺☺

I write down everything I want to remember. That way, instead of spending a lot of time trying to remember what it is I wrote down, I spend the time looking for the paper I wrote it down on.

☺☺☺

An old Swede told this story: "I was born twins. My brother died and somehow the records got mixed up. Now, I don't know if I'm Hans what's livin' or Jacob what's dead."

☺☺☺

If you could see your ancestors all standing in a row, there might be some among them that you wouldn't want to know. But here's another thought that commands a different view, if you could see your ancestors, would they be proud of you?

☺☺☺

Three wise monkeys sitting in a tree, discussing things as they're said to be. Says one to the other, "Now, listen, you monk, there's a rumor 'round that can't be true, that man descended from me and you.

What an idea, what a disgrace! No monk ever deserted his wife, starved her baby or ruined its life. And you've never known a mother monk to leave her baby with others to bunk. Or pass him on from one to another till he hardly knows who's his mother.

Another thing--you'll never see a monk who'll build a fence 'round a tree and let the coconuts go to waste, forbidding others a taste. And here's a thing a monk won't do: Use a gun or club or knife to take some other monk's life.

Yes! Man descended, the ornery cuss, but, brother, he didn't descend from us!"

☺☺☺

When I visited my mother last summer, I noticed that when she went to work in the temple on Tuesday and Thursday, she would always leave the Ensign by her favorite plant. When I asked her why, she replied very seriously:

"Plants grow better when you talk to them. Now that I work in the temple, I can't chat with them during the day, so I just leave them something good to read."

When the Mormon Bishop went to heaven, St. Peter gave him a Volkswagen for his personal use. The Bishop noticed, however, that the Catholic Priest had a Cadillac. When he complained, St. Peter explained that the Priest had lived his life on earth without a wife or family and, therefore, he was entitled to a luxury car in heaven. The Bishop, who accepted the fact that his family was more important than a luxury car, said he understood, and went on his way.

Several days later the Bishop noticed the Jewish Rabbi driving a Mercedes Benz sports car. He rushed up to St. Peter and said, "I understood when the Catholic Priest received a Cadillac, because he gave up a wife and family. But what about the Rabbi, he had a wife and children."

"True," said St. Peter. "But remember––he's a relative of the boss."

Young wife to her mother: "Oh, yes, things are much smoother here now that George has found the mistake in his genealogy that would have proven the theory of evolution."

Mark Twain: I spent $25 to research my family background, but once I found out who I descended from, it took $50 to cover it up.

A young fellow came rushing into the genealogical research offices requesting to see the chief genealogist right away.
"What's the problem?" inquired the researcher.

"I'm working on our family charts," he pleaded, "and it's driving me half crazy. Nobody was ever so mixed up. I need help and need it desperately."
"Let's see what you have written there," responded the sympathetic genealogist. This is what he read:

"I met a young widow with a grown-up stepdaughter and I married the widow. Then my father married our stepdaughter. That made my wife the mother-in-law of her father-in-law and made my stepdaughter my stepmother and my father became my stepson.

Then my stepmother, the stepdaughter of my wife, had a son. That child was my brother, as he was the son of my father, but he was also the son of my wife's stepdaughter, and therefore her grandson. Then my wife had a son, my nephew and my father's brother-in law.

The stepsister of my son is also his grandmother, because he is her stepson's child. My father is the brother-in-law of my child because the stepsister is my father's wife. I am the brother of my own son, who is also the child of my grandmother.

So I am my mother's son-in-law, my wife's child's uncle; my son is my father's brother, and I am my own grandfather.

"Now, let's see you put that down on a family group sheet!"

THOSE WHO MARRIED IN

Some ten or fifteen years ago
At a meeting of the Kin
Of my Hubby's ancestral family,
And those who'd married in,

I called attention to the fact
That for more than twenty years
I'd been listening to 'em whoop 'er up
With loud and noisy cheers--

About "Old Whiskers This or That",
And "Aunt Ellen", too,
The Wonders that they did and thought
And never failed to do.

But, with all their noisy cheerin'
About their kith and kin--
There never was a word of praise
For us who'd married in.

They didn't recognize the fact
That we brought in new life,
With every outside husband,
Or new and blushing wife.

They didn't know that long, long since
Their tribe would've faded thin
Except for those of us who'd had
The nerve to marry in.

We didn't often call it "nerve",
We often thought it love,
And had high-falutin' ideas
About the "powers" above--

But the family was the gainer
However it was done,
For new and outside breeding
Improved them--every one.

And so, at these here meetins'
My purpose is to say,
To those of you who've joined us
In any legal way,

We bid you welcome, one and all;
We hope you are as happy
As any other critter--with a
Hal er Del er Chuck as Pappy--

Er Kay er Lee er Lynn
Where e'er you trace your kin,
You really are a part of us
When you have married in.

And, if you came as strangers,
We too were strange to you;
We both had many things to get
Ourselves accustomed to.

To do it any different in this
    world of strife and sin--
You yet are of the Family--
For you have married in.

And we must all go forward
Not worshiping the past,
But building for the future
In worthwhile things that last.

Upon the old foundations
That have always been secure,
Of faith and hope and tolerance;
These things are always sure.

And we all will blend together
In a large and larger clan,
And be a mighty people,
So that any girl or man

May point with pride, and shout aloud,
Above the noisy din--
    "I am a Briggs!!!
    For I have married in."

-Written by J. P. Elder, adapted by the Briggs-

"Dad, what are ancestors?"
"Well, son, I'm one of your ancestors and so is your grandpa."

"Really, then why is it that people brag about them?"

It has been told that Brigham Young had lunch with a prominent Englishman noted for boasting of his ancestry. Taking a coin from his pocket, the Englishman said: "My great grandfather was made a lord by the king whose picture you see on this shilling."

"Indeed!" replied President Young smiling, as he produced an indian head penny from his pocket. "What a coincidence! My great grandfather was made an angel by the Indian whose picture you see on this penny."

Two old southern share croppers were rocking on the porch, discussing their genealogy.

"Yes, suh, man," said Ambrose, "I can trace my relations back to a family tree?"

"Chase 'em back to a family tree?" questioned Mose.

"Nah, man -- trace, not chase, trace 'em -- understand?"

"Well," said Mose, "they ain't but two kinds of things dat live in trees -- birds and monkeys -- and you sho' ain't got no feathers."

"One of my ancestors," a Mormon boasted to a Jew, "signed the Declaration of Independence."

"Congratulations, indeed," replied the Jew, "one of mine signed the Ten Commandments."

A Bishop, who was obsessed with genealogy, was asked by a large company to recommend a certain man for a job. The Bishop wrote back the following recommendation:

"Mr. Blank is an excellent young man. He is the son of Major Blank, the grandson of General Blank, the cousin of Sir Henry Blank, the nephew of Lord Blank, and he is otherwise well related."

The large company wrote back: "Thank you very much for your letter of recommendation concerning Mr. Blank. But we must point out that we are considering him for clerical work -- not breeding purposes."

"DON'T GIVE ME THAT. THE SACRED GROVE IS IN NEW YORK."

HOLIDAYS
TRAVEL
VACATIONS

The Relief Society President returned to Priesthood Executive Council after her vacation looking tired and haggard.

"What's the matter," asked the Bishop, "vacation too much for you?"

"I guess so," she replied, "with the kids taking vitamins and me taking tranquilizers it was a losing battle all the way."

Famous last words for Vacationers

"No, I didn't lock the back door. I thought you did."

"Don't worry about it. When it shows empty, there are at least two gallons left."

"So what if it's a nice restaurant? In this town they wear bathing suits everywhere. Besides what are they gonna do? Throw us out?"

"I don't care what the sign said. We don't get off until the next exit."

"Who needs sun block? I never burn!"

"How far to the next Rest Stop? 35 miles; why?"

Christmas is that magic time of year
When the year runs out,
The neighbors run in,
The batteries run down
And the bills run up!

My wife is the subtle type. This morning she told me that I really don't have to shop early for her Christmas present because -- Diamonds are forever.

On New Year's Eve, at the stroke of midnight, you're supposed to lean over and kiss the one you love most. With some, it's a husband; with others, it's a wife; with still others, it's a mirror.

☺☺☺

I went on a vacation for a change and a rest.
You know what? It worked!

The waiters got the change
And the travel agent got the rest.

☺☺☺

During a visit to the Holy Land, the guide explained how the country stretched from Dan to Beersheba. My wife, expressing some surprise, said to the lecturer,

"I didn't realize Dan and Beersheba were places. I always that they were man and wife, like Sodom and Gomorrah."

☺☺☺

Tourist: "What on earth did you put in your mattresses?"
Innkeeper: "Only the very finest straw, sir."
Tourist: "Well, at least now I know where the straw that broke the camel's back came from."

☺☺☺

"What state do you think Adam and Eve came from?" asked the Utahn. "Oh, there's no doubt they were from Utah," replied the Californian.

"They had nothing to wear, nothing to eat but an apple, and still thought they lived in Paradise!"

☺☺☺

Have you noticed how hypocritical people get about winter? They say the cold weather is good for you---it's healthy, invigorating, the best time of the year.

I'll believe all that nonsense, when they start running luxury winter cruises to Rexburg, Idaho.

☺☺☺

A businessman in Kansas City walked into a travel bureau. "I would like to make reservations for a trip around the world," he told the newly hired clerk.

"Yes, sir," replied the clerk cheerfully. "Will that be round trip or one way?"

☺☺☺

"All our visitors are welcome...
Some more than others."

141

When we went to Europe for a summer vacation, we took Luftansa, the German airline. About two hours out of New York, somewhere over the Atlantic Ocean, the plane developed engine trouble. The pilot spoke over the speaker system in a heavy German accent:

"Dis es your pilot, ve are havin' serious engine trouble. Ve are goin to 'ave to ditch de aeroplane. But don't vorry, der es an island on de right side of de aeroplane. Dows of you who can svimm, get on de right side of de aeroplane. Dows of you who can not svimm, get on de left 'and side of de aeroplane.

"Vhen ve hit the vater, dows of you on de right side of the aeroplane, jump out de vindow and svimm like mad for de island. Dows of you on de left side of de aeroplane...

(Pause) Ve vould like to thank you for flying Luftansa."

☺☺☺

Older Couple at Ticket Counter at Airport: Husband: "Is it at all possible to get two seats that are not together?"

☺☺☺

Mark Twain said, "The coldest winter I ever spent was the summer I spent in San Francisco." I would like to say, "The coldest winter I ever spent was the summer I went to Ricks College." I'm told Rexburg is blessed with a beautiful summer. Unfortunately, I've always been out of town that day.

☺☺☺

Every year it takes less time to fly around the world
And more time to get to work.

☺☺☺

An executive who had recently hired an English secretary went on a business trip to London. While away, a salesman who had never spoken to the new secretary, made one of his periodic calls to the executive's office.

"Mr. Allen is in the United Kingdom," the secretary told him. The salesman was shocked. "I'm terribly sorry," he said. "Is it too late to send flowers?"

☺☺☺

Family vacations are an educational experience. One of the first things you learn when taking your family to an exclusive, sophisticated, elegant restaurant is---that it's always the child with the loudest voice who has to go to the bathroom.

☺☺☺

NEW YEAR'S RESOLUTION

Make today as perfect as I can, and tomorrow will take care of itself, and yesterday will be another memorable event.

<u>Summer Vacation Advice:</u>
Take half the clothes you figured on--
And twice the money!

☺☺☺

Little Danny stayed with us while his parents took a second honeymoon to the Bahamas. To see if he understood what his parents were doing, I asked:

"Where are your mommy and daddy?" Without hesitation he replied: "They're vacationing in their Pajamas!"

☺☺☺

The Jet Age can be defined as a Lunch in London,
Dinner in Paris
And Baggage in Rome.

☺☺☺

Bargaining or haggling with street salesmen in certain countries is an old and ancient art, for both buyer and seller. Remember that the seller enjoys it as much as the buyer. For example, two American ladies were approached by such a peddler in Mexico City. The man was selling silver bracelets, all priced at 2,000 pesos.

One of the American women had been in Mexico long enough to negotiate intelligently and, after intensive bargaining--enjoyed to the hilt by both parties--she acquired a bracelet for 400 pesos.

"Now that's a genuine bargain," exclaimed the other lady. "I'll take a bracelet too, at the same price," she told the peddler. "No, no, Senora," protested the peddler. "for you ma'am, we must start all over again."

☺☺☺

A road map will tell us everything we want to know
Except how to fold it up again!

☺☺☺

A real friend is someone who takes a winter vacation on a sun-drenched beach and doesn't send a postcard.

☺☺☺

"I'm sorry, the manager isn't in," said the hotel clerk to the well-dressed lady who had just strutted in and insisted on seeing the manager. "Is there anything I can do for you?"

"No," snapped the pompous visitor. "I never deal with the hired help. I'll just wait until the manager returns!" About an hour later the society lady became impatient. "How much longer before the manager will be in?" she demanded. "About two weeks," replied the clerk. "He just left on his vacation."

This summer one third of the nation will be ill-housed, ill-nourished and ill-clad. Only they'll call it a vacation.

☺☺☺

Sign in a Travel Agency window:

"PLEASE GO AWAY!"

☺☺☺

The bigger the Summer vacation, the harder the Fall.

☺☺☺

Vacation is that time of year when the flowers in your garden are at their best and only the neighbors are around to enjoy them.

☺☺☺

"Last summer," said the old fisherman. "I was off the coast on a fishing trip, and while we were on deck early one evening, a great swarm of mosquitos, all of them as big as monstrous birds, came out from shore and settled on my sail boat.

And you know what? Within fifteen minutes those mosquitos had stripped it of every inch of canvas, and left the mast bare as beanpoles."

The tourists on the dock were inclined to scoff at the old fisherman's story, but one of the local citizens spoke up and confirmed his story saying: "It was only a week after that I was on a trip up the coast, and the same swarm of mosquitoes came out after us."

The fisherman didn't seem to appreciate his neighbor's unexpected support, for he said, "Humph! They did, eh? How did you know that they were the same mosquitoes?"

"How, did I know?" repeated the other with a chuckle. "Why, I recognized them because they all had on canvas overalls."

☺☺☺

A traveler just home from a vacation abroad was describing an earthquake to his friend. "Most amazing thing I ever saw," he said dramatically. "The hotel rocked. Cups and saucers were flying all over the room and --"

At this his meek-looking companion turned suddenly white. "Great Scott!" he cried. "That reminds me I forgot to mail a birthday card my wife gave me two days ago for her mother."

☺☺☺

The best place to spend your vacation this summer
Is somewhere near your budget.

THE W.C. LETTER

A lady from England, while visiting Switzerland, asked the local schoolmaster to help her find a place to stay where she could have room and board for the summer. He was most kind and took her to see several rooms. When everything was settled, the lady returned to England to make final preparations to move. When she arrived home, the thought occurred to her that she had not seen a "W.C." in the apartment. (For those who are unfamiliar with the term "W.C.". In many countries "W.C." stands for water closet or bathroom.)

So, she immediately wrote a note to the Swiss schoolmaster asking him if the was a "W.C." in the place. The schoolmaster was not very good in English and was not familiar with the term, so he asked the parish priest if he could help in the matter. Together, they tried to find the meaning of the letters "W.C." The only solution they agreed was that the letters must be an abbreviation for "Wayside Chapel". The schoolmaster then wrote the following letter to the English lady.

My Dear Lady,

I take great pleasure in informing you that the W.C. is situated nine miles from the house in the center of a beautiful grove of pine trees surrounded by lovely grounds.

It is capable of holding 229 persons and it is opened on Sundays and Thursdays only. As there are a great number of people expected during the summer months while you will be here, I suggest if you want to go that you go early, although usually there is plenty of standing room. This is an unfortunate situation, especially if you are in the habit of going regularly. It may interest you to know that my daughter was married in the W.C. and it was there that she met her husband. I can remember the rush there was for seats. There were ten persons to every seat usually occupied by one. It was wonderful to see the expression on their faces.

You will be glad to hear that a good number of people bring their lunch and make a day of it, while those who can afford to go by car arrive just on time. I would especially recommend your ladyship to go on Thursday when there is an organ accompaniment. The acoustics are excellent and even the most delicate sounds can be heard everywhere.

The newest addition to the W.C. is a bell donated by a wealthy resident of the district. It rings every time a person enters. A bazaar is to be held to provide for plush seats for all since the people feel it is a long needed. My wife is rather delicate so she cannot go regularly. It is almost a year since she last went and naturally it pains her very much not to be able to go more often.

I shall be delighted to reserve the best seat for you where you can be seen by all. For the children there is a special day and time so that they do not disturb the elders. Hoping to be of service to you.

Sincerely,

I can relate to the Christmas story in many ways. For instance, when Joseph and Mary went to Bethlehem, they had to stay in a stable, because there was no room in the inn. I've had travel agents like that myself.

☺☺☺

I just came back from Christmas shopping. I bought a football video game, a hockey video game, a Pac-Man video game, and a Donkey Kong video game. I also got something for the kids.

☺☺☺

CHRISTMAS MORN

The little boy-that-used-to-be
on Christmas morning watched the tree.
He hid beneath a man's disguise,
but oh, the sparkle in his eyes!

He watched his son with great delight,
And how his heart leaped at the sight
Of Junior opening up his toys,
And then--there were two little boys...

One half past three, and one--oh well,
His age in years, why need we tell?
It did not matter as they played
With auto, train and gay parade,

Circus and games and toy pop-gun...
I'm sure I do not know which one
was happier--the half-past-three
Or grownup lad that used to be.

-Della Adams Leitner-

☺☺☺

A Russian named Rudolf was arguing with his wife about the weather. "It's rain" said the husband. "It's snow" said the wife. Back and forth they argued..."It's rain...it's snow."

Finally the husband said "Rudolf the Red knows rain, dear."

☺☺☺

A man went to four stores to see what he could get for his wife.
And he didn't get one offer!

☺☺☺

Sign on a roadside shop:

"WE BUY JUNK AND SELL ANTIQUES."

A fisherman remembers longest the fish that got away.

☺☺☺

In some towns, a gourmet restaurant is a place where you leave the tray on the table after you eat.

☺☺☺

A loafer is a person who is trying to make both weekends meet.

☺☺☺

Man to travel agent: "I'm planning this trip as a surprise for my wife. I'll cable her from Paris."

☺☺☺

The best Christmas gift of all is --
The presence of a happy family all wrapped up in each other.

☺☺☺

When Danny was in first grade he got very excited about writing Christmas cards. He made everyone a handmade card with "I Love You", "You're Neat" or some other appropriate saying carefully written inside. He passed them out one night at the dinner table and we all enjoyed the messages. However, the one written to his mother, brought laughter to all, especially the older children. He wrote simply: "Mom, you are the Best! (B-E-A-S-T)."

☺☺☺

An elderly spinster took her first airplane trip, and as she got on the plane she went up to the pilot and said, "Are you sure this plane is safe to fly in?"

Nonchalantly he replied "Certainly, Ma'am, if it weren't safe do you think we'd let you use your credit card?"

☺☺☺

If you look like your passport photo,
In all probability you need a vacation.

☺☺☺

If all the cars in the United States were placed end to end,
It would probably be Labor Day Weekend.

☺☺☺

"I understand you're not going to get to vacation in Europe this summer," said one friend to another.
"No, that was last year," said the friend. "This year we're not going to Hawaii."

GOLD, CIRCUMSTANCE AND MUD
-By Rex Knowles-

It was the week before Christmas. I was baby-sitting with our four older children while my wife took the baby for his checkup. (Baby-sitting to me means reading the paper while the kids mess up the house). Only that day I wasn't reading. I was fuming. On every page of the paper, as I flicked angrily through them, gifts glittered and reindeer pranced and I was told that there were only six more days in which to rush out and buy what I couldn't afford and nobody needed. What, I asked myself indignantly, did the glitter and the rush have to do with the birth of Christ?

There was a knock on the door of the study where I had barricaded myself. Then Nancy's voice, "Daddy, we have a play to put on. Do you want to see it?" I didn't. But I had fatherly responsibilities, so I followed her into the living room. Right away I knew it was a Christmas play for at the foot of the piano stool was a lighted flashlight wrapped in swaddling clothes, lying in a shoe box.

Rex (age 6) came in wearing my bathrobe and carrying a mop handle. He sat on the stool, and looked at the flashlight. Nancy (age 10) draped a sheet over her head, stood behind Rex and began, "I'm Mary and this boy is Joseph. Usually in this play Joseph stands up and Mary sits down. But Mary sitting down is taller than Joseph standing up, so we thought it looked better this way."

Enter Trudy (age 4) at a full run. She never has learned to walk. There were pillowcases over her arms. She spread them wide and said only, "I'm an angel." Then came Anne (age 8). I knew right away she represented a wise man. In the first place she moved like she was riding a camel (she had on her mother's high heels). And she was bedecked with all the jewelry available. On a pillow she carried three items, undoubtedly gold, frankincense and myrrh. She undulated across the room, bowed to the flashlight, to Mary, to Joseph, to the angel and to me, and then announced, "I am all three wise men. I bring precious gifts: gold, circumstance, and mud."

That was all. The play was over. I didn't laugh. I prayed. How near the truth Anne was! We come to Christmas burdened down with gold--with the showy gift and the tinsely tree. Under the circumstances we can do no other, circumstances of our time and place and custom. And it seems a bit like mud when we think of it.

But I looked at the shining faces of my children, as their audience of one applauded them, and remembered that a Child showed us how these things can be transformed. I remembered that this Child came into a material world, and in so doing eternally blessed the material. He accepted the circumstances, imperfect and frustrating, into which He was born, and thereby infused them with the divine. And as for mud--to you and me it may be something to sweep off the rug, but to all children it is something to build with.

Children see so surely through the tinsel and the habit and the earthly, to the love which, in them all, strains for expression.

-The Guideposts Christmas Treasury-

LETTERS TO SANTA CLAUS FROM SALLY SIMPKINS

Dear Santa, I am only ten,
and much too young to think of men.
But, Santa, since I've been so good
I was hoping that you could
Place beneath my Christmas tree
A boyfriend who'll be good to me.
A boy with freckles and red hair,
I'll be so glad to see him there.

Dear Santa Claus, Did you forget?
Now I'm eleven, and no boyfriend yet.
So I'll expect a boy this year.
Not dolls and books and all that gear.
But I'd like a boy who's tall
'Cause since I'm growing, I don't go
for these short ones at all.

Well, hell–o, Daddy–o!!
How's it going for Old Kris Kringle??
I want a man who'll make me tingle!
You may have guessed, I'm now fourteen
And if you ask me, I'm the teen–age queen.
But man–oh–man, where is my guy?
Who's so groovy my friends'll die?
I'll expect him beneath my tree,
Make him as handsome as can be!!

Dear Mr. Claus, I'm now sixteen,
In the past, where have you been?
You've always brought me lots of toys
And all I want are lots of boys.
Because, Dear Santa, my nights get lonely,
I'm still waiting for my one and only.
Please make him tall, dark and athletic,
Captain of the ball team, and energetic.
A fabulous dancer, so light on his feet
Popular, kind , and in every way Neat!

Hi, Santa, College life is really great,
But now that I'm 19, I'd like a mate.
What I'd like is a returned missionary
Who's ready, willing and eager to marry.
It's not that I'm fussy, but how I'd adore
A man who's wealthy, intelligent, and witty,
Has a red BMW, with four on the floor.
And when the cold winter nights are long
He'll warm my heart with a romantic song.
So would you send this RM my way?
I'll be looking for him on Christmas day! ☺☺☺

My Dear Old Man, I'm now 22
And still have lots of faith in you.
I'd like a man with a Ph.D.
That's not much to ask, don't you agree
With a two car garage, a small estate
Who likes to sleep in and stay out late
Someone who can afford to travel a lot,
Give me this, and I'll bother you not!

Dear Santa Claus, Now I'm 35
Please, just send me anyone alive.

–Lonnie Hackworth–

A vacation consists of 2 weeks which are 2 short,
After which you are 2 return 2 work and are 2 broke not 2!

The department store Santa had a long line of children waiting to talk to him one afternoon before Christmas. Some of the children were more anxious than others to jump up on Santa's knee.

One little girl, who had been in the line for some time, eagerly jumped up on Santa's knee.

"Ho, ho, ho!" said Santa. "What do you want most of all , little girl?"

"I want to know where the bathroom is!" she replied.

DEAR SANTA,

Will you bring my dad a big
    Electric train?
Just like the one you brought to me,
    When Christmas comes again.

My daddy's head is getting gray,
    And yet I think that he;
Is just a little child inside
    About the size of me.

He gets down on the floor and plays,
    His eyes! Oh how they shine!
Please Santa bring a train to him.
    So I can play with mine!

Some people feel the world owes them a living.
The rest of us would settle for a small tax refund.

After a short courtship a young man married a young Italian exchange student. On their honeymoon, they went to Acapulco. At the hotel there was a demonstration of the famous Mexican high-divers, who would climb up about 100 feet in the air and dive into a shallow pool.

After they had finished, the groom climbed to the top of the little platform, did three triple somersaults, a reverse twist and dove into the water with hardly a splash. His bride was impressed. "Where did you learn to dive like that?" she asked. "Oh, didn't I tell you, I was a member of the U.S. Olympic Diving Team."

The bride quietly slipped off her cover-up, dove into the pool and quick as a wink, she did twenty-five laps without even breathing hard. The groom was excited. "Where did you learn to swim like that? Were you a member of the Italian Olympic Swimming Team?"

"No," replied the bride, "I was a beggar in Venice and learned to work both sides of the street."

MEN
FATHERS
HUSBANDS

The only difference between men and boys is --
The size of their costume and cost of their toys.

Policeman: "Didn't you suspect burglars had been in the house when you saw the drawers pulled out and the contents scattered all over the floor?"

Wife: "No, I just thought my husband had been looking for a clean pair of socks."

A tramp knocked on the door and asked the lady for something to eat. Not believing in handouts, she said, "Yes, I'll be glad to give you something to eat, if you'll chop a load of wood first."

"Ma'am," said the tramp with dignity, "I asked for a donation, not a transaction."

For his thirty years in the Navy, the Admiral had always carried a little book in his pocket. Every time, before he would leave the bridge, he would open his little book, mumble something under his breath and then go out with his men.

His fellow officers were always curious as to what special prayer this great man felt was so important that he read it every time before he would leave his post. At his retirement party they devised a plan to get a look at his book. Much to their surprise the only thing written in this little, well-worn book of advice was:

Remember, the right side of the ship is starboard; and the left side is port.

The rookie paratrooper, white in the face, came to his sergeant and asked for a transfer. "How come?" barked the sergeant.

"I-I-I just don't like parachute jumping," answered the rookie. "Why?" insisted the sergeant.

"Well," answered the rookie, "I guess I just don't like to practice at anything where I have to be perfect at it the first try."

Fathers are large people who frequently declare
That other children eat their meals and sit straight upon a chair.
Other children wash their hands, according to my father
They never yell, or lose their toys, or fight or be a bother.
Other children, father says, speak when spoken to;
They answer please and thank you, the way I'm supposed to do.
I'm sorry for my father, just as sorry as can be,
He knows so many lovely children 'n gets stuck with one like me!
–Zoa Sherburne–

When someone sings his own praises,
He always gets the tune too high.

Husband, wearing an apron, to his sick wife in bed: "That loud crash you just heard in the kitchen is nature's way of saying, 'Get well soon.'"

On his death bed the husband made the wife promise she would buy a double cemetery space and put two tombstones side by side. On his, she was to write "Follow me," then every time she visited she would remember their love and remain faithful.

Well, the wife followed her husband's wishes completely, but on the second tombstone she wrote: "To follow thee I'm not content, until I know which way you went."

Those who get too big for their britches --
Will be exposed in the end.

A young mother looked in the bedroom one evening and saw her junior executive husband standing silently by the baby's crib, looking down thoughtfully. In his face she could read his wonder and admiration. She went to him softly and took his hand in hers. "A penny for your thoughts," she said.

He turned and looked at her with wonder in his eyes. "I can't understand it," he said. "How on earth can the manufacturer make a crib like this for $49.95?"

A Pessimist is a man who, when he smells flowers --
Looks around for the coffin.

Some of the greatest contributions to literature were made by people who threatened to write a book but never got around to it.

"Have any of your childhood dreams ever been realized?" said the psychologist to the business executive laying on the couch.

"Yes," came the pensive reply. "When my mother used to cut my hair, I often wished I didn't have any."

☺☺☺

I'm not bald.
I'm just too tall for my hair.

☺☺☺

Men can be divided into three groups:
Those who make things happen,
Those who watch things happen
And those who wonder what happened.

☺☺☺

A father is a guy who has snapshots in his wallet
Where his money used to be.

☺☺☺

When people disagree with me
I don't argue very long.
For I believe, it's their sacred right
To be bullheaded, blind and wrong!

☺☺☺

A self-righteous man is one who listens to a sin-condemning sermon, and then tells his companions, "Gosh, the speaker sure did give it to them, didn't he?"

☺☺☺

Man believes not only that "He who laughs last, laughs best,"
But that "He who laughs, lasts."

☺☺☺

A very melancholy man, who was always up on the latest accident and death statistics, once cornered Mark Twain. "Mr. Clemens, do you realize that every time I breath, an immortal soul passes into eternity?"

"Have you ever tried cloves?" asked Twain.

☺☺☺

It is human nature to think wisely --
And to act in an absurd fashion.

-Anatole France-

154

I try to maintain a positive attitude toward all things. For instance, there are some who might say I'm bald. On the other hand, I have a naturally curly scalp.

☺☺☺

Isn't he great? He's a man of a thousand Jokes--
If you count the 500 times he's told the two of them!

☺☺☺

You can tell so much about a man just by observing the way he dresses. For instance, just looking at that outfit he's wearing tonight tells us four things about our guest of honor: He's neat, tidy, affluent and color blind.

☺☺☺

The day (John) was born, his destiny was determined.
His mother didn't quite make it to the hospital,
So he was born in the family car -- an Edsel.

☺☺☺

Nowadays it's very hard to be a deep thinker. Every time I sit down to ponder the meaning of life, the riddle of the universe, or the complexities of human life---my wife asks me to take out the garbage.

☺☺☺

He has always followed one guiding principle:
"Lead me not into temptation--I can get there quicker myself!"

☺☺☺

The start of the deer hunting season in Utah is an event of special significance. Each year, on opening day, a substantial portion of the male population retires to outlying cabins and lodges, where they eat, drink, and play cards. Any deer foolish enough to bust in the door or poke his head through the window is shot on the spot!

☺☺☺

Woman describing her husband to a friend

"He's the kind of man who always hits the nail right on the thumb!"

☺☺☺

My husband never loses his temper.
He can always find it right when he needs it.

☺☺☺

A conviction is that splendid quality in ourselves --
Which we call bullheadedness in others.

Optimists say things can't get any worse.
Pessimists say they don't have to.

☺☺☺

A truck driver, hauling a new load of cars, was having headlight trouble. Unable to fix the headlights on his truck, he decided to climb on top of the truck and turn on the lights of the front car of his load.

Pulling his rig back on the highway, the trucker saw an approaching car suddenly swerve, smash through the guardrail and skid into a cornfield. He stopped the truck, ran back to the overturned car and pulled out two stunned but uninjured occupants. "What happened?" asked the trucker.

"Well, as I was telling Sam," explained the slightly drunk motorist, "If that thing is as wide as it is high, we'd better get off the road!"

☺☺☺

Amos: My heavens, it's been five years since I've seen you. You certainly do look older.

Andy: Really? That's funny. I doubt if I would have even recognized you if it hadn't been for your suit.

☺☺☺

Husband: Where in heavens name does all that grocery money go I give you.

Wife: I'll give you just one hint. Stand sideways and look in the mirror.

☺☺☺

Husband: I was a fool when I married you.

Wife: I guess you were, but I was so infatuated at the time that I didn't seem to notice.

☺☺☺

The grieving widow went to a spiritualist to try to get into contact with her dead husband. "Charley," she asked, "Are you happy now?"

"I'm very happy," was his reply. "Are you happier than you were with me on earth?" "Yes, far happier," came the voice. "Tell me, Charley, what is it like in heaven?"

"Heaven?" declared Charley..."Who's in heaven?"

☺☺☺

I do all of my planning while I'm shaving...
That's why I'm so sharp with my answers!

The tired businessman's day at the office was capped by his wife's announcement that their cook had walked out. "Oh, no," groaned the husband. "What was the trouble this time?" "You were," charged the wife.

"She said you used insulting language to her over the phone this morning." "Good heavens," confessed the husband, "I'm really sorry. I thought I was talking to you!"

People who snore always fall asleep first.

Women scream a lot about equal rights, but if I must say so myself, life appears to be very cruel to men. When they are born, their mothers are the ones who get the compliments and the flowers.

When they get married, their bride gets the presents and the publicity. When they die, their wives get the insurance and winters in Florida.

The farmer asked his young son whether he was the one who had pushed over the family outhouse. When the boy admitted that he had, his father took him to the woodshed and gave him a sound whipping.

The boy was indignant. "You told me about George Washington, and how he never told a lie, even about the cherry tree, and everyone loved him for his honesty. Then when I tell the truth, you whip me!"

"That's true," said his father. "but there was no one in the cherry tree when George Washington chopped it down."

Mel was quite conceited as a young man.
He always knew he could come out on top.
He just never realized it would be a combfull at a time.

A good father never puts off until tomorrow
What he can get his kids to do today.

An old mountaineer from West Virginia was celebrated for his wisdom. "Uncle Zed," a young man asked, "how did you get so wise?"

"Twern't hard," said the old man. "I've got good judgement. Good judgement comes from experience. And experience....well, that comes from having bad judgement."

Shortly after WW II, a refugee from a displaced persons camp finally got his visa and sailed for America, faithfully promising to send for his wife the moment he had the money. He got a job, but after several months still had not been able to save enough to send for her.

One day he received a letter from her. It was written in English. Unable to read English yet, he asked a neighbor to read it to him. This man was an ill-tempered, mad-at-the-world type with a gruff voice. "Why haven't you sent for me?" he read angrily. "I need the money right away."

The immigrant snatched the letter from his neighbor's hands, and stuffed it angrily in his pocket. She had no right to speak to him like that; he was doing the best he could.

A few weeks went by and he received a second letter. This time he asked a gentle, compassionate young priest to read the letter for him. "Didn't you get my letter? Why haven't you sent for me?" read the priest in his soft, modulated voice. "I need the money right away."

"Well," said the man, "that's better. If she hadn't changed her tone, I never would have sent for her."

☺☺☺

Any father who thinks he's all-important should remind himself that this country honors father only one day a year, on Father's day. On the other hand, pickles get a whole week!

☺☺☺

A Quaker was milking his cow and it kicked over the bucket. "Thou must not do that," he said patiently.

It happened again. "Must I remind thee again, thou must not do that."

When it happened the third time, the Quaker said, "It is against my religion to curse thee or smite thee, but if thou doest that again, I shall sell thee to a Methodist down the street who will beat the devil out of thee."

☺☺☺

Some men attempt to run their home, their wife and their children on the following management principle:

        Rule 1: Father is always right.
        Rule 2: If Father is wrong, go back to rule 1.

☺☺☺

Mark Twain reflected: "When I was 18 I was appalled by how little my father knew or understood, but by the time I reached 21, I was amazed at how much he had learned in just three years!"

On one of his visits home, a traveling salesman volunteered to give his wife a night out while he kept the kids. Having sent the children up to bed, he settled down to read. Like a yo-yo, one kid kept bouncing to the bottom of the stairs, but dad kept sending him back up.

At 9:30, the next door neighbor called to inquired if her son were there. The father promptly informed her that he hadn't seen any extra little boys.

Then suddenly, over the bannister popped a little head and a voice shouted, "I'm here, Mom, but he won't let me go home!"

☺☺☺

No female vanity exceeds the audacity of the male ego. I heard about a man recently who saw his wife reading a book entitled "What Twenty Million American Women Want." Seeing the title he grabbed the book out of her hand and started thumbing through the pages.

Astonished, and not just a little bit irritated, she stared up at him and said, "What in the name of heaven are you doing?" He simply told her, "I just want to see if they've got my name spelled right."

☺☺☺

Fifth grade son: "Dad, you know that problem you helped me with last night? It was all wrong."

Father: "Oh, I'm sorry, I can't seem to catch on to this modern math."

Son: "That's all right, none of the other fathers got it right either."

☺☺☺

Three men were engaged in one of those profitless conversations that involve all of us at one time or another. They were considering the problem of what each would do if the doctor told him he had only six months to live.

Said one man: "If my doctor said I had only six months to live, the first thing I would do would be to liquidate my business, withdraw my savings, and have the biggest fling on the French Riviera you ever saw. I'd play roulette, I'd live like a king!

Said another, "If my doctor said I had only six months to live, the first thing I would do would be to visit a travel agency and plot out an itinerary. There are a thousand places on earth I haven't seen, and I would like to see them before I die, the Grand Canyon, the Taj Mahal, Angkor Wat....all of them."

Said the third, "If my doctor said I had only six months to live, the first thing I would do would be to get another doctor."

☺☺☺

Be tolerant of those who disagree with you --
After all, they have a right to their ridiculous opinions.

An elderly gentleman was riding on the bus the other day. A young boy who was sitting near him began to laugh, and laughed so hard that he couldn't stop.

Irritated the elderly gentleman told the young man's mother that the boy needed a good spanking to teach him proper respect. The mother undisturbed by the whole thing replied. "He has had nothing to eat today, and I don't believe in spanking on an empty stomach."

Whereupon, the elderly gentleman said, "Neither do I; here let me help you turn him over."

☺☺☺

When our second daughter was born, my mother came to help me with the new baby and my 14 month old toddler. On one occasion, when both children were fussing and wet, my husband remarked, "At times like this I think God should have made mothers with four arms."

"He did," replied mother, "but two of them are on the fathers."

☺☺☺

My husband never loses his temper --
He always has it!

☺☺☺

Three fellows who thought they were great hunters (they had many trophies) were trying to determine what they wanted to do one fall. They decided that they all wanted to go get a Caribou in Alaska!

So they went to Alaska and hired an airplane with pontoons on it, and had the pilot fly them into the bush. He landed on a little lake and promised them he would be back in three days. He warned them, however, that with the size airplane he had, he could only take back three hunters and one Caribou.

Three days later when the pilot came back for them, there were not only three hunters, but three Caribou. The pilot was very upset and said, "I told you, there is no way in he world I can get off this lake with three hunters and three Caribou!!! The hunters said, well, we did it last year! Well, you aren't going to do it in my plane," said the pilot. "That's the same thing the guy said last year, they replied, but when we offered him $100 extra bucks he changed his tone." "Well, not in my plane," said the pilot. Well, to make a long story short, he finally agreed to take all three hunters and their Caribou for $500.00.

So they loaded everything on the plane and after great difficulty, they got off the ground. Suddenly, CRASH!!! into the trees! One of the hunters, dangling from the tree, cried out, "Where are we?" Another hunter, crawling out of the plane said "Oh, about 100 yards from where we crashed last year!!"

☺☺☺

I owe, I owe...
So off to work I go!

160

Show me a man who is a good loser
And I'll show you a man who plays golf with his boss.

☺☺☺

The state of Matrimony is --
One of the United States

☺☺☺

An Austrailian was trying to explain the game of rugby to his American friend. "This is a tough game," said the Aussy, "And a lot of shins get kicked before it's over."

Not to be out done, the American replied, "We have a game like that in America. We call it poker."

☺☺☺

I dreamed I died and went to Heaven. I thought it was a little premature and so I asked St. Peter if he would explain to me how the system worked. He took me into a great big room filled with clocks. There were small clocks and large clocks. Each clock represented the life of a person still on earth. Some were ticking very slow and some were running fast. I asked St. Peter why they weren't all moving at the same rate.

St. Peter said, "Let me explain the system. Each person on earth has a clock. When you do something good, it moves a little slower. If you do something bad, it moves faster."

I looked around and saw the clocks of all of my brothers except my brother, Kay. So I asked St. Peter, "Where's the clock for my brother, Kay?" He said, "Oh, his clock goes so fast we moved it into the office and are using it for a fan."

☺☺☺

In the middle of his sermon the preacher gripped the pulpit hard and said, "The bible says, 'Be ye therefore perfect, even as your Father in Heaven is perfect.' Now for most of us we have a long way to go. Is there anyone in the congregation that thinks he is perfect? If there is, would he please stand up?"

Then as he took a long pause for effect, a middle aged gentleman near the back stood up. "Brother," asked the preacher, "do you seriously consider yourself to be perfect?"

"No," replied the man, "I'm standing in proxy for my wife's first husband."

☺☺☺

The high priest teacher asked, "Who can tell me who was most upset when the Prodigal Son returned home after wasting his father's money on riotous living?"

The class was quiet, then suddenly from the back came an unacknowledged grumble, "the fatted calf!"

I'M GLAD YOU'RE MY DAD

Some Dads are serious and
Some Dads are funny.
Some Dads give kisses and
Others give money.
Sometimes they're happy and
Sometimes they're mad.
No matter what. . . I'm glad you're my Dad!

Some Dads have grey hair and
Some Dads are so tall.
Some Dads are skinny and
Have no hair--at all.
Sometimes they're smiling and
Sometimes they're sad.
No matter what. . . I'm glad you're my Dad!

Some Dads like ice cream and
Others like beef steak.
Some Dads love hot dogs and
Others like cheese cake
Some Dads eat anything
Tasty or bad.
No matter what. . . I'm glad you're my Dad!

When I'm stubborn
When I'm naughty
When I'm feeling mad
Just simply remember I'm glad you're my Dad
And then you won't feel. . . so bad!

Sung to the tune of "My Favorite Things"
From: "The Sound of Music"
-By Cheryl Briggs-

A wealthy easterner who had grown up in Utah before going east to make his fortune, decided to return to Utah for the deer hunt. So he called an old family friend to see if he would act as a guide.

The man replied, "Sorry, I don't guide hunters any more. I only take out fishing parties."

Why's that?" asked the wealthy easterner. "Getting a little too old for the trails?"

"Nope," replied the guide, "I've never had a fisherman mistake me for a fish!"

I'm not going bald!
I'm developing a solar panel for a sex machine.

MISSIONARIES

It was a gorgeous October day. My husband Art and I were down at the boat landing helping our friend Don drag his skiff up on the beach. Art remarked wistfully that it would be a long time before next summer, when we could all start sailing again.

"You folks ought to take up skiing like our family and have fun the year round." Don said.

"Doesn't that get pretty expensive?" I asked?

Don straightened up and smiled. "It's funny," he said. "We live in an old-fashioned house---legs on the tub, that sort of thing. For years we've been saving up to have the bathroom done over. But every winter we take the money out of the bank and go on a couple of family skiing trips.

Our oldest boy is in the mission field now, and he often mentions in his letters what a great time we had on those trips. You know, I can't imagine his writing home to say: 'Boy, we really have a swell bathroom, don't we, dad?'"

☺☺☺

Missionary's Farewell Prayer:

"Lord, please bless the Mia Maids,
They will be just about the right age when I get home."

☺☺☺

Comment made by father at missionary farewell:

"Our son's greatest strength, other than his choice of parents,
Is his faith in the Lord."

☺☺☺

Hotel Clerk: "I hope you enjoyed your stay with us, sir."
Optimistic Mission President: "Well, the bed was too hard, the
price too high, the food lousy, the service slow, and there was too much noise....but by golly, I sure enjoyed your ice water."

☺☺☺

Over-weight Elder: "But President, my mother was an excellent cook."
Mission President: "Elder, you're a living testimony of that fact."

☺☺☺

A mission may be the only vacation a fellow gets
between his mother and a wife!

My wife wrote me a letter in Hawaii, where I was undergoing a very accelerated training course in the Navy. In her letter she said two young men had come through the neighborhood and knocked on the door. Mormons, they were, which of course meant nothing to me because I'd never heard of a Mormon. I really had no idea what a Mormon was.

The only thing that registered on me was that two young men had knocked on my door with my wife at home and me 2,000 miles away. I didn't care what they called themselves. What were they doing calling on my wife? In her letter she said, "You know, it is rather strange. They both have the same first name -- Elder."

-Hartman Rector-

☺☺☺

Vatican guide to missionaries: "It took Michelangelo four years to get that ceiling painted."

Junior companion: "He must have had the same landlord we've got now."

☺☺☺

Priest to missionaries: "Good Morning. How are the sons
     of the devil this morning?"

Missionaries' reply: "Just fine, how are you Father?"

☺☺☺

The missionaries converted a successful young butcher who tired to persuade his partner to join the Church, but to no avail. "Why won't you listen to the lessons," the newly converted member asked.

"Because," his partner said, "if I get religion, too, who would weigh the meat?"

☺☺☺

A call to serve in a foreign mission was the first time the Idaho farm boy had ever been in an airplane. Shortly after take-off there was a large flash of light, an explosion and engine number 4 quit. The pilot came back and reassured the passengers that the plane was perfectly capable of flying on the remaining three engines; however, this would delay arrival time by about one hour.

After a short while, engine number 3 also quit. Again the pilot told the passengers they had nothing to worry about, but their arrival would be delayed another hour. When engine number 2 gave out, the pilot told everyone that this was a very modern aircraft and it was perfectly capable of flying on only one engine. But again, the loss of power would result in further delays in the arrival time.

The missionary from Idaho who had been very courageous about the whole problem, whispered to his companion, "Gee, I hope engine number 1 doesn't burn up or we could be up here all day."

A non-member boy wanted to marry a Mormon girl. Her parents felt that it would be advisable for the lad to listen to the missionary lessons and accept the family religion. Accordingly he began to read the Book of Mormon and attend the lessons. All went well, until one day the mother came home to find her daughter lying on the sofa crying her heart out.

"It's awful," the girl cried. "There isn't going to be any wedding."
"What's the matter, darling, doesn't he love you anymore?"

"It isn't that," the daughter cried. "We oversold him. He's going on a mission."

A concerned mother put her arms about her missionary son for a last hug before he boarded the plane, and said, "Now son, remember, don't eat the food or drink the water."

Tommy had a little lamb,
He also had a sheep.

It followed him to the MTC,
Where it died from lack of sleep.

President Tanner related an incident which occurred while he was in England: Two missionaries were conversing with a minister. They didn't agree on very many things.

Finally the minister said, "Well, on this one thing we can agree. We are all trying to serve the Lord." The missionaries replied, "Yes, you in your way and we in His."

When my friend and I paid a visit to the Missionary Training Center, the elder at the information desk handed us a descriptive pamphlet. As my friend glanced at it, his mouth suddenly dropped open in surprise. "This must be a mistake!" he exclaimed. "It says the missionaries rise each morning at 5:00 a.m." The elder at the desk smiled. "It's definitely a mistake," he said, "but it's true."

Missionary Safety Slogan: Drive carefully. Remember it's not only the car that can be recalled by its maker.

At a missionary welcome home: "It's so good to be back and see everyone here, my relatives, my friends, my girlfriend.... and her husband."

When a missionary gets discouraged, he should remember that Noah preached for 120 years and every single contact drowned.

Heaven's Gate is closed to him who comes alone --
Save a friend and save yourself!

A young missionary once had a chat with a French monk who argued the fact that missionaries were not as famous as the Jesuits for scholarship or the Trappists for silence and good works.

"But," commented the missionary, "when it comes to humility, you've got to admit, we're tops."

A missionary in France received a package from his fraternity brothers. It contained what appeared to be a very plain and ordinary necktie, suitable for wearing on a mission.

He wore it often. One evening when he went calling on a very straight family, in the middle of a very deep religious discussion, the lights went out. It was pitch dark--except for the missionary's plain tie, on which gleamed the request in bright, florescent colors, "KISS ME!"

An Idaho farm boy who was raised on a dairy farm, went on a mission. "Dear parents," he wrote, "I sure like the missionary life. It's nice to lie in bed every morning until 6:00."

A young missionary, who was more handsome than brainy, was visiting with his companion one day. The companion asked to be shown through the greenhouse of one of their investigators. Pausing a moment before one plant he asked its name.

"It belongs to the begonia family," was the investigator's answer. "Oh," said the missionary, "how nice of you to look after it while they're away."

Missionary giving door approach: "My companion and I have traveled over two-thousand miles to bring you this message."

Lady at door: "Then why have I seen you going from door-to-door all morning?"

Missionary: "Why, we didn't know where you lived!"

My companion always has his own way.
He writes in his journal two weeks ahead of time.

☺☺☺

Mission president to lazy elder: "Elder, have you ever been to the zoo?"

"No, sir," said the elder.

"Well, you ought to go," said the mission president. "You'd get a real kick out of watching the turtles zip by."

☺☺☺

Zone leader: "Elder, did you shave this morning?"
New Missionary: "Yes, sir."

Zone Leader: "Well, next time stand closer to the razor."

☺☺☺

Missionary: "Don't bother me, Elder, I'm writing to my girl."
Companion: "Then, why are you writing so slowly?"

Missionary: "Oh, she can't read very fast."

☺☺☺

Mission President: "Why are you scratching your head, Elder?"
Elder: "I've got arithmetic bugs on my head."

Mission President: "What are arithmetic bugs?"
Elder: "Fleas!"

Mission President: "Why on earth do you call them arithmetic bugs?"
Elder: "Because they add to my misery, subtract from my pleasure, divide my attention and multiply like the dickens!"

☺☺☺

A missionary stationed in a far away land was noted for his loyalty to his fiancee. Then one day he received a 'Dear John' telling him that she was going to marry a fellow who had never gone on a mission, and would he please return her picture.

He was so upset that the missionaries in his apartment rallied to avenge their companion. A collection of photographs and snapshots of girlfriends and sisters was taken from every missionary in the zone. They were packed in a huge package and shipped to the elder's former fiancee.

Upon opening the package she found the following note: "Please pick out your picture and return the rest to me. This is a little embarrassing, but I can't seem to remember which one is yours."

An investigator was trying to explain to the missionary how tough life is: "When things go against you, life is awful. For example, the stock market is down, my boy broke his leg today, my wife's father died today, etc."

"You think you've got problems," said the missionary. "I just bought a suit with two pairs of pants and tore a hole in the coat."

☺☺☺

The mother of a young missionary in Iceland knitted him a warm jacket which she airmailed with the following letter:

"Postage costs so much for every little ounce, that I cut off the buttons. Love and kisses, Mother.

P.S. the buttons are in the right-hand pocket."

☺☺☺

Investigator response to Missionary:

Young man, I don't want to be rude, I really think the world of what you're saying--but before you go any further, maybe I'd better tell you what I think of the world.

☺☺☺

Missionary: "All that I am, I owe to my mother."

Companion: "Why don't you send her 30 cents and square the account?"

☺☺☺

MISSIONARY'S FIRST DOOR APPROACH

"Good Madam morning, I'm a mission mormonary traveling without body parts or passion, representing a God with purse or script. I'm here to heal the dead, cast out the sick and raise the devil.

As John looked down the creed of time he saw Miss Heaven flying with an angel while he was on the patmos Island.

Now the world has misconstructed this passage and the correct interpretation is that in 1920 a 15 year old boy was born in 1805. He became interested in religion because of the many different religious sexes. One night a 14 year old angel appeared to him and gave him the gospel.

Thank you for your kind attention and hope you got your money's worth as we preach for nothing. I bid you a good night."

☺☺☺

A smile is a curve that can set a lot of things straight.

Comments from an Elder at his farewell: The Bishop has been very persistent in his efforts to get young men to go on missions. He asked the most handsome young man in the ward to go, and he turned him down.

Then he asked the most intellectual young man to go, and he turned him down. So he asked the young man with the most potential, and he turned him down, too.

So the Bishop, not discouraged nor shaken by what had happened, decided to ask me. And as you can see, I decided I should accept the call of the Lord and go on a mission.

After all, how could I turn the Bishop down, when he asked me for the fourth time?

A missionary sister, white of hair, is stooped over her cane.
Her footsteps, uncertain, need guiding.

While down the church aisle with a wan, toothless smile,
Her companion in his wheelchair comes riding.

And who is this elderly missionary couple thus met?
You'll find when you've closely explored it.

That here is that rare, most conservative pair,
Who waited 'till they could afford it.

Comments to a new mission president: "A mission president's assignment is like going on an overnight camp-out with 200 overgrown boy scouts.

Comments from a visiting General Authority: "It is a pleasure to be here with you today Elders and Sisters. As I look out over this group of missionaries I'm awed by the responsibilities God has given you. I realize that you represent the finest minds and talents the church has to offer your investigators and the good people of this country...

Therefore, before we begin I'd like to ask President Jones to say a short prayer for your investigators and this country."

Investigator: "I'm from New York. I suppose you know where New York is?"
Southern Utah missionary: "Oh, yes, our ward has a missionary there."

Be pleasant until ten o'clock in the morning, and the rest of the
day will take care of itself.
-Elbert Hubbard-

Four missionaries went out to the airport in Rome to see a companion off for home. Unfortunately, the Elder was short $1.00 from having enough to pay his airport tax. So in desperation he decided to ask the two Nuns who were waiting for a different flight, if they would lend him one dollar so he could return to America.

The one Nun looked at him rather suspiciously and asked, "Young man, do you mean to tell me that you can go to America for only one dollar." The Elder assured her that he could. "Here then," was her reply, "have this five dollar bill and take your four friends with you."

☺☺☺

Father's advice to his missionary son:

Write to your mother once a week.
Write to your Bishop once a month

Write to your Stake President once a year.
Write to your girlfriend once.

☺☺☺

Finnish Mission Slogan: "Many are cold, but few are frozen."

☺☺☺

You may have read in Time magazine several years ago that a Priest was advocating the unionization of Priests. He wanted to call the union the "National Association for the Advancement of Collared People", and they wanted the same advantages as everyone else -- Sundays off.

☺☺☺

A mother sat sobbing as the Bishop explained that a letter had been received from her son's mission president in Brazil indicating that her missionary son had been eaten by cannibals on the Amazon.

Trying to console her the Bishop responded, "Yes, it is terrible, Sister Tyler, but just think, your son gave them their first real taste of religion."

☺☺☺

Four missionaries were hiking over primitive trails in Indonesia. One of the missionaries was constantly joking and ribbing one of the other elders who was a little overweight and not well coordinated.

Then suddenly as they crossed a narrow bridge, the loud mouth elder slipped and fell face first into a muddy pond. The mud was only about knee deep, but the more he struggled, the more stuck he became.

As two of the elders got a branch to pull him from the muddy mire, the long-suffering overweight elder looked heavenward and said, "Thanks, Lord. You can let him up now."

A missionary from Salt Lake City was sent to New York on his mission. Rather than preach the gospel, the missionary spent most of his time telling the New Yorkers how beautiful Salt Lake City was with its large, beautiful boulevards, clean, neat industrial parks, and its wonderful parks and playgrounds.

One day while the missionary was having dinner at a member's home, the New Yorker became tired of listening to the missionary brag about the beauty of Salt Lake City. Finally he said, "The only thing I can think of that would improve Salt Lake City would be to make it a seaport."

The missionary looked puzzled for a moment and then asked him, "How in the world could you make Salt Lake City a seaport being so far from the ocean?"

The New Yorker replied, "That would be a very easy task to accomplish. The only thing that you would have to do is to lay a ten-inch pipeline from Los Angeles to Salt Lake City. Then, if you can suck as hard as you can blow, you'll have it a seaport inside of half an hour!"

Two missionaries were asked by the mission president to travel the mission and visit all the elders. One night they stopped at a motel. The motel keeper said, "I'll have to put you two fellows in the same room."

"That's all right," said the elders.

"Well, I'm sorry for the inconvenience," said the hotel keeper, "but you should have a comfortable night's sleep. It has a feather bed."

At two o'clock in the morning, one of the elders woke up his companion. "Elder, please change places with me," he groaned, "It's my turn to sleep on the feather."

In the Alaskan Missions they refer to Eskimo Saints as:

"One of God's frozen few."

A missionary in the South Pacific was captured by cannibals and placed in a large pot to cook. When the chief appeared he talked to the missionary in perfect English. When the missionary asked him where he had learned such good English, the chief replied, "I'm a graduate from BYU Hawaii."

"You're a BYU grad?" said the missionary, "and you still eat your fellow man?"

"Yes," the chief responded, "but now I use a knife and fork."

The best way to make your dreams come true...
is to wake up.

COURAGE

When PARLEY P. PRATT was on one of his missionary journeys. He was once falsely accused of not paying his bills and was locked in a hotel over night until he could be taken to the prison, which was some distance away. The next morning, a very special story unfolded that helps us understand the courage and ingenuity of this early apostle:

"In the morning the officer appeared and took me to breakfast; this over, we sat waiting in the inn for all things to be ready to conduct me to prison. In the meantime my fellow travelers came past on their journey, and called to see me. I told them in an undertone to pursue their journey and leave me to manage my own affairs, promising to overtake them soon. They did so.

After sitting awhile by the fire in charge of the officer, I requested to step out. I walked out into the public square accompanied by him. Said I, 'Mr. Peabody, are you good at a race?' 'No,' said he, 'but my big bull dog is, and he has been trained to assist me in my office these several years; he will take any man down at my bidding.' 'Well, Mr. Peabody, you compelled me to go a mile, I have gone with you two miles. You have given me an opportunity to preach, sing, and have also entertained me with lodging and breakfast. I must now go on my journey; if you are good at a race you can accompany me. I thank you for all your kindness--good day, sir.'

I then started on my journey, while he stood amazed and not able to step one foot before the other. Seeing this, I halted, turned to him and again invited him to a race. He still stood amazed. I then renewed my exertions, and soon increased my speed to something like that of a deer.

He did not awake from his astonishment sufficiently to start in pursuit till I had gained, perhaps, two hundred yards. I had already leaped a fence, and was making my way through a field to the forest on the right of the road. He now came hallooing after me, and shouting to his dog to seize me. The dog, being one of the largest I ever saw, came close on my footsteps with all his fury; the officer behind still in pursuit, clapping his hands and hallooing, 'stu-boy, stu-boy--take him--watch--lay hold of him, I say--down with him,' and pointing his finger in the direction I was running. The dog was fast overtaking me, and in the act of leaping upon me, when, quick as lightening, the thought struck me, to assist the officer, in sending the dog with all fury to the forest a little distance before me. I pointed my finger in that direction, clapped my hands, and shouted in imitation of the officer. The dog hastened past me with redoubled speed towards the forest; being urged by the officer and myself, and both of us running in the same direction.

Gaining the forest, I soon lost sight of the officer and dog, and have not seen them since."

May we learn from this experience the necessity of being courageous and recalling that man's extremities are God's possibilities. Parley P. Pratt did everything within his own power to continue his missionary work and in the end, through inspiration, the Lord sustained him and allowed him to continue his labors.

While I was on my mission I faithfully wrote my girl friend every week, telling her how much I missed her. When I came home, I found out she was going to marry the postman!

☺☺☺

A new missionary was awakened the first morning in the missionfield by his District leader. Who with his loud booming voice was yelling, "Elder, it is 5:30 in the morning!"

The new elder simply rolled over and said, "Elder, if it is 5:30, you had better get to bed we have a rough day ahead of us!

☺☺☺

Success is just a matter of luck.
Ask any failure.

☺☺☺

Seven prayerless days
Make one weak.

☺☺☺

In our mission we insist on old fashioned alarm clocks with their earth shattering ring to get us up in the morning. The Mission President won't allow those modern clock radios that awaken you with soft music and gentle whispers.

He says if there is anything he can't stand in the morning, it's hypocrisy!

☺☺☺

President: "You look a little tired today!"
Overweight Elder: "Yeh, guess I am. This morning I finished fifty
(50) push-ups.

President: "Really?"
Elder: "Yup, didn't think I'd ever make it. Started 'em in 1974!"

☺☺☺

Zone Leader: "I hear you've started an excercise program?"
Lazy Elder: "Yup, soon I'll be able to touch my toes without
bending my knees!"

Zone Leader: "That's remarkable!"
Lazy Elder: "Yup, been a long struggle, but I'll make it... soon
as my fingernails grow another 24 inches!"

☺☺☺

If you're to busy to laugh, you're too busy!

"SING A HYMN, ELDER... SING A HYMN."

MUSIC

THE LORD LOVES A LAUGHIN' MAN

THE LORD LOVES A LAUGHIN' MAN, YES
THE LORD LOVES A LAUGHIN' MAN
FITS RIGHT INTO HIS HEAVENLY PLAN
THE LORD LOVES A LAUGHIN' MAN.

THE LORD LOVES A MAN WHO SINGS
SINGIN'S ONE OF HIS FAVORITE THINGS
COME ON AND SING WHENEVER YOU CAN
THE LORD LOVES A SINGIN' MAN.

A MAN WHO LAUGHS AND A MAN WHO SINGS
LEAVES HAPPINESS EVERYWHERE
HE WHO HAS A HAPPY HEART
IS RICHER THAN A MILLIONAIRE.

SO LAUGH, SING AND PRAISE THE LORD
THESE ARE THINGS ANYONE CAN AFFORD
COME ON AND LAUGH WHENEVER YOU CAN
THE LORD LOVES A LAUGHIN' MAN.

-Sy Miller/Jill Jackson-

The Primary chorister was teaching the three year olds the song-- "Popcorn Popping on the Apricot Tree." She asked the children to crouch down on the floor until they sang the line, "I looked out the window and what did I see, popcorn popping on the apricot tree." At that point all of the children were to jump up off the floor like popcorn popping.

All went as planned except for one of the children who remained crouched on the floor. When the chorister asked why he didn't pop up like the other children, he said, "I'm burning on the bottom of the pan."

Remember the tea kettle:

Though up to its neck in hot water, it continues to sing.

Even though I can't carry a tune in-a-bucket, I know the Lord wants me to sing in church. In fact he wrote a scripture just for me.

PSALMS 98:4 -- Make a joyful noise unto the Lord...make a loud noise, and rejoice, and sing praise.

Chorister to Organist:

Somehow this is not what I pictured when I was told
I would someday be the leader of many.

The little boy sitting next to me in Church whispered in his mother's ear, "What's that man next to me singing?" "Bass," she whispered back.

"That's why it sounds so funny. We're singing 'Silent Night.'"

I was invited to be the speaker at a Regional Single Adults Relief Society fireside on marriage one evening. As I read the program I had to chuckle because the opening hymn was "The World has Need of Willing Men," and the closing hymn was "Unanswered Yet, the Prayer."

My husband: I want to sing but I don't know what to do with my hands.
Choir director: Hold them over your mouth.

When I was young my mother always sang 'Silent Night,' instead of a lullaby. It wasn't so much that I liked the song, but she was always praying that I would let her have one.

After reminding the brethren of their welfare assignment to haul hay the next morning at 4:00 a.m., the closing hymn was announced as "I Have Work Enough To Do."

A very athletic-looking man escorted his wife to the concert. They arrived late, pushing their way into the middle of the row. He asked the man sitting next to him, "What are they playing?"

"The Fifth Symphony," was the reply.
"Well, thank goodness," he said, "I've missed four of them already."

A young composer who had written a piano sonata played it for elderly Camille Saint-Saens. It was a work of little merit, but Saint-Saens listened grimly to the end. When the other asked for his opinion, he sighed and said:

"When I was your age, some fifty years ago, I wrote music like that. And now the good Lord has sent you to punish me for it."

This is a very musical time of year.
It's when they play "The Wedding March" for brides,
"Pomp and Circumstance" for graduates,
and "Brother, Can You Spare a Dime" for parents.

☺☺☺

A young lady asked Arthur Rubenstein, the piano virtuoso, to listen to her playing. He consented. When she had finished, she asked, "What do you think I should do now?" His reply: "Get married."

☺☺☺

I used to teach an early morning Seminary class, and I always had a hard time to get anyone to sing. One day I asked my children if they would record for the class, "I Am a Child of God.

"Although they weren't to enthusiastic about the request, my wife promised they would have it ready before they went to bed. That evening I had to go off to a Church meeting, and when I returned the tape recorder was on the table and the instructions were clear that they had recorded it.

I took it to class the next morning without checking the tape, when I turned on the recorder my nine year old daughter said, "We thought we'd better sing for you, because mother says, if we don't our daddy will."

☺☺☺

"Daddy, would you buy me a trumpet?" asked the little boy.
"I should say not," answered the father. "A trumpet is altogether too noisy."
"Come on, Dad," compromised the lad. "I promise I'll only play it when you're asleep."

☺☺☺

On the bulletin board in the foyer a special fireside was announced as: "Do You Know What Hell Is?" Directly underneath someone had posted the sign, "Come and Sing in Our Ward Choir."

☺☺☺

During the Vietnam conflict, the Viet Cong tricked many a Yankee by shouting in English: "Charlie, please help, I'm wounded, let me come in!" Then when the sentry would let him come into the perimeter, he would start shooting or throw a grenade into the camp. One night as a young sentry stood watch, out of the dark came the pitiful cry, "Charlie, please help! I'm wounded, let me come in. "How do I know you're an American?" asked the sentry. "Trust me; please, I need help," came the reply.

Well, the young sentry didn't want to be tricked. So before he would let the man come close to camp, he decided to ask him a question. "All right! If you're a yank, tell me who wrote the 'Star Spangled Banner'?" There was a pause. Finally the soldier responded, "Simon and Garfunckel." There was another pause, then --"That's right, come on in!"

A violinist is a man who is always up to his chin in music.

☺☺☺

"I know only two tunes, one is 'Yankee Doodle' and the other one isn't."

–Ulysses S. Grant–

☺☺☺

When I was younger I started to take lessons on the saxophone, then one day my dad traded it in for a cow.

When my mother complained, he said, "I jest figured that they both made about the same noise, but at least the cow gave milk."

☺☺☺

Every person in the world may not become a personage. But every person may become a personality. The happiest people are those who think the most interesting thoughts. Interesting thoughts can live only in cultivated minds. Those who decide to use leisure as a means of mental development, who love good music, good books, good pictures, good plays at the theater, good company, good conversation -- what are they? They are the happiest people in the world; and they are not only happy in themselves, they are the cause of happiness in others.
–William Lyon Phelps, Readers Digest–

☺☺☺

I spent my days stringing and unstringing my instrument,
And the song I came to sing remains unsung.

☺☺☺

Introduction for a pianist, violinist, singer, drummer, etc. -- "She (He) is the product of a very expensive musical education -- her (his) father was sued by three different neighbors at the same time."

☺☺☺

Last night our high school band played Beethoven.
Beethoven lost.

☺☺☺

We had Ward Conference at the Singles Ward last week. The sacrament meeting program was most interesting. It contained the name, address and telephone number of every girl in the choir.

☺☺☺

Hula Dancer: A shake in the grass.
–Wall Street Journal–

The ward music director's first name was Hope. She was a gregarious person who enthusiastically smiled and maintained eye contact with the congregation as she led the hymns at church.

Hope was a petite little mother, who was expecting another child soon. In fact, she was several weeks overdue and the whole ward was anxiously awaiting the arrival of the new baby. Every week we expected to see a substitute chorister. But surprisingly, one Sunday morning Hope was still there at the front of the congregation, leading the music in her cheerful manner.

On this particular Sunday, the Bishop had selected one of the wards favorite hymns, "We thank Thee, O God, For a Prophet." Suddenly in the middle of the hymn the congregation burst into laughter, as they sang:

"There is Hope smiling brightly before us,
and we know that deliverance is nigh!"

☺☺☺

"Let us remember that it takes both the white and black keys of the piano to play the Star-Spangled Banner."
-Dr. Frank P. Graham-
(addressing Southern Conference of Human Welfare)

☺☺☺

Visitor: "Your son is making good progress with his voice lessons. He carries the tune nicely."
Parent: "Do you really think so? We were afraid that we were merely getting used to it."

☺☺☺

Bishop: "Are you sure you are ready to lead a regional Primary Choir?"
Elderly Primary Chorister: "Absolutely. I've had two nervous breakdowns, was shell-shocked in France, and I live in an apartment above a family with twelve noisy children."

☺☺☺

"Did you say your son plays the piano like Liberace?"
"Yes, They both use two hands."

☺☺☺

Little Kate came home from primary one day and announced that she had learned a new song--"God Bless America". To demonstrate, she sang a few bars:
"God bless America, land that I love;
Stand beside her and guide her,
Through the night with a light
from a bulb."

POLITICS
and
GOVERNMENT

Democracy means the right to do whatever you please without asking permission of anybody except your boss, your doctor, your lawyer, your landlord, your bank, your city, state and federal authorities and your wife and children.

☺☺☺

Even if the majority agrees on an idiotic idea,
it is still an idiotic idea.

☺☺☺

A real American is a man who prefers the front of the bus, the back of the Church and the middle of the road.

☺☺☺

It would be useless to bomb Washington. If you destroy one building, they already have two other buildings completely staffed with people doing exactly the same thing.

☺☺☺

An America saved is an America earned.

☺☺☺

Once when Abraham Lincoln was visiting the Union front during the Civil War, a young aide-de-camp was showing him around. Lincoln wanted to take a look at the enemy, so he stood up, top hat and all.

As musket fire began coming his way, the aide-de-camp, named Oliver Wendell Holmes, took Lincoln's arm and dragged him to safety, saying, "Get down, you fool!"

Later the young aide worried about his hasty remark. How would the Commander in Chief react to such disrespect? His concern evaporated when President Lincoln sought him out before departing, and said, "Good-bye, Colonel Holmes. I'm glad to see you know how to talk to a civilian."

☺☺☺

I look forward to the day when schools have unlimited funds to spend,
and the Pentagon has to hold bake sales to buy tanks.

I've often wondered why in "uncivilized countries" they sleep in open huts, while in the "civilized countries" we have to lock our doors and bar our windows.

☺☺☺

When Congress gets the Constitution all fixed up, they are going to start in on the Ten Commandments.....just as soon as they can find somebody in Washington who has read them!

-Will Rogers-

☺☺☺

Politics is like being a turtle. You'll find out fast enough who your enemies are, if you'll just stick your neck out a little.

☺☺☺

The dove of peace comes not only with an olive branch in her bill, but with a bill in her olive branch.

☺☺☺

An ounce of private enterprise is worth
A pound of Government aid.

☺☺☺

The government report says there is no unemployment in the U.S...it is just a rumor started by a bunch of people out of work.

☺☺☺

Most people would be willing to mind their own business,
If the government would give it back.

☺☺☺

Paradise: Where the only government collection agency
Is the Department of Sanitation.

☺☺☺

Conservative politicians are enamored with existing evils,
while Liberals wish to replace them with others.

☺☺☺

Have you noticed how many parents are bringing their babies to hear the political candidates speak? Helps them to sleep.

☺☺☺

God bless America; it needs all the help it can get.

183

The mayor took his wife to visit a town construction project. They stepped into the construction elevator and on the way up the mayor's wife waved to one of the workmen, and he waved back.

The mayor inquired into the matter and his wife explained that the man had dated her before she had married. The mayor thought on this and on the way back down he said "You're sure lucky you married me instead of him."

"You've got it all wrong," she replied. "If I had married him, you'd be working here and he'd be the mayor."

☺☺☺

You have to admire the Republicans for astuteness. Yesterday a Republican began a speech to his supporters by saying..."As I look out over this dense crowd..." and right away I figured he knew his audience.

☺☺☺

When I look at most politicians....
I'm glad that only one of the candidates can be elected.

☺☺☺

November is when we close our eyes, bow our heads and give thanks for the turkeys we are about to receive. Then we vote.

☺☺☺

This just in from Illinois:

With six cemeteries still to be heard from---
The election is still too close to call.

☺☺☺

A political pollster knocked on the door and a sour-faced lady answered. "What party does your husband belong to?" he asked. The lady responded curtly, "I sir, am the party he belongs to."

☺☺☺

Whatever happened to the good old days--
When we had presidents we could afford?

☺☺☺

All creatures have natural enemies to keep their population under control. For mice, it's cats. For insects, it's birds. For democrats, it's voters.

☺☺☺

Whenever I hear that some bit of information comes from a reliable source, I always think of the derivation of the word "reliable." It consists of "liable" as in being able to lie---and "re" as in time and time again.

A local politician sent out thousands of letters to the voters in his county requesting funds to help finance his re-election. The letters were addressed simply "Occupant."

A few days later he received one check for $100,000. He could hardly believe his eyes. Who was this benefactor? Quickly he looked at the name on the check. It was signed "Occupant."

☺☺☺

Jimmy Carter, then governor of Georgia, was running hard for a second term in office. One day, after a busy morning chasing votes (and no lunch) he arrived at a church barbecue. It was late afternoon and he was famished. As he moved down the serving line, he held out his plate to the woman serving chicken. She put a piece on his plate and turned to the next person in line.

"Excuse me," said the Governor, "do you mind if I have another piece of chicken?" "Sorry," said the woman, "I'm supposed to give one piece of chicken to each person."

"But I'm starved," the governor said. "Sorry," the woman said again, "only one to a customer."

Now the governor was a modest and unassuming man, but he decided that this time he would throw a little weight around. "Do you know who I am?" he said. "I am the Governor of this state!"

"Do you know who I am?" the woman said. "I'm the lady in charge of the chicken. Move along mister!"

☺☺☺

How many bureaucrats does it take to change a light bulb?
Fifteen. One to change it and fourteen to be named to a
commission to see if it should be changed!

☺☺☺

When Harry Truman was thrust into the presidency at the death of F.D.R., Sam Rayburn gave him some fatherly advice:

"From here on out you're going to have lots of people around you. They'll try to put a wall around you and cut you off from any ideas but theirs. They'll tell you what a great man you are, Harry. But you and I both know you ain't."

☺☺☺

A man received a "second notice" from the tax bureau that his tax was overdue. The letter threatened suit if the man did not pay up at once. The fellow got the money together hastily and rushed to the tax office. "I would have paid earlier, but I honestly didn't get your first notice," he told them.

"Oh," replied the clerk, "we've run out of first notices, and besides, we find that the second notices are a lot more effective."

I'm against three-day weekends for Federal Employees. I don't mind all the extra money it costs to give them three days off, but what bothers me is all the money it costs to retrain them when they get back.

☺☺☺

You have to be impressed by Utah County. Where else can you see kids stand up in class and recite: "I pledge allegiance to the Flag of the United States of America---and to the Republicans for which it stands..."

☺☺☺

The gravity of the situation is impossible to exaggerate, but I'll try.
-British Diplomat-

☺☺☺

Albert Einstein once admitted that figuring out his U.S. income tax was beyond him....he had to go to a tax consultant. "This is too difficult for a mathematician," said Einstein. "It takes a philosopher."

☺☺☺

A real patriot is the fellow who gets a parking ticket
and rejoices that the system works.

☺☺☺

Just be glad you're not getting all the government you're paying for!
-Will Rogers, Jr.-

☺☺☺

The late Senator Theodore Green, a Democrat from Rhode Island, perfected a technique for winning votes. While campaigning he would never tip waiters, cab drivers, etc. Instead he would tell them, "Be sure and vote Republican."

☺☺☺

A Republican was on his deathbed and he called his son in and said "Son, I want you to go downtown and change my registration from Republican to Democrat."

"Why!" exclaimed his son, "would you do such a terrible thing, you've been a Republican all your life?!" "Son," he replied, "it's better for one of them to die, than for one of us."

☺☺☺

Heckler: "I wouldn't vote for you if you were St. Peter!"
Politician: "If I were St. Peter, you couldn't vote for me! You wouldn't live in my district!"

☺☺☺

Blessed are the Young -- For they shall inherit the National Debt!

President Theodore Roosevelt, while making a whistlestop speech, was repeatedly interrupted by a belligerent Irishman who kept shouting, "I'm a Dimmycrat! I'm a Dimmycrat!" Losing his patience, the President interrupted his speech and asked the heckler why he was a Democrat. "Because me grandfather was a Dimmycrat, me father was a Dimmycrat, and I'm a Dimmycrat," the man answered.

With elaborate sarcasm, Teddy asked, "Suppose your grandfather had been a jack-ass and your father had been a jack-ass. What would you be?" Without hesitation, the man replied, "A Republican."

☺☺☺

"In Germany, under the law everything is prohibited except that which is permitted. In France, under the law everything is permitted except that which is prohibited. In the Soviet Union, everything is prohibited, including that which is permitted. And in Italy, under the law everything is permitted, especially that which is prohibited."
-Time Magazine, March 1985-

☺☺☺

Lee Iacocca: Whenever I was asked if I intended to run for President, I would say: "Let me get those rumors out of the way. I find them unjustified and unsettling. Besides, they stir up a lot of unrest in my campaign staff."

☺☺☺

Some congressmen think that government waste is a dollar spent in another congressman's district.

☺☺☺

Thieves once broke into the Kremlin, and were said to have stolen the complete results of the next election.

☺☺☺

Death has some advantages over taxes.
Death doesn't get worse every time Congress convenes.

☺☺☺

Taxes remind me of the game of golf.
You can drive your heart out for the green, and then end up in the hole!

☺☺☺

The modern patriot is the man who is sorry that he has only one income to give to his country.

☺☺☺

"Dad, do all fairy tales begin with 'ONCE UPON A TIME?'"
"No Son, some begin with 'WHEN I AM ELECTED!'"

187

Nothing makes it harder for politicians to remember campaign promises than getting elected.

☺☺☺

A wise woman is the one who makes her husband feel as if he is the head of the household when actually he is only chairman of the entertainment committee.

☺☺☺

Mail order ad for wierd looking tinkertoy

Mothers, this toy prepares children for today's world,
No matter how you put it together it won't work.

☺☺☺

Government is like a strong medicine with major side effects.
It should be used sparingly and only as a last resort!

☺☺☺

Beating swords into plowshares and spears into pruning hooks has now become only a Senior Citizens' Arts and Crafts activity.

☺☺☺

Although it sounds ridiculous to say it,
This country was originally founded as a protest against taxation.

☺☺☺

The Republican Convention (1928) opened with a prayer. If the good Lord can see his way clear to bless the Republican Party the way it's been carrying on, the rest of us ought to get it without even asking for it.
   —Will Rogers—

☺☺☺

At a Democratic National Convention, Will Rogers wrote: Ah! They was Democrats today, and we was proud of 'em. They fought, they fit, they split, and adjourned in a dandy wave of dissension. That's the old Democratic Spirit. A whole day wasted and nothing done. I tell you, they are getting back to normal...

☺☺☺

"Papa, what is a traitor in politics?"
"A traitor son, is a man who leaves our party and goes over to the other one."

"Well, then, what is a man who leaves his party and comes over to yours."
"A convert, my boy, a convert."

" AND YOU HAD TO PRAY FOR A <u>BIG</u> FAMILY. "

PRAYER

Too many members of the church expect a million dollar answer
to a ten cent prayer!

-Spencer W. Kimball-

Our leaders have demonstrated that one can enjoy both faith and humor. It has been said of Heber C. Kimball, counselor to Brigham Young, that he prayed and conversed with God "as one man talketh to another." However, on one occasion, while offering an earnest appeal on behalf of a certain one of his fellow creatures, he startled the kneeling circle by bursting into a loud laugh in the very midst of his prayer. Quickly regaining his composure and solemn address, he remarked apologetically, 'Lord, it makes me laugh to pray about some people.'"

-Heber C. Kimball-

What shall we give to the children? Pray for a sense of humor. "Laughter leavens life" and brings a sunny spirit.

-Marion D. Hanks-

It was thrilling to listen to a father relate this story about his three-year-old youngster recently, as they knelt by the crib in the usual manner for the little fellow to say his simple bedtime prayer. Eyes closed, heads bowed, seconds passed, and there were no words spoken by the child.

Just about the time Dad was going to open his eyes to check the lenghty delay, little Tommy was on his feet and climbing into bed. "How about your prayers?" asked Dad. "I said my prayers," came the reply. "But son, Daddy didn't hear you."

Then followed the child's classic statement: "But Daddy, I wasn't talking to you."

-Robert L. Simpson-

I don't know of a single foreign product that enters this country untaxed except the answers to prayer.

-Mark Twain-

"During the dark days of the Civil War, an incident occurred that gave insight into Lincoln's belief that God is omnipotent. A prominent minister, hoping to cheer up the weary president, assured Lincoln that the Lord was on Lincoln's side. To which President Lincoln responded:

"I am not at all concerned about that, for I know that the Lord is always on the side of right. But it is my constant anxiety and prayer that I and this nation should be on the Lord's side."

AN INFORMAL PRAYER

"The proper way for a man to pray,"
said Deacon Lemuel Keys,
"And the only proper attitude,
is down upon his knees."

"No, I should say the way to pray"
said Reverend Dr. Wise,
"Is standing straight with outstretched
arms and rapt and upturned eyes."

"Oh, no, no, no," said Elder Snow;
"Such posture is far too proud.
A man should pray with eyes fast closed,
and head contritely bowed."

"It seems to me his hands should be
austerily clasped in front,
With both thumbs pointed toward the ground"
said Reverend Dr. Hunt.

"Last year I fell in Hodgskins's well,
head first," said Cyrus Brown.
"With both my heels a-strikin up,
my head a-pointin' down."

"And I made a prayer right then and there;
best prayer I ever said...
"The prayin'est prayer I ever prayed,
was a-standin' on my head."

A man was stranded on his rooftop as dangerous floodwaters rose around him. Lots of people came to offer help, but he refused to leave his home, saying, "I'm a good man. God will save me."

Unfortunately, he drowned, and was he annoyed! When he went to heaven, he complained, "Why didn't you save me?"

And God said, "I sent you a log, two boats, and a helicopter...with some people, it's never enough."

A man in a large eastern city wrote to the local newspaper to report that the country is in far worse shape than most people suspect. His evidence: "Every time I call Dial-a-Prayer, I get a busy signal."

☺☺☺

When we were being transferred to New York, our small daughter, having lived all her short life where we were, was very unhappy about the move.

The night before the moving vans came, she was saying her prayers. She went through the usual, "God bless Mommy and Daddy," then added, "I guess I'd better tell you that this is good-bye. I won't be able to pray to you anymore---we're moving to New York."

☺☺☺

Courage is fear that has said its prayers.

☺☺☺

Unselfish young woman praying: ". . and I ask nothing for myself, but my brother sure wants a brother-in-law."

☺☺☺

A man was nailing tin roofing on a very high barn, when he slipped and started to slide toward the edge.

"Oh, Lord," he prayed, "I have never bothered you before, but please help me now."

Suddenly his pants caught on a nail and he stopped right by the edge. "Never mind Lord," he added, "I don't need your help now."

☺☺☺

The newly licensed teenage daughter had run the family car into a ditch on the side of the road. As father surveyed the situation, he asked, "How did you do that? You said there was no traffic, and it was daylight and I know you're a competent driver. What happened?"

Reluctantly, the daughter replied, "I had my eyes closed--just for a second---while I prayed I'd get there safely."

☺☺☺

Billy had invited two of his young non-member friends to dinner. As the rather large family and friends sat down to the table, one non-member turned to the other and said, "They always say a blessing on the food. It gives everyone a fair start."

☺☺☺

Life is fragile -- Handle with prayer.

Years ago an old lady down South had no money to buy food. But with complete trust in God, she got down on her knees and prayed aloud: "Dear Lord, Please send me a side of bacon and a sack of corn meal."

Over and over again, the old lady repeated the same plea in a loud voice. One of the town's worst characters, overhearing her supplication, decided to play a trick on her. Hurrying to the nearest store, he bought a side of bacon and a sack of corn meal. Upon his return to the cabin, he dropped the food down the chimney. It landed right in front of the hungry woman as she knelt in prayer.

Jumping to her feet, she exclaimed jubilantly: "Oh, Lord, you've answered my prayer!" Then she ran all around the neighborhood telling everyone the good news.

This was too much for the scoundrel. He ridiculed her before the others by telling how he had dropped the food down the chimney himself.

The wise old woman quickly replied: "Well, the devil may have brought it, but it was the Lord who sent it!"

A motorcyclist had his front tire blow out, which threw him in the air and over a high cliff. By luck, he caught a little bush and held on for dear life. Realizing he had only two choices: Let go of the bush and fall to sure injury or maybe death, or hang on to the bush until he could attract someone's attention and be saved. He began to shout and shout for help, but nobody heard. Finally he began to pray.

"Lord, please help me." After a while a voice said "I hear you. What do you want?" "Please help me Lord, I don't want to die." "Do you believe that I am the Lord?" "Yes, yes, Lord, I believe." "Then let go of the bush." "But Lord," said the cyclist, "isn't there another way?" "No," said the voice, "if you have faith, you'll let go."

After thinking about it for a moment the cyclist shouted, "Isn't there anybody else up there?"

Do you say your individual prayer every night, Robby," asked the Home Teacher. "No, Mommy says them for me," was Robby's reply.

"Indeed. And what does she say?" asked the Home Teacher. "She says, 'Thank God you're in bed!'"

Our son had only heard his grandfather pray at Thanksgiving, New Year's and on special occasions when he typically said a long prayer over the food. One night after a fun campout and fishing trip, grandfather, to our son's surprise, asked a very brief blessing on the food.

With a gleam in his eye, our son grinned at his Grandfather and said "You don't pray so long when you're hungry, do you Grandpa?"

193

A minister, a doctor, and a lawyer were involved in a shipwreck. Fortunately while they were drifting in the life raft, they sighted a distant island. There were signs of human habitation, but no people were in view.

Since the currents were drifting them away from the island, the lawyer volunteered to swim ashore and bring help. Just as he was about to dive into the sea, the minister urged that they have a parting word of prayer, so a brief prayer was said.

Eagerly the two remaining voyagers watched their companion swim toward shore. Suddenly they were horrified to see a huge shark making directly for the lawyer. At the last moment, however, the shark ducked and the swimmer was saved. Later, another shark came into view and made a pass at the lawyer, but he too, ducked just as he approached the struggling swimmer.

"There!", boasted the minister triumphantly, "We have just observed an answer to our prayers. Because of the prayer we said, the Lord has seen fit to save our lawyer friend from the hungry sharks."

"Well, that may be," said the doctor dubiously, "but personally I'm inclined to believe it was simply an expression of professional courtesy."

Joseph Smith sat down to eat a scanty meal of corn bread, and prayed, "Lord, we thank Thee for the Johnny cake, and ask Thee to send us something better... Amen."

Before the bread had been eaten, a man came to the door and ask if Joseph were home, and upon being informed that he was, said, "I have brought you some flour and ham."

After thanking the man and blessing him for the gift, the Prophet turned to his wife and said, "I knew the Lord would answer my prayer."
–Joseph Smith, The Man and the Seer p. 59–

My words fly up, My thoughts remain below;
Words without thoughts, never to heaven go!
–Shakespeare--Hamlet-

I can't blame God for what I am,
Nor for the troubles that surround me;
He did his best with what I was
When he found me!
–Carol Lynn Pearson--Beginnings-

SIGN IN HIGH SCHOOL FACULTY LOUNGE
In case of nuclear attack, the Supreme Court's ruling on prayer...
Will be temporarily suspended!

A NASA official at Cape Kennedy was explaining to a TV announcer how a module carrying humans had been successful in landing men on the moon.

The reporter asked: "That must have been a most complex plan, one of the greatest ever designed by man. Could you explain to our listeners how such a wonderful plan got started?"

"True, it has been a most complex plan," the space agency representative said. "We began with the words, 'Our Father who art in Heaven.'"

☺☺☺

One night when our son Jeff was only three years old. I knelt with him to hear his prayers. First his introduction brought a chuckle, then a tear. He began in all seriousness:

"Our Father who Art in Heaven, how do You know my name?"

☺☺☺

An elderly gentleman passed his granddaughter's room one night and overheard her repeating the alphabet in an oddly reverent way. "What on earth are you up to?" he asked.

"I'm saying my prayers," explained the little girl. "But I can't think of exactly the right words tonight, so I'm just saying all the letters. God will put them together for me, because he knows what I'm thinking."

☺☺☺

Self-discipline is when your conscience tells you to do something
and you don't talk back.

-W. K. Hope-

☺☺☺

Two missionaries were walking along the street, when they found a large dog blocking the sidewalk. "Don't be afraid," said one of the elders to his frightened companion. "Look at his tail, see how it wags. When a dog wags his tail, that means he won't bite you."

Unimpressed by his companion's seeming knowledge of "Canine Psychology," his frightened companion said, "That may be, but look at that fierce gleem in his eyes. To me he looks like he would enjoy eating us alive. Which end are we supposed to believe?"

☺☺☺

To live is to go on a long journey.
To pray is to call home!

Unfortunately, some never call, even though it is toll-free!

If today, you find yourself farther away from God than yesterday,
You can be sure who has moved.

☺☺☺

When your lips are close to God,
But your heart is far away;

No matter if your voice is loud,
He will not hear you pray.

You must have a sincere heart.
And in Jesus Christ believe.

From all deception stay apart,
For God, you don't deceive.

☺☺☺

A missionary took his girl out soon after he returned home from his mission. When he took her to the door he shook hands and said good night.

His girl said, "Didn't you forget something?" "Oh, yes," said the Elder, "Let's kneel and have a word of prayer."

☺☺☺

Sinning keeps you from praying --
Praying keeps you from sinning.

☺☺☺

There are those in this life that feel that it's good enough just to be good, you know, if you're good that's all that's necessary. But it isn't. You've got to be good for something.

This is God's work and those who do God's
work will get God's pay.

No matter how long may seem the day,
No matter how weary be the way.

He does not pay as others pay,
With silk and gold and raiment gay

But his high wisdom knows the way.
And this is sure that come what may

Who does God's work will get God's pay!

☺☺☺

No matter where you stand on the prayer-in-school issue, one truth cannot be denied: Children will pray as long as they get math tests.

"HOW CAN YOU SLEEP WITH SO MUCH SIN & PERVERSION IN THE WORLD ?"

REPENTANCE
and
SIN

Perhaps I could begin with an interesting question posed recently and an equally interesting answer. The question was, "Don't you think the commandments should be rewritten?"

The answer was, "No, they should be reread."

-Richard L. Evans-

Probably the most famous law of living is Murphy's Law:
"If anything can go wrong it will."

My wife's not so famous corollary is just as simple:
"If anything can't go wrong, it will anyway!"

A man consulted his doctor. "I've been misbehaving, Doc, and my conscience is troubling me," he complained.

"And I suppose you want me to prescribe something that will strengthen your willpower?" asked the doctor.

"Well, no," said the fellow. "I was thinking more of something that would weaken my conscience."

The creator of the Wizard of Id comic strip summed up the morality of our age when he had the priest ask the Little King:

"Of all the major sins, Sire, which do you consider to be the number one?"

"Well," said the Little King, "they're all bad, but I like greed best."

I am reaping rewards for years of thought,
I am harvesting seeds I have sown.

And as I look at what I've wrought,
I find it's weeds I've grown!

Women flee temptation, but men crawl away from it
In the cheerful hope that it may overtake them.

☺☺☺

Classified Ad in Campus Newspaper
Bill G. contact me right away. Bring three rings:
Engagement, Wedding, and Teething. Have news for you. Martha.

☺☺☺

Phone call to the Salvation Army
"Do you save bad girls?"
"Why certainly!"
"Good! Would you save me one for Saturday night?"

☺☺☺

You must learn from the mistakes of others.
You can't possibly live long enough to make them all yourself.

☺☺☺

You're only young once.
After that it takes some other excuse for behaving like an idiot.

☺☺☺

Note found under a windshield wiper
I have just smashed your car. The people who saw the accident are watching
me. They think I am writing down my name and address. They are wrong.
Good luck.

☺☺☺

Lead us not into temptation.
Just tell us where it is; we'll find it.

☺☺☺

Different people look for different things in the Ten Commandments. Some
look for divine guidance, some for a code of living and some...for loopholes.

☺☺☺

A man was accused of stealing a tire, but the evidence was so sketchy the
judge had to dismiss the case, even though he felt in his heart that the man
was guilty.

"You're discharged," said the judge. The man just stood there.
Angrily the judge shouted, "I said you were discharged, acquitted, you're free.
Get out!"

"Scuse me, Judge," the man asked, "does that mean I gotta give the tire back?"

Bishop: "What must we do before we can expect forgiveness of our sins?"
Young Priest: "Sin!"

☺☺☺

On Sunday, as we sat down to eat our dinner, our ten year old son asked: "Dad, what does it mean when they say, "Thou shalt not commit agriculture."

Hardly missing a beat between spoonfuls, my husband answered, "That just means that you shouldn't plow another man's field."

☺☺☺

"There is no honesty these days," complained the wealthy lady. "My maid ran off with my best dress...you know, the one I smuggled through customs from my trip to Paris."

☺☺☺

Profanity is the effort of a feeble brain
To express itself forcibly.
-Spencer W. Kimball-

☺☺☺

It is hard to believe a man is telling the truth when you know that you would lie if you were in his place.

☺☺☺

An Illinois preacher compiled a list of 457 sins. He was swamped with requests for the list by people who were afraid they had missed something.

☺☺☺

Three students arrived at the gates of heaven together, one from BYU, one from Utah State, and one from University of Utah. St. Peter met the young men and asked each one where he was from.

"BYU," said the first young man. "Sorry son," St. Peter said, "you haven't had enough trial in life, so we're sending you down below for some experience."

"Utah State," answered the second young man. This time St. Peter sent him back to earth for a longer trial period.

"U of U," said the third young man. "Come right in," motioned St. Peter, "you've been through Hell already."(Feel free to change the names)

☺☺☺

Someone said, "They're liable to cut you off the Church." Guess maybe some of them would like to. But they can't cut me off the Church....I repent too fast.
-J. Golden Kimball-

A president of an elders quorum told this story of a man whom they had called on many times....a good man who had good intentions. He welcomed them to his home, listened to them, and then he would usually say, "Well, I will. I intend to. I will do it. I will come to church when I get straightened out."

Then they would go back another time. The same story..."Well, when I get straightened out, I'll come to church."

Then the Elder's president said, "I was called on to speak at the man's funeral. Well....he was in church all right, and he was surely straightened out!"

-ElRay L. Christiansen-

☺☺☺

If opportunity came disguised as temptation,
One knock would be enough.

☺☺☺

If you make a mistake, all is not lost.
You can always be used as a bad example.

☺☺☺

If God seems so far away,
Ask yourself who moved?

☺☺☺

Most people justify the way they live; that is to say, instead of fitting their lives to a philosophy, they invent a philosophy to fit their lives.

☺☺☺

Live your life so that you
don't have to hide your diary.

☺☺☺

Half a truth is a whole lie.

☺☺☺

One has to wonder where mothers learned all about the things they tell their daughters not to do.

☺☺☺

The Lord was good enough to give us two ends to use in this life; one to think with, the other to sit on. Which one we choose to use will determine our success in life.

The simple truth is this: HEADS YOU WIN -- TAILS YOU LOSE!

Two preachers and a taxi cab driver went up to heaven at the same time. St. Peter met them at the pearly gates and asked the first minister, "Who are you and what have you done?"

"I'm a minister and I've preached the gospel for some twenty-five years." "Well, stand over to one side there," ordered St. Peter. He then questioned the second clergyman. "I've been a pastor for twenty-five years," was his reply.

"Ok, please stand over there by that other fellow," said St. Peter. Then he asked the last man, "What about you?" "Oh, I'm a taxi driver," the cabbie answered. "Been drivin the streets of New York for about ten years."

"Glad to have you," replied St. Peter, "pass through the gates."
"Why have you allowed that man to go in before us?" protested the preachers.

"Because," said St. Peter, "in ten years he has scared the devil out of more people than both of you have in half a century."

TEN REASONS WHY I SWEAR

1.   It pleases my mother so much.
2.   It is a fine mark of manliness.
3.   It proves I have self-control.
4.   It indicates how clearly my mind operates.
5.   It makes my conversation so pleasing to everyone.
6.   It leaves no doubt in anybody's mind about my good breeding.
7.   It impresses people that I have more than an ordinary education.
8.   It is an unmistakable sign of culture and refinement.
9.   It makes me a very desirable personality among children and women and in respectable society.
10. It is my way to honor God who said, "Thou shalt not take the name of the Lord, thy God, in vain."

ADVICE TO HENRY FORD FROM HIS MOTHER.

"Bite off more than you can chew... and chew it.
Dare to do more than you can do... and do it.
Hitch your wagon to star, keep your seat and there you are!"

The Briggs' have long admired the epitaph in Boot Hill Cemetery in Arizona, which reads "HERE LIES JACK WILLIAMS. HE DONE HIS DAMNDEST!"

Hopefully, when all is said and done, the world will feel the same about us!!!"

It is easier to ask forgiveness,
Than to ask for permission!

THE CALF PATH
-Sam Foss-

One day this calf walked home, as good calves should. And it made a crooked trail, as all calves do. But still he left behind his trail and thereby hangs my moral tale.

The trail was taken up next day by a lone dog, and then sheep. Through those old woods a path was made. And many men wound up, in and out, and dodged and turned, and bent about, and uttered words of righteous wrath because "twas such a crooked path."

But still they followed, do not laugh, the first migrations of that calf. The forest path became a lane, the lane became a road and the years passed on in swiftness fleet. The road became a village street and this, before men were aware, the city's crowded thoroughfare.

Each day a hundred thousand route, following this zig-zag calf about. And o're his crooked journey went the traffic of a continent. A hundred thousand men were led by one calf near three centuries dead.

They followed still his crooked way and lost one hundred years a day. For thus such reverence is lent to well established precedent. A moral lesson this might teach, were I ordained and called to preach, for men are prone to go it blind along the calf paths of the mind. And work away from sun to sun to do what other men have done.

They follow in the beaten track and out and in and forth and back and still their devious course pursue to keep the path that others do. They keep the path a sacred groove, along which all their lives they move. But how the wise old wood gods laugh who saw that first primeval calf. How many things this tale might teach, but I am not ordained to preach.

A FENCE OR AN AMBULANCE
-Joseph Malius-

'Twas a dangerous cliff as they freely confessed,
    Though to walk near its crest was so pleasant.
But over its terrible edge there had slipped
    A Duke and full many a peasant.

So the people said something would have to be done.
    But their projects did not at all tally.
Some said, "Put a fence round the edge of the cliff."
    Some, "An ambulance down in the valley."

But the cry for the ambulance carried the day,
    For it spread through the neighboring city,
A fence may be useful or not, it is true,
    But each heart became brimful of pity,

(Continued)

203

For those who slipped over that dangerous cliff;
    And the dwellers in highway and alley
Gave pounds or gave pence, not to put up a fence,
    But an ambulance down in the valley.

"For the cliff is alright if you're careful," they said.
    And if folk's even slip or are dropping.
It isn't the slipping that hurts them so much,
    As the shock down below when they're stopping."

So day after day as these mishaps occurred,
    Quick forth would their resources rally
To pick up the victims who fell off the cliff,
    With their ambulance down in the valley.

Then an old sage remarked, "It's a marvel to me,
    That people give far more attention
To repairing results than to stopping the cause,
    When they'd much better aim at prevention."

"Let us stop at its source all the mischief," he cried,
    "Come neighbors and friends, let us rally.
If the cliff we will fence, we might almost dispense
    With the ambulance down in the valley."

"Oh, he's a fanatic," the others rejoined,
    "Dispense with the ambulance, Never!
He'd dispense with all charities, too, if he could.
    No, no we'll support them forever.

Aren't we picking up folks just as fast as they fall?
    And shall this man dictate to us? Shall he?
Why should people of sense stop to put up a fence,
    While the ambulance works in the valley?"

But a sensible few who are practical, too,
    Will not bear with such nonsense much longer.
They believe that prevention is better than cure
    And their party will still be the stronger.

Encourage them with your purse, voice and pen,
    And while other philanthropists dally,
They will scorn all pretense and put up a fence
    On the cliff that hangs over the valley.

Better guide while they're young than reclaim them when old,
    For the voice of true wisdom is calling,
"To rescue the fallen is good, but 'tis best
    To prevent other people from falling."

Better close up the source of temptation and crime
    Than deliver from dungeon and galley.
Better put a strong fence round the top of the cliff,
    Than an ambulance down in the valley.

"When in doubt, tell the truth."
-Mark Twain-

☺☺☺

Women fret and fret about their faults,
Until they seem to double.

Men forgive themselves their faults,
And save the Lord the trouble!

☺☺☺

Women have long been door mats,
And the years these mats have been trod;

They have kept men from going in,
With muddy feet to God.

☺☺☺

If you were accused of being a Christian
Would there be evidence enough to convict you???

☺☺☺

"Imagine yourself as a living house. God comes in to rebuild that house. At first, perhaps, you can understand what He is doing. He is getting the drains right and stopping the leaks in the roof and so on. You knew that those jobs needed doing and so you were not surprised.

But presently He starts knocking the house about in a way that hurts and does not seem to make sense. What on earth is He up to?

The explanation is that He is building quite a different house from the one you thought of -- throwing out a new wing here, putting on an extra floor there, running up towers, making courtyards. You thought you were going to be made into a decent little cottage; but He is building a palace."

-C.S. Lewis-

☺☺☺

If you could give the person responsible for most of your problems a good swift kick in the pants, you wouldn't be able to sit down for months.

☺☺☺

A halo only has to slip a few inches
To become a noose.

☺☺☺

Purchasing Agent: "Ma'am, how much do you take off for cash?"
Saleslady: "Sir, of all the nerve!"

THE QUITTER
-Edgar A. Guest-

Fate handed the quitter a bump, and he dropped;
The road seemed too rough to go, so he stopped.
He thought of his hurt, and there came to his mind
The easier path he was leaving behind
"Oh, it's all much too hard," said the quitter right then;
"I'll stop where I am and not try it again."

He sat by the road and he made up his tale
To tell when men asked why he happened to fail.
A thousand excuses flew up to his tongue,
And these on the thread of his story he strung,
But the truth of the matter he didn't admit;
He never once said, "I was frightened and quit."

Whenever the quitter sits down by the road
And drops from the struggle to lighten his load,
He can always recall to his own peace of mind
A string of excuses for falling behind;
But somehow or other he can't think of one
Good reason for battling and going right on.

Oh, when the bump comes and fate hands you a jar,
Don't baby yourself, boy, whoever you are;
Don't pity yourself and talk over your woes;
Don't think up excuses for dodging the blows.
But stick to the battle and see the thing through.
And don't be a quitter, whatever, you do.

I'LL GO WHERE YOU WANT ME TO GO

I'll go where you want me to go dear Lord,
Real service is what I desire.
I'll say what you want me to say, dear Lord,
But don't ask me to sing in the choir.

I'll say what you want me to say dear Lord,
I like to see things come to pass,
But don't ask me to teach boys and girls dear Lord,
I'd rather just stay in my class.

I'll do what you want me to do dear Lord,
I yearn for the Kingdom to thrive.
I'll give you my nickels and dimes dear Lord,
But please don't ask me to tithe.

I'll go where you want me to go dear Lord.
I'll say what you want me to say,
But I'm busy just now with myself, dear Lord.
I'll help you some other day.

With thoughtless and impatient hands,
    We tangle up the plans, the Lord hath wrought.

And when we cry to Him in pain,
    He saith, be quiet man, while I untie the knot!

A young primary teacher was trying to teach the children the importance of obedience. To illustrate her lesson she told them the story of a little lamb that strayed from the flock and was eaten by the big bad wolf.

"You can see," she said, "if the lamb had been obedient and stayed with his mother and friends, he wouldn't have been eaten by a wolf."

"No, ma'am," answered one small child. "He would have been eaten by people."

The shortest sermon in the world is seen everyday on the common road sign:
KEEP RIGHT!

Humans are funny animals --
We would rather play in someone else's sandbox than our own.

The chains of habit are too weak to be felt:
Until they are too strong to be broken.
-Samuel Johnson-

I don't have a psychiatrist and I don't want one for the simple reason that if he listened to me long enough he might become disturbed.

Two skeletons were locked in the closet. One rattled to the other, "How did we get in here?"

The other said, "I don't know, but if we had any guts we would get out."

"Discipline is the training that make punishment unnecessary."

TO ERROR IS HUMAN,
But when the eraser wears out before the pencil,
<u>You are over doing it!</u>

THE TOUCH OF THE MASTER'S HAND

'Twas battered and scarred, and the auctioneer
    Thought it scarcely worth his while
To waste much time on the old violin,
    But he held it up with a smile.
"What am I bidden, good folks," he cried,
    "Who'll start bidding for me?
A dollar, a dollar--now who'll make it two--
    Two dollars, and who'll make it three?

"Three dollars once, three dollars twice,
    Going for three". . . but no!
From the room far back a gray-haired man
    Came forward and picked up the bow;
Then wiping the dust from the old violin,
    And tightening up all the strings,
He played a melody, pure and sweet,
    As sweet as an angel sings.

The music ceased and the auctioneer
    With a voice that was quiet and low,
Said: "What am I bidden for the old violin?"
    And he held it up with the bow;
"A thousand dollars--who'll make it two?
    Two thousand once--and who will make it three?
Three thousand once, three thousand twice
    And going--and gone" said he.

The people cheered, but some of them cried,
    "We do not quite understand--
What changed its worth?" The man replied:
    "The touch of the master's hand."
And many a man with life out of tune,
    And battered and torn with sin,
Is auctioned cheap to a thoughtless crowd.
    Much like the old violin.

A "mess of pottage," a glass of wine,
    A game and he travels on,
He's going once, and going twice--
    He's going--and almost gone!
But the MASTER comes, and the foolish crowd,
    Never can quite understand,
The worth of a soul, and the change that's wrought
    By the touch of the Master's hand.

Uncle Mike: "Robby! How old are you now?"
Robby: "I'm at that awkward age."

Uncle Mike: "What is the awkward age?"
Robby: "I'm too old to cry and too young to swear!"

" BRETHREN, IF YOU FEEL THAT YOU CAN'T ACHIEVE EAGLE
SCOUT, BROTHER CHANG HERE HAS BEEN CALLED TO HELP YOU."

SCOUTING

A good man had been given the assignment in his ward of arranging the Boy Scout banquet. He had worked hard, made his choices and carried them through. The tables were set, the food was in the pot, and the hour was drawing nigh.

His wife came over early to check things out. Everything seemed in order, but it looked mighty colorless to her trained "Relief Society" eye. She turned to him and said, "It looks okay, Honey, but what are you going to use for the centerpieces?"

Surprised, he looked the situation over and considered the matter seriously for a moment. Then in the full agency and wisdom of his manhood, he replied, "Butter--squares of butter should do just fine!"

"What a fine looking youngster," said the elderly gentleman to the young mother. "I hope you're starting while he's young to encourage him to be an Eagle Scout and go on a mission."

"Yes," smiled the fond mother, "But I'm afraid it's going to be a bit difficult, as ----"

"Oh, nonsense!" interrupted the older gentleman. "As the twig is bent, so is the tree inclined."

"I know that," agreed the young mother, "But this twig is bent on being a girl. And we're inclined to let her be just that!"

While serving as Scoutmaster, I lay awake listening to the boys in the tent next to mine one night:

"There's something hard under my sleeping bag," said a voice. "That's nothing," said another, "my bag got wet in the creek and my air mattress is flat. I wish I was home in my nice soft bed." "Yeah, me too." cried another. "I'm hungry and cold. Let's go home!"

"Are you crazy?" said the Patrol Leader. "If we go home now, they'll never let us do this again!"

The trouble with being a scoutmaster today
Is that you can't be sure whether the kids
Are following you or chasing you!

Having just returned from scout camp, little Brian was enthusiastically telling his mother all of the wonderful things they had done at camp. His mother smiled and asked, "After all of that time away from home, I'll bet you were glad to get home weren't you?"

"Well, not 'specially," replied Brian, "but some of the other fellows were---those that had dogs at home."

☺☺☺

Your nobody 'til somebody loves you
And the next thing you know you're a den mother!

☺☺☺

The Boy Scouts were out collecting bottles for a fund raising activity. One ambitious young man knocked on a door and a sour-faced lady came to the door and asked: "What da ya want, Sonny?"

"D-d-do you have any beer bottles for the Boy Scouts M-m-m-ma'am?" he asked. "Look here young man, do I look like the kind of lady who would drink beer?" replied the lady.

"S-s-sorry, Ma'am," was his reply. "D-d-do you have any vinegar bottles you could spare?"

☺☺☺

SCOUTMASTER'S LAMENT

If I hadn't let the bishop in
When he came to call that night;
If I hadn't made the promise
That I'd strive with all my might
To inspire those scouts,
To get their projects done,
To urge, incite and stimulate
And encourage every one;

If I hadn't made this statement:
"My sustaining membership will not be late.
That I'll surely have it handed in
On the appointed date."
If I did not have the knowledge
That on judgement day I'd find
That the boys had gone ahead
And left me far behind,

Then tonight I'd just relax a bit,
And from all my worry cease,
Turn on TV, then settle back
And go to hell in peace!!

-Adapted from a poem by Karl Mitchell-

Son: "Father, did you ever go to Scouts when you were a boy?"

Father: "Why, certainly. I never missed a Tuesday!"

Son: "See, Mother, I told you it wouldn't do me any good."

☺☺☺

Mother: "Son, that's the fifth time you've gone back for ice cream and cake. As a Scout doesn't that embarass you?"

Scout: "Why should it. I keep telling them it's for you."

☺☺☺

Our scout meetings may be the only fight in town that starts and ends with prayer.

☺☺☺

Bishop: "How was the campout?"

Scoutmaster: "Fine, but I've renamed the boys in the Snail Patrol. Instead of Johnny, Robby, Derek, and Jake; I call them Everybody, Somebody, Anybody, and Nobody.

Whenever, there was an important job to be done, like dishes, Everybody was asked to do it. Everybody was sure Somebody would do it. Anybody could have done it, but Nobody did it. Somebody got angry about that because it was Everybody's job. Everybody thought Anybody could do it, but Nobody realized that Everybody wouldn't do it. So it ended up that Everybody blamed Somebody when Nobody did what Anybody could have done!

☺☺☺

SIGN ON THE WALL OF THE YMCA

"Don't wait to be a great man. Be a great boy!"

☺☺☺

Summer Camps are those places where little boys go for mother's vacation.

☺☺☺

A mother sent her young son to the store for two pounds of plums. When he returned the mother called the grocer to complain that she had weighed the plums and found only a pound and a half.

"I'm sure my scales are correct," said the grocer, "have you weighed your son?"

☺☺☺

They nicknamed the assistant scoutmaster "Sanka"
Because he had "no active ingredient in the bean."

One night as I lay in the tent listening to the scouts talk and laugh back and forth, I heard the following little argument:

"A little bird told me today what kind of a lawyer your dad is."
"What did the bird say?"
"Cheep, cheep."
"Well, a duck told me what kind of a doctor your old man is. Quack, Quack!"

☺☺☺

Up to sixteen, a lad is a Boy Scout.
After that he is a girl scout.

☺☺☺

On an NBC television broadcast, Lewis B. Hershey, as Draft Director was discussing the question of when a boy becomes an adult.

"A boy becomes an adult," he said, "three years before his parents think he does -- and about two years after he thinks he does."

☺☺☺

Youth may be glorious, but you can't make it a career!

☺☺☺

"Something about Blazer Scouts quite unpins a teacher's poise
For even when they're quiet, she can hear them thinking noise."

☺☺☺

SCOUTER'S MOTTO

"An ounce of motivation is worth a pound of threats,
Ten pounds of pressure and a ton of reminders."

☺☺☺

The scoutmaster stopped at a roadside ice cream shop to buy the boys a treat. Each of the boys quickly told the attendant what kind of ice cream they wanted. But when it came to Robbie, the scoutmaster said, "Robbie, I think you should have vanilla."

"Why?" queried Robbie, "I like chocolate best."

"Yes, I know," said the wise scoutmaster, "but I think vanilla will look better on your uniform."

☺☺☺

"Scientists say that ants are the hardest workers in the world, but somehow they find time to attend all of our campouts."

"A scout with the right kind of stuff in him preaches harder to himself than anyone else can."

☺☺☺

"A wise scout is like a straight pin
His head keeps him from going too far in."

☺☺☺

Boy's are born with two eyes, but with one tongue,
In order that they might see twice as much as they say!

☺☺☺

The older generation thought nothing of getting up at six in the morning... I can assure you that the younger generation doesn't think much of it either.

☺☺☺

Advice to Scoutmasters: If you're able to play with the kids and enjoy it, that is a sure sign that you are still young.

☺☺☺

Last night I had a funny pain
And to the Doc I flew.
Said he, "That comes from overwork,
There's nothing I can do."

"You need a month of quiet rest."
He added with a smile.
"You'd better drop the scouts and try
Your office for a while."

☺☺☺

Teacher: "Now, Jimmy, explain the difference between 'sufficient' and 'enough'."

Jimmy: "If mother gives me cake and ice cream, I get sufficient. If I help myself, I get enough."

☺☺☺

"Johnny, I'll have you behave yourself when you're at home! What would your scoutmaster say if you acted like that at scouts?"

"He'd say, 'Behave yourself Johnny--remember you're not at home now!'"

☺☺☺

Deacon's quorum teacher: "Which of all the parables do you like best?"
Deacon: "The one where everybody loafs and fishes."

Leadership is somewhat like the small boy who was trying to lead a large dog. "Where are you taking that big dog?" asked a neighbor.

"Don't know yet," replied the boy, "but when he decides where he wants to go, I'll take him there."

☺☺☺

BUILDING BOYS IS BETTER THAN MENDING MEN!

☺☺☺

THE MANLY LEADER

He readies each assignment
    With vigor and with vim;
He gets it clearly in his head
    Until it's a part of him.
When he gives a lesson,
    His eyes know where to look.
They like to meet a young man's eyes --
    Not pages of a book.

The conscientious leader
    Is much concerned for youth.
His lips and tongue and vocal cords
    Will always speak the truth.
Because he is a gentleman,
    His knees you seldom see,
But you can tell he has them
    For he's on them frequently.

His legs may not be muscles great;
    They're fit, though, for the climb.
And one thing's sure: they'll get him there,
    Every time -- on time.
In the reach for something better
    It is just as you suppose:
This super he-man leader
    Is always on his toes!

☺☺☺

The four goals of an effective Scoutmaster

    (1)   to inspire;
    (2)   to instruct;
    (3)   to illustrate; and
    (4)   to ignite.

☺☺☺

If you want to recapture your youth --
    Just cut off their allowance!

Son: "How much am I really worth, Father?"
Father: "Well, you're worth at least a million dollars to me."
Son: "Would you mind advancing me ten dollars on your account?"

Son: "Dad, can I use the car."
Father: "No, but help yourself to the lawn mower."

MY CHUM

He stood at the crossroads all alone,
The sunlight in his face.
He had no thought for the world unknown --
He was set for a manly race.
But the roads stretched east and the roads stretched west,
And the lad knew not which road was best,
So he chose the road that led him down,
And he lost the race and the victor's crown.
He was caught at last in an angry snare
Because no one stood at the crossroads there
To show him the better road.

Another day at the self-same place,
A boy with high hopes stood.
He too, was set for a manly race;
He too, was seeking the things that were good.
But one was there who the roads did know.
And that one showed him which way to go.
So he turned from the road that would lead him down,
And he won the race and the victor's crown.
He walks today the highway fair
Because one stood at the crossroads there
To show him the better way.

BOYS BUILD CHARACTER BY OBSERVING THE OUT-OF-DOORS

The tree that never had to fight
For sun and sky and air and light
But stood out in the open plain
And always got its share of rain,
Never became a forest King,
But lived and died a scrubby thing.

The boy who never had to fight
To win his share of sun and sky and air and light,
Never became a manly man,
But lived and died as he began.
Good timber does not grow in ease --
The stronger the wind, the tougher the trees.

" , AND YOU TOLD HIM, WE'D PLACE THREE THOUSAND 'BOOKS OF MORMON' IN ONE DAY. ELDER, YOU'RE INSPIRING."

SCRIPTURES

A young child was being examined by the court to test her reliability as a witness in a very important trial.

"Do you know anything that is in the Bible?" "Oh," said the child, "I know everything!" "What!?" the judge asked in astonishment. "Can you tell us some of the things that are in there?"

"Sure," the child stated confidently. "There's a picture of Aunt Hazel, a lock of Jenny's hair, Mom's favorite recipe for apple pie, and a parking ticket daddy refused to pay."

Sometimes we are quick to judge others. One night while I was hometeaching, I learned a great lesson. I knocked on the door of one of my home teaching families, but received no response. I was annoyed because I could hear the vacuum and knew the mother of the family was home. Somewhat irritated that I would have to return again another night, I wrote a short scripture and put it under the door:

> Revelations 3:20
> "Behold, I stand at the door and knock:
> If any man hear my voice, and open the door,
> I will come in to him."

The next Sunday, when I met the lady at church, she acted somewhat embarrassed. And well she should be I thought. It is difficult to make an extra appointment, and my time is valuable. When I tried to talk to her, she quietly slipped me a note: "Please read Genesis chapter 3 verse 10. I could hardly wait to look up in my scriptures what kind of an apology could she possible give for being what I considered a bit rude. So I opened and read:

> Genesis 3:10
> "I heard thy voice in the garden,
> And I was afraid because I was naked;
> And I hid myself"

My wife and I have recently taken up jogging. One morning I tried unsuccessfully to awaken my wife, who had been up several times during the night with a fussy baby.

Standing by the bed, I said cheerfully, "The scriptures say early to bed and early to rise..."

From far under the covers came the reply, "How do you know they have been translated correctly?"

"I've told you," said the housewife to the door-to-door salesman, "I don't need a dictionary. We already have one. There it is, lying over there on the dresser."

"Lady, you can't fool me" retorted the salesman. "That's no dictionary; that's a Bible."

"How can you tell?" asked the lady in amazement.
"That's easy," said the salesman. "Look at the dust on it!"

☺☺☺

Two little girls were talking about their grandparents.
"Why does your grandmother read the Bible so much?" asked one.
"I think she is cramming for her finals," replied the other.

☺☺☺

"I would like a nice book for a friend in the hospital," said the elderly lady.
"Something religious?" asked the salesclerk.
"Er–no," replied the lady, "the doctor told her this morning she is going to get well."

☺☺☺

One of the sisters, gathering the little tots around her on the stand, told the story of Jesus feeding the multitude in the miraculous manner set forth in the New Testament.

Going home that afternoon, one of the mothers, anxious to impress the lesson upon the mind of her little son, asked him certain questions concerning it. "What did Sister James tell us today?" The boy replied: "She told us how the Savior fed the people." "How many people?" "Five thousand." "And what did he feed them with?" "Five loaves of bread and two fishes."

"Well, now," said the mother, "How do you suppose he could do that?" The little fellow mused a moment, and then blurted out: "Well, I don't believe those in the middle got any."
–Orson F. Whitney , April 1926–

☺☺☺

Two friends were seated next to each other in the congregation when, to the surprise of one, he was asked to sustain the other as the new Sunday School Teacher.

Quietly, he leaned over to his friend and said, "I'll bet you don't even know the Lord's Prayer!"

"Everyone knows that," his friend answered. "It's 'Now I lay me down to sleep.'"

"I guess I will sustain you," said the friend admiringly. "I didn't know you knew that much scripture."

A man whose consuming love of money was ruining his life, asked the Bishop for an interview. He explained to the Bishop that he felt something was missing in his life, and he rationalized that if he had more money he would become a better Christian. "Yet," he said, "even though I'm generous with my funds and a good provider for my family, something seems to be missing. What could it be?"

Perceiving the man's difficulty, the Bishop opened the Bible, pointed to the word "God," and asked, "Can you see that?"

"Certainly," the man replied.

The Bishop placed a coin over the word, and asked, "Can you see it now?"

The man didn't answer, but smiled and said, "Thanks Bishop, I understand."

Two BYU coeds were comparing notes about their previous night's date. "The night was beautiful, the moon was so romantic and bright you could read the scriptures by it." said one.

"Yeah?" swooned the other excitedly. "What did he do?"

"He read the scriptures."

SIGN ON BACK OF MISSIONARY'S BATHROOM DOOR

"Can you think to sit upon your thrones in a state of thoughtless stupor,
While your enemies are spreading the work of death around you?
–Alma 60:7–

YOUR OWN VERSION OF THE GOSPEL

You are writing a Gospel,
A chapter each day,
By deeds that you do,
By words that you say.

Men read what you write,
Whether faithless or true:
Say –– What is the Gospel
According to you?

Today is the day of bargain hunters. If it had been this way in biblical times, the Lord would probably have offered another commandment free if we would accept the first ten.

SCRIPTURAL QUOTATIONS SHOWING
THE LORD'S ATTITUDE REGARDING JOY, HAPPINESS AND GLADNESS

GOD HATH MADE ME TO LAUGH, SO THAT ALL THAT HEAR
WILL LAUGH WITH ME.
-Genesis 21:6-

ALL THE SONS OF GOD SHOUTED FOR JOY!
-Job 38:7-

THOU LOVEST RIGHTEOUSNESS, AND HATEST WICKEDNESS:
THEREFORE GOD,THY GOD, HATH ANOINTED THEE WITH
THE OIL OF GLADNESS ABOVE THY FELLOWS.
-Psalms 45:7--Hebrews 1:9-

SERVE THE LORD WITH GLADNESS
-Psalms 100:2-

HAPPY IS THAT PEOPLE...WHOSE GOD IS THE LORD
-Psalms 144:15-

A MERRY HEART MAKETH A CHEERFUL COUNTENANCE
-Proverbs 15:13-

WHOSO TRUSTETH IN THE LORD; HAPPY IS HE
-Proverbs 16:20-

A MERRY HEART DOTH GOOD LIKE A MEDICINE
-Proverbs 17:22-

A TIME TO LAUGH...AND A TIME TO DANCE...
-Ecclesiastes 3:4-7-

REJOICE AND BE EXCEEDING GLAD
-Matthew 5:12--Revelation 19:7-

FOR GOD LOVETH A CHEERFUL GIVER
-II Corinthians 9:7-

BE OF GOOD CHEER
-John 16:33--Acts 27:25--D&C 78:18-

AND AGAIN I SAY REJOICE
-Philippeans 4:4-

MEN ARE THAT THEY MIGHT HAVE JOY
-2 Nephi 2:25-

WICKEDNESS NEVER WAS HAPPINESS
-Alma 41:10-

THERE COULD NOT BE A HAPPIER PEOPLE AMONG ALL THE PEOPLE
WHO HAD BEEN CREATED BY THE HAND OF GOD
-4 Nephi 1:16-

CANST THOU READ THIS WITHOUT REJOICING
AND LIFTING UP YOUR HEARTS FOR GLADNESS.
-D&C 19:39-

INASMUCH AS YE DO THESE THINGS WITH THANKSGIVING,
WITH CHEERFUL HEARTS AND COUNTENANCES,
NOT WITH MUCH LAUGHTER, FOR THIS IS SIN,
BUT WITH A GLAD HEART AND A CHEERFUL COUNTENANCE --
...THE FULNESS OF THE EARTH IS YOURS.
-D&C 59:15-16-

LET THY HEART BE OF GOOD CHEER BEFORE MY FACE
-D&C 112:4-

WE HEAR IN THE GOSPEL....A VOICE OF GLADNESS
-D&C 128:19-

HAPPINESS IS THE PURPOSE OF LIFE.

"Happiness is the object and the design of our existence; and will be the end thereof, if we pursue the path that leads to it; and this path is virtue, uprightness, faithfulness, holiness, and keeping all the commandments of God...

In obedience there is joy and peace unspotted, unalloyed; and as God has designed our happiness -- and the happiness of all His creatures, He never has -- He never will institute an ordinance or give a commandment to His people that is not calculated in its nature to promote that happiness which He has designed, and which will not end in the greatest amount of good and glory to those who become the recipients of His law and ordinances.

-Joseph Smith, Jr.-
-Teachings of the Prophet Joseph Smith p. 255-

BIBLE QUIZ

1. WHEN WAS THE FIRST RADIO MADE?
    When God took a rib from Adam and made a loud speaker!

2. WHY DID MOSES LOSE THE RACE?
    He was told to come fourth.

3. WHEN WAS ADAM BORN?
    Just before Eve.

4. WHO WAS THE FIRST FINANCIER?
    Noah. He floated a company when the world was in
    a state of liquidation.

5. WHO WAS THE FIRST MAN IN THE BIBLE?
    Chap number 1

6. WHY COULDN'T THEY PLAY CARDS ON THE ARK?
    Noah was sitting on the deck.

7. WHEN WAS THE FIRST AUTOMOBILE MENTIONED?
    When Elijah went up on high.

8. WHEN WAS MONEY MENTIONED FIRST IN THE BIBLE?
    When the dove brought the green leaf to Noah.

9. WHERE DID NOAH KEEP THE BEES?
    In the Arc-hives.

10. WHEN WAS BASEBALL FIRST MENTIONED?
    Gen 1:1   In the Big-inning

11. WHAT DID THE EGYPTIANS DO WHEN IT GOT DARK?
    They turned on the Israelites.

12. WHO WAS THE GREATEST PHYSICIAN?
    Job. He had more patience than anyone.

13. WHEN WAS THE LONGEST DAY?
    When there was no Eve.

14. WHO WAS THE FIRST AND LARGEST GUARDIAN?
    The big fish. He brought up Jonah.

15. WHY DID THEY NOT USE PAPER AND PENCILS IN BIBLE TIMES?
    The Lord told them to multiply on the face of the earth.

16. WHO WAS THE FIRST ELECTRICIAN?
    Noah. He made the ark light on Mount Ararat.

17. WHY WAS MOSES THE WORLD'S MOST WICKED MAN?
He broke all of the commandments at once.

18. WHO WAS THE FIRST BUSINESS WOMAN?
Pharoah's daughter. She saved a little prophet
from a rush on the bank.

19. HOW MANY PEOPLE SLEPT IN MOSES BED?
Five. He slept with his forefathers.

20. WHEN WAS TENNIS FIRST MENTIONED?
When Joseph served in the Pharoah's court.

21. WHO WAS THE GREATEST ACTOR?
Samson. He brought down the house.

22. FOR WHAT WAS EVE MADE?
For Adam's express company.

23. WHEN WAS THE FIRST MEAT MENTIONED IN THE BIBLE?
When Noah took Ham on the ark.

24. WHY DIDN'T EVE GET THE MEASLES?
She'd 'Ad-am.

25. HOW DO WE KNOW THAT ADAM HAD SUGAR?
He raised Cain.

26. WHO WAS THE WORLD'S FASTEST RUNNER?
Adam. He was the first in the race.

27. WHEN WAS MEDICINE FIRST MENTIONED?
When the Lord gave Moses two tablets.

28. WHAT TYPE OF COAT DID ADAM AND EVE WEAR?
Bare skin.

29. WHEN WAS THE FIRST FAMILY QUARREL?
When Adam and Eve raised a little Cain.

30. WHO WAS THE FIRST WOMEN MENTIONED?
Genne's sis.

31. WHEN WAS THE BANKING BUSINESS FIRST MENTIONED?
When Moses issued a note to Pharoah on the Bank
of the Red Sea.

32. WHEN WAS THE FIRST MENTION OF CONSTIPATION?
King David sat on the thrown for 40 years and nothing
could move him.

33. WHAT WAS THE TELEPHONE NUMBER IN THE GARDEN OF EDEN?
ADAM-8-1-2.

"FOR YEARS MARVIN AND I HAVE BEEN RATING THE TALKS FROM ONE TO TEN. WOULD YOU LIKE TO KNOW YOUR SCORE?"

SPEAKERS

"I would like my preaching to have color, thrill, feel homelike, and revive old memories; and, if I can't feel that way among the Latter-day Saints, where on earth can I go to feel that free."

-J. Golden Kimball-

☺☺☺

"I will take the liberty of suggesting to my brethren who address this congregation that our sermons should be short, and if they are not filled with life and spirit, let them be shorter."

-Brigham Young-

☺☺☺

A mother and her young daughter were listening to a public speaker when the child said to her mother, "Isn't that man happy?" The mother replied, "I guess so." To which the girl remarked: "Why doesn't he tell his face?"
-Paul H. Dunn-

☺☺☺

"...a fool's voice is known by his multitude of words."
-Eccles. 5:3-

☺☺☺

I have found that public speaking is much like the oil business.
If you don't strike oil on your first few tries, stop boring.

☺☺☺

There are only three ingredients to a good speech.
First, it must have a good beginning.
Second, it must have a good ending.
Third, keep the first two close together.

☺☺☺

The economies of good speech dictate that the mind cannot accept
What the seat cannot endure.

☺☺☺

"I always enjoy one of Brother Briggs' speeches.
They're like a big red balloon -- 99 percent hot air,
But beautifully packaged!"

I was at a meeting where the speaker asked for a donation. I decided to donate $100 to the cause. As the speaker droned on, however, I decided to cut it to fifty dollars.

When the speaker continued, I cut again the intended contribution to $10. Finally, the speaker finished and the collection plate was passed around. When it reached me, I took a dollar out.

-Mark Twain-

☺☺☺

Once upon a time there was a lion so ferocious that he ate a bull. He felt so great that he roared. A hunter heard him roar and shot him.
MORAL: If you are full of bull, keep your mouth shut.

-Updated Aesop's Fabel-

☺☺☺

A man cut himself shaving while he prepared a talk. His wife asked him what happened. "I was concentrating so hard on my talk I cut myself while shaving."

His wife replied, "You should have concentrated on your shaving and cut your talk."

☺☺☺

The guest speaker rose and addressed his audience:
"Now, before I start, I want to say something."

☺☺☺

All good speakers should say this little prayer before giving a talk in Church:
Lord, fill my mouth with worthwhile stuff,
And nudge me when I've said enough.

☺☺☺

One evening I was asked to speak to a conference of Women Executives. Realizing how attentive women are to physical things, like hair style, gestures, shoe shine, etc., I decided before I spoke to find a room where I could look myself over to insure that every thing was alright. So I found a room with a large mirror on the wall where I could look myself over and practice my gestures.

After I had been practicing for awhile, this lady came up to me and asked if I ever get nervous before speaking. I said, "That's ridiculous. I never get nervous before I speak."

She said, "Are you sure?" "Yes," I replied, "why do you ask?" "Oh," she replied, "I just wondered what you were doing here in the ladies room?"

☺☺☺

Don't make the mistake of throwing your mouth into high gear
Until you're sure your brain is turning over.

A man was speaking at the mental institution. An inmate in the back stood up and said, "Throw the bum out. He's rotten." After this had happened three or four times, the speaker was noticeably upset and asked the director if he should quit.

The director quickly responded, "No, please continue. That man has been here 15 years and that is the first intelligent thing he has ever said."

While campaigning for the presidency, Mr. Stevenson gave a very impressive speech to an audience in the Midwest. Trying to impress Mr. Stevenson with her education, a society matron approached him and said, "Oh, Mr. Stevenson, your speech was just superfluous."

With his wry, little grin he responded quite sarcastically, "Madame, I am glad you liked it. I am thinking of having it published posthumously." To which she replied, "Oh, great, the sooner the better."

After a flowery introduction the visiting General Authority started his sermon with the following comment: "May the Lord forgive this good brother for his flowery introduction, and me for enjoying it so much."

The sacrament meeting speaker stopped in the middle of his sermon and leaned over to the bishop and asked: "Why is it that everybody in the congregation has a cough?"

"Those aren't coughs," said the bishop, "Those are time signals."

"How was your talk, dear?" asked the high councilman's wife. "I held the congregation open-mouthed," he replied. "They all yawned at once."

A General Authority had agreed to be the featured speaker at a Chamber of Commerce luncheon. A news photographer was observed vying for a vantage point to get an action shot.

The M.C., fearing that the speaker would be annoyed, called to the photographer and said, "Don't take his picture while he's speaking. Shoot him before he starts!"

The other night I was introduced as the speaker to a small group. The man who introduced me apologized for asking a man of my position to speak before such a small group, but he added, "I tried to find a speaker with less talent, credentials, etc., but I couldn't."

One evening the Preacher got carried away with his sermon and began to preach as the Bible tells us to pray—"without ceasing."

As he rambled on and on, the congregation began to leave. Observing the most patient person in the audience leave, the janitor, who was sitting out on the front step of the chapel, inquired, "Isn't he through yet?"

The patient man, who was heading for his car, paused long enough to reply, "Oh yes, he's through all right, but he won't quit."

A long-winded lecturer had been holding forth for more than an hour, except for brief pauses from time to time to gulp a hasty drink of water.

Finally, during once such break in the vocal barrage, an old gentleman in the audience leaned toward his neighbor and said in a loud whisper, "First time I ever saw a windmill run by water!"

An Indian named Big Smoke was employed as a preacher to his tribe. A visitor encountered Big Smoke at the trading post one day and asked him what he did for a living.

"Umph," replied Big Smoke, "me preach."
"That so? What do you get for preaching?"

"Me get two dollars every time for preaching."
"Well," said the visitor, "Isn't that darn poor pay for preaching?"

"Umph!" said Big Smoke, "me darn poor preacher!"

A guest speaker at Yale University devotional exercises took as his text the four letters "Y-A-L-E." "Y," he said, "means youth," and he talked about that for 15 minutes. "A," he continued, "stands for ambition," and that took another 15 minutes. "L is for life,"---another 15 minutes. "E" is for Enthusiasm," ---another 15 minutes to fill out the full hour.

As soon as the lecture was finished the students rushed to their classes as fast as they could go---all except one. He knelt, apparently in prayer. The speaker was deeply touched that he had so influenced at least one listener. He went down into the chapel seats, touched the lad on the shoulder and inquired why he was praying so earnestly.

He lifted his face and said "I'm giving thanks that this is not the Massachusetts Institute of Technology!"

Chinese Proverb: He who gives short speech,
Still has friends when meeting is over.

FOR SPEAKERS AND TOASTMASTERS

As you know, our Program Committee is always on the lookout for speakers who can capture your imagination, stimulate your intellect, captivate your good sense and rivet your attention. And so, while this search continues, tonight we've settled for (Mr. Briggs).

☺☺☺

FOR WHEN THE MICROPHONE SQUEALS

If you had to listen to as much nonsense as this mike,
You'd squeal too!

☺☺☺

If all the people who sleep in sacrament meeting were to lay end-to-end on the floor, they would be more comfortable.

☺☺☺

I love to speak so much that occasionally I get carried away. Now I'm aware of the problem, but if I should ever forget it, my wife will always be there to remind me.

She contends that people may not be a great deal wiser after my talks, but they are always a great deal older!

☺☺☺

A new convert was asked to give his first sacrament meeting talk. He was frightened, so he went to the Bishop to see what he should do. The bishop said, "Well, it's only a short talk, so just stand up, grasp the pulpit hard and say in a loud voice; 'I come unto you today,' then the spirit will guide you into your testimony. Don't worry!"

So the good brother stood up, gripped the pulpit hard and said in a loud voice, "I come unto you today." Nothing happened, so he thought "Well, maybe I didn't grip the pulpit hard enough or maybe the Lord didn't hear me." So he gripped the pulpit harder and shouted, "I come unto you today..."

Again, no response, so he tried a third time even harder and louder, but this time the pulpit broke and he fell directly into the lap of a little old lady in the front row. Embarrassed, he got up, picked up the lady and apologized. "That's all right," she said. "You warned me three times and I should have moved!"

☺☺☺

The biggest handicap some people have is their mouth.

☺☺☺

Speakers are a lot like mushrooms.
You never know if you're getting a bad one until it's too late.

Last night as I read over my talk, I fell asleep...
So you know what you're in for.

☺☺☺

The mind is a wonderful thing. It starts working the minute you're born and never stops until you get up to speak in public.

☺☺☺

RESPONDING TO A NEEDLING INTRODUCTION: "I'd like to just say one thing about that introduction: They say that humor is a gift--and I guess (name) just hasn't gotten around to unwrapping his.

☺☺☺

Long-winded speakers exhaust their listeners long before they exhaust their subjects. Recognizing this danger, one speaker began his talk this way:

"I understand that it's my job to talk to you. Your job is to listen. If you quit before I do, I hope you'll let me know.

☺☺☺

Sometimes when I am called on extemporaneously, I feel like President Truman must have felt in one of his speeches to the economic advisors and analysts of Wall Street. Truman had just fired his speech writer because the speech writer told the press that all of Truman's good ideas were his and that Truman really didn't understand anything he said.

The next morning Truman was scheduled to give his speech before the geniuses of Wall Street. He didn't have time to rewrite the speech, and because it was very technical in nature, he decided he would use the speech that had been written by the fired speech writer.

As he got into the speech, he explained how the multiplier effect of new purchases for government defense spending could continue to pull us out of the depression and perhaps help us avoid additional taxes.

The speech was tremendous. He received continuous ovations, and President Truman quietly thought to himself, "My speech writer has really outdone himself on this one. Perhaps I should reconsider. "He was not sure what all the economic garbage meant, but the analysts loved it.

Then, as he got into the most technical part of the speech, the room became very still as the audience tried to understand every word. At last the moment came and the audience breathlessly waited for a new announcement of economic policy. Truman turned the page of the speech and written in bold letters across the top of the page were the following now famous lines: "O.K., fathead, you're on your own."

☺☺☺

A yawn may be bad manners
But at least it's an honest opinion.

I'm happy to be here. I don't know that I'm particularly nervous;
But I've been incredibly alert all morning.
-J. Richard Clarke-

☺☺☺

I've been given a $5.00 introduction for a 15 cent talk.

☺☺☺

Why is it that those who have something to say can't say it,
While those who have nothing to say keep saying it.

☺☺☺

The High Councilman was trying to explain the relationship between fact and faith. "That you are sitting before me in this congregation," he said, "is a FACT. That I am standing before you, speaking from this pulpit, is FACT. That I believe anyone is listening to me is FAITH."

☺☺☺

A Relief Society President, a High Councilman, and an Elder's Quorum President in a foreign land were caught in a revolution and ordered to face a firing squad for their religious beliefs.

Each was granted one final request. The Relief Society President's only request was that the room in which she was to be shot have a nice table with a clean white table cloth and a center piece of flowers.

The High Councilman requested that since it was early in the month and he hadn't yet given his sacrament meeting talk for the month that he be granted the opportunity to give his last sermon before he be put to death.

Upon hearing the High Councilman's request the Elder's Quorum President said, "Yes, I have one last request please shoot me first--I couldn't stand to hear one more talk from the High Council."

☺☺☺

Child's Poem on High Council Sunday

If the world were to be flooded, to this meeting I would fly.
For the world could be flooded, and this meeting would still be dry.

☺☺☺

The football fan will give anything for seats on the 50-yard line on Saturday, but on Sunday is content with the pew closest to the back door. Our speakers must be throwing interceptions.

☺☺☺

It has been truly said
That a smile speaks in all languages.

Some talks are like a long-horn steer:
Two widely separated points with a lot of bull in between.

☺☺☺

A speech instructor once advised me that an after dinner speech should always be short. He said: Be accurate! Be brief! And then Be seated!

Ladies and gentlemen, I promise you that I shall be as brief as possible---no matter how long it takes me.

☺☺☺

A good speech is one that offers faith, hope and hilarity.

☺☺☺

Remember, a speech doesn't have to be eternal to be immortal.

☺☺☺

I'm reluctant to accept after-dinner talks, when the fellow who invites you says, "There isn't any special topic, just give us some good advice."

Socrates was a Greek philosopher who went around giving good advice. And the people poisoned him!

☺☺☺

Better to be silent and thought a fool --
Than to speak out and remove all doubt.

☺☺☺

ADVICE TO SOMEONE WHOSE PERFORMANCE HAS BEEN SUB-PAR

It is easy to be pleasant
When life flows by like a song,
But the man worthwhile is one who will smile,
When everything goes dead wrong.

For the test of the heart is trouble
And it always comes with the years,
And the smile that is worth the praises of earth
Is the smile that shines through the tears.

☺☺☺

One time in Brazil, I had to give a talk through an interpreter. The audience seemed to enjoy my talk and I felt good about the message. After the meeting, a person who I knew spoke English approached me and said:

"You gave a good talk, but (pointing to the interpreter), he gave a better one!"

The Lord doesn't ask about our inabilities or abilities;
He only asks about our availabilities.
If we show our dependability,
He will help us in our capability.

☺☺☺

One Sunday I asked my fifteen year old what he thought of the High Council speaker. His comment caught me by surprise, he simply said, "He is the kind of person who couldn't lead a group in silent prayer."

☺☺☺

In church many people fear being on the program with a good speaker. I've often given the following advice: "Don't try to beat the other speaker; just try not to beat yourself".

☺☺☺

"I like the silent church before the service begins
better that any preaching."
-Ralph Waldo Emerson-

☺☺☺

"The only difference between the pros and the novices is that the pros have trained the butterflies to fly in formation."
-Edwin Newman-

☺☺☺

Be careful of the words you say,
Make them soft and sweet.

You never know from day to day,
Which ones you'll have to eat!

☺☺☺

One night as I sat in my study, I received a call from the Daughters of the Utah Pioneers. The caller introduced herself and asked if I believed in "free speech?"

When I said "Yes," she said, "Swell, we'll put you down to give us one at our 24th of July celebration!"

☺☺☺

In a letter to the editor of Capper's Weekly, a man wrote: "When I asked a friend of mine the secret of his popularity, he attributed it to one particular word. 'Years ago,' he said, 'upon hearing a statement with which I disagreed, I used to say baloney, and people began to avoid me like a plague.

Now I substitute the word AMAZING for BOLONEY, and my phone keeps ringing and my list of friends continues to grow.'"

SERMONS WE SEE

I'd rather see a sermon than hear one any day;
I'd rather one should walk with me than merely show the way.

The eye's a better pupil and more willing than the ear;
Fine counseling is confusing, but example's always clear.

And the best of all the preachers are the men who live their creeds,
For to see the good in action is what everybody needs.

I can soon learn how to do it if you'll let me see it done;
I can watch your hands in action, but your tongue too fast may run.

And the lectures you deliver may be very wise and true,
But I'd rather get my lesson by observing what you do.

Or I may misunderstand you and the high advice you give,
But there's no misunderstanding in how you act and how you live.

Apologizing for his speaking ability, General Dwight D. Eisenhower once said the following:

My speaking ability reminds me of my boyhood days on a Kansas farm. An old farmer had a cow that we wanted to buy. When we asked him about the cow's pedigree, the old farmer said he didn't know what pedigree meant. So we asked him about the cow's butterfat production. Again he said that he had no idea what it was.

Finally, we asked him if he knew how many pounds of milk the cow produced each year. Again the old farmer just shook his head and said, "I don't know, but she's an honest cow, and she'll give you all the milk she has."

One evening a speaker at Sacrament Meeting was annoyed by a fly that kept buzzing around his head. Finally in the midst of a very important point the fly flew right into his mouth, and before he knew it, he had swallowed it.

He choked and sputtered right during what should have been the most serious part of his presentation. The situation was humorous for the congregation, and it could have destroyed some speaker's patern of thought.

However, the speaker, after he had coughed and sputtered, regained his composure and simply said, "Huh, serves that darn fly right. He should have watched where he was going."

A good storyteller is a person who has a good memory
And hopes that other people haven't!

GET THE AUDIENCE'S ATTENTION

A farmer went to the mule auction one day and bought himself a big, beautiful mule. The auctioneer said, "This mule is a beautiful animal, but you do have to treat him gently. Treat him like a baby and he'll do anything for you."

So the farmer bought the mule, walked out, and hitched him up to his wagon. The mule wouldn't budge. The farmer kissed him on the cheek, whispered sweet things in his ear, and patted him on the back, but the mule wouldn't pull the wagon.

So he went running back into the auction and said, "You lied to me! You sold me a mule and told me if I handled him like a baby he'd do anything for me. I can't get him to do a single lick of work."

"H-m-m-m, that's funny," said the auctioneer. "Let's go take a look." The auctioneer walked out, talked gently to the mule, tried to get the mule to move, but the mule wouldn't budge. So he jumped down off the wagon, grabbed a great big stick, and broke it right over the mule's head. "Now give him a try," he said.

"Giddy-up," said the farmer, and the mule started right off.

"I don't understand," the farmer said. "You told me to treat this mule gently, like a baby."

"You do," said the auctioneer, "but first you have to get his attention."

OVERCONFIDENCE CAN KILL A GOOD SPEAKER

The lion met the fox on the trail one day. He stared at the fox and roared as loud as he could, "Mr. Fox, who is the King of the Jungle?"

"Why, you are!" said the fox. "What a smart fox," thought the lion as he walked down the path. Later he met a monkey. "Who is the King of the Jungle?" roared the lion.

"No question," said the monkey, "you're the King of the Jungle." "That's a smart monkey," said the lion as he strutted through the jungle. Suddenly in the trail the lion met a large gorilla. "Who's the King of the Jungle?" roared the lion.

Quickly the gorilla grabbed the lion by the tail. Twirled him around his head several times, threw him against a tree, jumped up and down on his head, and then without a word walked off down the path.

The lion still dazed by the blows, meekly shouted after him, "You didn't have to get so upset just because you didn't know the right answer."

If you want to soar with the eagles on the morrow,
you shouldn't hoot with the owls all night.

One day I decided that I would speak strictly by inspiration. So I thought I would just open the Bible and put my finger on a scripture and talk about whatever the scripture said.

So I stood up at the pulpit, opened the Bible and touched my finger to a scripture. The scripture (Matt:27-5) said "Judas went and hanged himself."

Well, As I stood there, stumbling and fumbling about for a few seconds, I decided to tell a few jokes and try it again. So I opened up the Bible, closed my eyes, and put my finger on another verse (Luke 10:37) which says "Go and do thou likewise."

☺☺☺

I wish my wife where here tonight.
If she were, you would like me a lot better!

☺☺☺

If you count to ten before you speak,
You'll never say a word in pique.

In fact, the chance is very small
You'll ever get to talk at all.

☺☺☺

A WISE OLD OWL

A wise old owl
Sat on an oak.

The more he saw,
The less he spoke;

The less he spoke,
The more he heard;

Why aren't we like
That wise old bird?

☺☺☺

An American buyer visiting in Korea told a long but amusing anecdote at a luncheon in Seoul. The translator repeated it to the non-English speaking group in just a few words and the audience laughed and applauded.

Later the American buyer commented, "I think it was wonderful the way they appreciated my joke. It's amazing how you were able to shorten it into Korean and still have them understand the point."

"Oh, it was simple," the interpreter replied, "I merely said, 'American with big checkbook has told funny story. You do whatever you think is appropriate.'"

-Funny Funny World-

"Tonight, I've entitled my talk "THIS AND THAT"
So I won't get off the subject."

☺☺☺

If you ever get in a situation where your hands are wet and your mouth is dry:
Just put your hands in your mouth and you'll never go wrong!

☺☺☺

Your Stake is a great Stake. Why the President knows how to preside,
the Teachers know how to teach, and even the Ushers know how to ush!
–Elder Spencer H. Osborne–

☺☺☺

Our Stake Presidency is like the bottom half of a double boiler, they let off a
lot of steam, but they rarely know what is cooking.

☺☺☺

Sometimes when I hear people say how grateful they are for the opportunity to
speak, it reminds me of the story of the race horse.

A race horse was running in a big race, suddenly he stumbled and fell
spilling his rider. The horse's owner ran out on the track and checked
the horse. Finding him with a broken leg, the owner pulled out a gun
and shot the horse right between the eyes.

The rider who was lying in the mud, gasping for breath and wincing
from pain, watched the whole event quietly. Then the owner turned to
the rider and asked, "How are you?"

Quickly, the rider answered. "Oh, don't worry about me, I've never
felt better in my whole life!"

☺☺☺

Never try to walk up a wall that's leaning towards you...
Never try to kiss a person that's leaning away from you...
And never speak to a group that knows more about a subject than you do.

–Winston Churchill–

☺☺☺

"The truth requires constant repetition
Because error is being preached about us all the times."
–Goethe–

☺☺☺

Behold the turtle, he makes progress...
Only when he sticks his neck out!
–James B. Conant––Former Pres. of Harvard University–

"It's working, Elder. The cougar basketball is breaking the ice."

SPORTS

To have your name inscribed up there is greater yet by far,
Than all the Halls of Fame down here and every man-made star.
This crowd on earth, they soon forget the heroes of the past,
They cheer like mad until you fall and that's how long you last.

I tell you friend, I would not trade my name however small,
If written there beyond the stars in that Celestial Hall,
For any famous name on earth or glory that they share,
I'd rather be an unknown here and have my name up there.

–John Wooden–

NOTE: At the time, John Wooden was the only person to be honored by the Basketball Hall of Fame as an All-American, both as a coach and as a player.

☺☺☺

Man blames fate for other accidents,
But feels personally responsible when he makes a hole-in-one.

☺☺☺

It's amazing how creative you can get when playing golf with your boss. You find yourself saying things like: "Golly gee, you hit that ball well! Did you see how high the water splashed?"

☺☺☺

Dear Abby: "I'm married to a football coach, but during the football season he doesn't pay any attention to me. What can I do?

"Dear Wife of Football Coach: Try putting a big number on your back."

☺☺☺

Last season we couldn't win at home and we were losing on the road. Our coach was willing to accept the blame...he couldn't think of anyplace else to play.

☺☺☺

Every employee who golfs knows how important the fundamentals are. Like keeping your head down---when the boss throws his ball out of the rough.

☺☺☺

Two things kept me from a career as a professional athlete: When we played baseball I could never hit a curve ball, and in golf, I could.

The psychology instructor had just finished a lecture on mental health and was giving an oral test. Speaking specifically about manic depression, she asked, "How would you diagnose a patient who walks back and forth screaming at the top of his lungs one minute, then sits in a chair weeping uncontrollably the next?

A young man in the rear raised his hand and answered, "A basketball coach?"

☺☺☺

A ten-year-old protested vigorously when his mother asked him to take his younger sister with him when he went fishing. "The last time I took her with me," he said, "I didn't catch a single fish."

"Well," said his mother, "I'll talk to her. I promise you this time she won't make any noise." "It wasn't the noise, Mom," the boy said. "She ate all the bait."

☺☺☺

Once upon a time there was a man who was such a golf addict that he was neglecting his job. Frequently he would call in sick as an excuse to play. One morning, after making his usual call to the office, an angel up above spotted him on the way to the golf course and decided to teach him a lesson. "If you play golf today, you will be punished," the angel whispered in his ear.

Thinking it was only his conscience, which he had successfully ignored in the past, the fellow just smiled . "No," he said, "I've been doing this for years. No one will ever know. I won't be punished."

The angel said no more and the fellow stepped up to the first tee where he promptly whacked the ball 300 yards straight down the middle of the fairway. Since normally he was a real duffer, and had never driven the ball more than 200 yards, nor shot under ninety in his life, he couldn't believe it. Yet, there it was.

And his luck continued. Long drives on every hole, perfect putting. By the ninth hole he was six under par and was playing near perfect golf. The fellow was walking on air. He wound up with an amazing 61, about 30 strokes under his usual game. Wait until he got back to the office and told them about this! But, suddenly, his face fell. He couldn't tell them. He could never tell any one! The angel smiled.

☺☺☺

Symbols are devices that enable people to immediately identify with a particular subject or organization. Take sports. If you see a bat, it means baseball. If you see goalposts, it means football. If you see crutches, it means skiing.

☺☺☺

Each year the Jazz (any pro team with a poor record) spend money, work hard, do their best and still end up way behind. That's why we love 'em. They're just like us.

A newspaperman, visiting the Raider's football training camp in California, had just come from the Jack London Historic Monument. He read a sample of London's prose to quarterback Marc Wilson:

"I would rather be ashes than dust! I would rather that my spark should burn out in a brilliant blaze than it should be stifled by dry rot. I would rather be a superb meteor, every atom of me in magnificent glow, than a sleepy and permanent plant. The proper function of man is to live, not to exist. I shall not waste my days in trying to prolong them. I shall use my time."

"What does that mean to you?" the newspaperman asked the quarterback. "Throw deep," said Wilson.

The bishop was invited to participate in the ward golf tournament. He was most anxious to do well. So on the first hole he took out a new ball, and put it on his tee. Then before he hit he walked to the back of the tee and offered a quick prayer. When he returned to hit the ball, a voice from Heaven said, "Try a practice swing."

Thinking this was good advice, he stepped back and took a swing or two for practice. Then as he approached the ball again, the voice from Heaven said, "use an old ball."

Do you ever have the feeling that you'd need a head start
just to finish last?

When a little known rookie with the Milwaukee Braves came up for his first time at bat in a major league game, the catcher said to him mockingly, "Hey kid, you're holding your bat all wrong. You should hold it with the label up so you can read it."

"I didn't come up here to read," retorted the young Hank Aaron. Fifteen years later, Aaron passed Babe Ruth to become the greatest home run hitter in major league history.

Sports Illustrated writer, Jeannette Bruce, once spent two-and one-half years taking judo lessons, progressing steadily through the entire spectrum of self-defense belts.

"I kept on out of my inability to give up a losing battle," she said, "and on a rainy night, it all seemed worthwhile...the thing every judo student dreams of, happened to me. I was walking down Sixth Avenue about 9:00 p.m. when a man stepped out of a dark doorway and tried to snatch my purse. How prepared I should have been! How ready to smash him to the pavement with a flourishing foot sweep! Instead--what did I do? I hit him over the head with my umbrella."

To cut 10 strokes off your golf score,
All you have to do is get rid of one thing---
WITNESSES.

☺☺☺

The Russians are really going to be hard to beat in the next Olympics. I saw a picture of a Russian shotputter who had to be the biggest, toughest, meanest, ugliest athlete I have ever seen. I don't remember her name.

☺☺☺

The older a man gets,
The better he was as an athlete in his youth.

☺☺☺

A doctor, specializing in internal medicine, had a simple formula for disposing of businessmen with certain types of nervous indigestion. He would ask them if they played golf. If so, he told them to give it up. If not, he told them to take it up.

☺☺☺

On activity night the Laurel class went horseback riding. One of the young ladies that had never been on a horse before said, "That's an adorable horse over there."

"Yes," said the stablemaster, "he is a beautiful animal, but that horse has never been ridden." "Oh, goodie," was her excited reply. "We can both learn together."

☺☺☺

My boy Jeff, sat dejected after losing a little league soccer match 3-2. His hometeacher, who also had a boy on the team tried to console him. "Jeff," he said, "winning isn't everything. Remember, when the 'Great Scorer' comes to write down the outcome of this game, he will not remember whether you won or lost, but how you played the game."

"I guess so," said Jeff half-heartedly.

"You know who the 'Great Scorer is don't you?" asked the hometeacher. "Sure," Jeff answered sadly. "Timmy Green. He scored all three goals."

☺☺☺

My friend, who is an avid golfer, took up skiing last winter. One day, while coming down the slope, he lost control. Realizing he was about to crash into the skier in front of him and not knowing what to do, he yelled, "fore!"

About a second later he ran over the poor guy in front of him. "Gee," the victim moaned apologetically, "I would have moved out of your way, but I was looking for a golf ball."

I went golfing with my wife. On the tee she took a putter and drove two hundred and fifty yards onto the green. Then she took an iron and putted the ball to within two feet of the cup. Then she asked for a wood and got the ball into the cup.

"Now," she said disgustedly, "I'm in real trouble." "Why?" I asked. "I don't know what club I'll use to get it out of the hole."

☺☺☺

Kramer's fishing trip had been a flop, and on the way home he entered the local fish market. The merchant asked Kramer what he'd like. "Just stand over there and throw me five of the biggest trout you have," he replied.

"Throw 'em? What in the world for?" the merchant asked in amazement. "So I can tell my wife I caught them," replied Kramer. "I may be a poor fisherman, but I'm no liar."

☺☺☺

At a certain university, two football players found themselves in academic trouble and on probation. The coach arranged with the Academic Dean for a special competency test. The exam, which consisted of only one question, read: Old MacDonald had a (blank) .

The one athlete said to the other in a whisper, "What's the answer?" "Farm," answered the other. "How do you spell it?" asked the first. "Don't you remember?" answered the brighter one, "ei-ei-o."

☺☺☺

The devil challenged St. Peter to a football game.
St. Peter accepted saying, "You don't have a chance,
we have all the good players."

The devil replied, "But we have all the refs."

☺☺☺

The paper says our coach retired because of illness and fatigue...
Which is simply a kind way of saying the fans are sick and tired of him.

☺☺☺

The trouble with being a good sport is that
you have to lose to prove it.

☺☺☺

Be cautious with people who say they jog every day.
Chances are they will lie about other things as well.

☺☺☺

Life is like an archery contest---one shaft after another.

When Roger Blough, Chairman of U.S. Steel Co., accepted the National Football Foundation and Hall of Fame gold medal for his alma mater, he told the audience:

"In the three years I played football we won 7, lost 17 and tied 2 games. A sports statistician with a great capacity for charity calculated that we won better than 75% of the games we didn't lose."

☺☺☺

A batter let a fastball go by. The plate umpire remained silent, thinking about it. Finally the batter could stand it no longer.

"What is it?" he shouted, "a ball or a strike?" "Sorry," the umpire said. "A pitch ain't nothin' 'til I call it somethin'."

☺☺☺

Two men argued about which would take the only taxi in sight. One returned to his wife at the curb. "Why did you let him have the cab?" she asked. "He needed it more than I did," the husband explained weakly. "He was late for his karate lesson."

☺☺☺

Last fall, a friend of mine went back to Princeton (his alma mater) to visit his son on a big football weekend. The football at Princeton may not be all that big, but I'm told the weekends are!"

☺☺☺

I love to take my young men to sports banquets. It is always an inspiration to hear famous athletes speak on, "What stealing bases, throwing spitballs and beaning batters have taught me about honesty and fair play."

☺☺☺

A fellow got up one Saturday morning with the odd feeling that something about this day was to be different. Something unusual was going to happen.

He glanced out the window at the thermometer: 33 degrees. He went downstairs----strange, the clock had stopped at 3 o'clock. He picked up the paper and read the date: The third of the month. Threes---that was it!

He grabbed the paper and flipped it open to the racing section. Sure enough, in the third race there was a horse named Trio! The fellow hurried to the bank, drew out his life savings and bet it all on the horse to win. It ran third.

☺☺☺

Occasionally, my wife convinces me to attend a ballet. Now I really don't understand the ballet. No matter how much I pay for the tickets, I never hear what they say. Last time I went to the ballet, I noticed the girl danced around on her toes for the whole evening and so I asked my wife, "Why don't they just get a taller girl.

If a man's golf scores range in the high nineties, friends say he neglects his golf. When, after considerable effort, he brings those scores down into the low eighties, they say he neglects his business. You can't win!

The little league coach called one of his players over to him and said: "We don't believe in temper tantrums, screaming at the umpire, and tossing things onto the field. Do you understand that?"

"Yes, sir," answered the boy. "Well, then," sighed the coach, "please try to explain it to your father."

A football coach called his players together in the locker room before the first big game of the season. "Now, remember, men," he said, "football is a game which develops courage, leadership and, above all, individual initiative. Now get out there and don't forget to do exactly what I tell you!"

An executive who passed an asylum on his way to work, used to stop every once in a while to watch one of the inmates going through the motions of winding up and pitching an imaginary ball. A friend asked the executive what he found so interesting about the man's performance.

"Well," said the executive, "if things keep on going the way they are, I'll be in there some day catching for that guy, and I want to get on to his curves."

It doesn't matter whether you win or lose, until you lose---
Then it matters.

A certain freshman was promised that if he would join the local athletic fraternity, he would be granted a permit allowing him to buy a football ticket without having to stand in line. One day he went to the stadium and presented his precious permit.

"Get in that line over there," he was told. "But," protested the freshman, "this permit allows me to buy a ticket without standing in line." "I know that," said the ticket taker. "That is the line for people who don't have to stand in line to buy tickets."

"Did you fish with flies?" asked a neighbor to the returning fisherman. "Fish with flies?!" exclaimed the vacationer. "I hope to tell you we did. We camped, dined, fished and slept with 'em!"

A coward, in an emergency, thinks with his legs.

☺☺☺

A sweet old Norwegian lady always followed our cross-country ski team. One day she knitted a pair of socks specifically for our star skier. Gratefully he put them on, then limped through almost an hour of torturous skiing.

When the race was finally over, he sat down, pulled off his shoes, peeled the socks off his aching feet, and found a wad of paper rolled up in the toe. Opening it he read a well-intended note saying, "God bless your tired feet."

☺☺☺

When glory comes, loss of memory follows.
-French Proverb-

☺☺☺

Little League Soccer Coach: We have a great team this year. So far we've had no losses, no forfeits, and no points scored against us.
Friend: That's fantastic!
Coach: Yes...the first game is next Saturday.

☺☺☺

The Primary teacher asked Robby why he was late. "I was going to go fishing this morning with my dad and Uncle Lynn," he answered, "but dad wouldn't let me go."

"How fortunate you have such an understanding father," commented the teacher. "I hope he also explained why you shouldn't fish on Sunday."

"He sure did," Robby replied. "He said there wasn't room enough in the boat for all of us."

☺☺☺

There is a football story about a high school team which is losing 6-0 late in the game. The coach, desperate for any chance of winning, sends in a young and inexperienced quarterback and tells him to do whatever he can.

The quarterback calls play No. 11, and the team scores a touchdown on a 90-yard run. They kick the extra point and win the game as the gun goes off. After the cheers subside, the coach asks the quarterback why he chose play No. 11, which the team never practiced.

The quarterback replied "I looked in front of me and saw our best player, and he was No. 7. I saw our second best player and he was No. 6. When I put them together, I called play No. 11."

The coach said, "Son, don't you know that 7 and 6 make 13?" The quarterback paused for a moment and replied, "Boy, coach, if I was as smart as you are, we never would have won the game."

You can discover more about a person in an hour of play
Than in a year of conversation.
-Plato-

☺☺☺

"I'd move heaven and earth to break 100," the golfing duffer said as he swung at his ball. "Concentrate on heaven," pleaded his friend. "You've moved enough earth already!"

☺☺☺

Time was passing slowly on Noah's ark, so the lion suggested to the giraffe that they choose sides for a football game. The giraffe agreed. The lion's team kicked off and on the first play from scrimmage the monkey handed off the ball to the rhino, who charged up the middle for 10 yards.

On the next play, the rhino scrambled all the way for a touchdown. At halftime the giraffe's team was leading 42-0. Early in the second half the monkey again handed off to the rhino. The rhino headed for a hole in the line, but the centipede, who was playing defensive tackle, reared up, grabbed the rhino and threw him to the deck, causing a fumble. The rabbit, who was playing free safety, picked up the ball and scored for the lion's team.

The lion was elated. "Fantastic tackle!" he exclaimed to the centipede. "Where were you during the first half?!" The centipede replied, "I was lacing up my shoes."

☺☺☺

As the king came to a small city near Nottingham, England, he noted that an archer had used the city wall as a backdrop for his targets. To the surprise of the King, all the arrows were right in the center of the targets.

The king, in his speech at the great banquet that evening, asked for the archer to come forward . As the man came forward the audience all laughed and cheered. The King decided to knight the archer for his great talent. As he finished his speech he "Dubbed" the archer as a knight of the round table. The audience laughed, some booed and many just looked stunned. The King asked the local sheriff why the people were so rude.

"You see Sir," said the Sheriff, "the man you've just knighted is not really a great archer, but the town idiot. He shoots the arrows first, and then draws the target."

☺☺☺

Parents and Children are in a constant battle,
If either ever wins, they both lose forever.

☺☺☺

Golf is a game in which a ball less than 2 inches in diameter is placed on a ball more than 8,000 miles in diameter. The objective of the game is to hit the small ball, not the large one.

My father was describing the toughest fish he had ever caught to his grandchildren. "It took me three hours to land this terrific sea monster," he said. "Grandpa!" said one of the grandchildren, "I've seen the pictures....that fish was only six inches long."

"Sure," admitted their grandfather, "but after three hours of fighting, a fish can loose a lot of weight."

Before going into college basketball coaching, Dick Shultz, head coach at the University of Iowa, was a minor league baseball catcher. He once had a manger who was given to eccentric lineup changes.

The manager decided one night to put a rookie third baseman at first base, a position he had never played before. The inevitable happened. a left-handed batter drilled a grounder to the neophyte first baseman, who grabbed the ball and, instead of stepping on the base for the out, reflexively began to throw, quite as if he were playing third. But halfway through the throwing motion he realized where he was and fell into a series of contortions in an effort to keep from throwing the ball away. The runner was so startled by this that he stopped on the baseline. The first baseman finally fired the ball to home plate, where Catcher Schultz made a startled grab.

"I didn't want the ball," Schultz says, "so I threw it back to him." Although the runner had stopped, the first baseman still did not think to step on first. Instead, he did what a third baseman would do. He cut him off and started a rundown play. The runner, by now as confused as anyone, fell into the act as the first baseman and Schultz began throwing the ball back and forth. Finally the runner made his break back to his last base, which happened to be home. Schultz tagged him and the umpire bellowed, "You're out!"

Schultz had only one question. He turned to the umpire and inquired innocently: "What would you have done if he had been safe?"

–Sports Illustrated, April 1971–

Pro football is like nuclear warfare.
There are no winners, only survivors.

A coach is a fellow who will gladly lay down YOUR LIFE for the school.

A little boy went to the Psychiatrist and said "Everybody hates me and I get beat up by everybody. I'm going to run away."

The psychiatrist said "If you run away, where will you go?" The little boy said, "I'm going to run away to the University of Utah football team...they don't beat anybody."

WHY A MINISTER QUIT SPORTS

According to the Rev. Arthur C. Johnson of the Cottonwood Presbyterian Church, there are 12 reasons why he quit sports. Any similarities between these reasons and why his members didn't attend Church services seem more than coincidental. The reasons:

(1) Every time I went, they asked me for money.
(2) The people with whom I had to sit didn't seem very friendly.
(3) The seats were too hard and not at all comfortable.
(4) I went to many games, but the coach never came to call on me.
(5) The referee made a decision with which I could not agree.
(6) I suspected that I was sitting with some hypocrites. They came to see their friends and what others were wearing, rather than to see the game.
(7) Some games went into overtime, and I was late getting home.
(8) The band played some number that I had never heard before.
(9) It seems that the games are always scheduled when I want to do other things.
(10) I was taken to too many games by my parents when I was growing up.
(11) I recently read a book on sports and now I feel that I know more than the coaches do.
(12) I don't want to take my children to any games because I want them to choose for themselves what sport they like best.

☺☺☺

Highway sign just out of Yellowstone Park

Fishermen, do you have worms?
Smile anyway!

☺☺☺

You can tell our Bishop is a sports fan.
He always reminds us that Heaven is the goal--but Satan is the goalie!
☺☺☺

"Jog??? Who Me???
Heavens no! I want to be sick when I die!

☺☺☺

"Do I jog?
No, I'm too busy speaking at the funerals of my friends who do!"
-Gordon B. Hinckley-

☺☺☺

A modest way to accept a generous introduction

"I want to thank you for that glowing introduction. I think some of your statements were overly generous--but as a poor golfer, I always appreciate a good lie."

My neighbor is a physical fitness buff. The other day as I was leaving for work he came jogging by and asked: "Why don't you drive by my side and see how fast I can run."

So I started at 10 MPH and he stayed right with me. I sped up to 20 MPH, looked out my window and he was still there. The same thing happened at 30, 35 and 45 MPH. Then there was a large bang, and he disappeared.

Quickly I stopped and went running back to find him. He was hanging in a tree, looking something awful. "What happened?!" I asked. Feebly he replied, "Have you ever blown a sneaker at 45 MPH?"

One jogger, huffing and puffing, to another: "The doctor was certainly right when he said that jogging would add years to my life. I feel ten years older already."

While driving through the desert one day, we saw a man running down the road with a bottle of juice, a loaf of bread and carrying a car door. Curious, we stopped and asked, "What are you doing?"

"I like to jog," was his answer. "Then why are you carrying all of that stuff." "Well," he explained, "When I run long distances, I need to stop and drink and eat occasionally." "But why the car door?" we asked. "When it gets hot," the jogger answered, "I just roll down the window."

I used to worry about my health--
but that was back when I had some.

My husband never took up jogging until he passed a weighing machine in Las Vegas that said I SPEAK YOUR WEIGHT. So he put a dime in the slot and stepped on the platform. A voice spoke up and said, "One at a time, please."

Whenever I get the urge to jog
I go lie down until it passes.

Studies show that, on average, anyone who runs ten miles a day, every day, in good weather and bad, in the blazing summer heat and in the frigid winter cold---will live to the age of 90.

And if they don't live 'til 90---they'll look 90!

During quail season in Georgia, an Atlanta journalist met an old farmer hunting with an ancient pointer at his side. Twice the dog ran rheumatically ahead and pointed. Twice his master fired into the open air. When the journalist saw no birds rise, he asked the farmer for an explanation.

"Shucks," grinned the old man, "I knew there weren't no birds in that grass. Spot's nose ain't what it used to be. But him and me have had some wonderful times together. He's still doing the best he can -- and it'd be mighty mean of me to call him a liar at this stage of the game!"

☺☺☺

"I'd rather watch a winner than hear one any day!!"

☺☺☺

"If you're ten minutes early, you're five minutes late!

-Vince Lombardi-

☺☺☺

"WINNERS MAKE IT HAPPEN.
LOSERS LET IT HAPPEN."

☺☺☺

"Doing nothing is one of the hardest of all jobs.
When you get tired, you can't rest."

☺☺☺

"I am sorry," said the dentist, "but I can't give you an appointment this afternoon. I have eighteen cavities to fill." And with that he picked up his golf bag and out of the office he went.

☺☺☺

And when that One Great Scorer comes
To mark against your name,

He writes not that your won or lost
But how you played the game.
-Grantland Rice-

☺☺☺

He lost the game
    No matter for that --
He kept his temper,
    He swung his hat
And cheered the winners --
    A better way,
Than to lose his temper
    And win the day.

BABE RUTH

Let me give you a quick little Babe Ruth story to show you the kind of man he was. The great New York Yankees went into Philadelphia one day to play a very important three-game series with the old Philadelphia Athletics. They had a left-handed pitcher, named Robert Moses Grove or "Lefty" Grove. A member of the Hall of Fame, 6 feet 4 inches tall, about 220 pounds and could throw harder than anyone in baseball at that time. Lefty Grove was a little bit mean, too. Someone said that Lefty Grove wouldn't give his mother a good pitch to hit. He was just mean; when he missed, he missed high and inside all the time. He just wasn't going to be beat by the Yankees.

So on this day, with 35,000 fans screaming in that little shy, intimate park where the stands are right near the playing surface, Babe Ruth and the Bronx Bombers came to town. At the top of the first inning--the Babe always hit third in the line-up...the Babe digs in with the fans just booing something terrible. Grove throws three fast balls by him, just bing, bing, bing, and he's out. As he turns to go to the dugout, with 35,000 fans booing him, the Babe tipped his hat, smiled, put his bat in the rack, and took a drink at the fountain.

Undisturbed about failure, Babe came back in the third inning and Grove struck him out again on three straight pitches...The Fans booed louder. The Babe tipped his hat, smiled, put his bat in the rack and had a drink at the fountain. Babe came up in the seventh and Grove got him out again, and now the fans were getting a little personal. The Philadelphia fans were terrible, and they were calling him names. Babe just tipped his hat, smiled, put his bat in the rack and got a drink at the fountain. The old Babe had that quiet confidence: "I'm gonna get ya, I'm gonna get ya, if I keep at it long enough."

He got up in the top of the ninth, and the score was 4-2 for the Athletics. Top of the ninth, Yankees behind, two men on base. The Babe digs in, and 35,000 fans were just sure that he was going to be a failure again. Out on the mound, Lefty Grove was thinking, "What am I going to throw him now?" At the plate Babe says, "He has thrown fast balls by me all day; he's going to try and throw another fast ball by me." So he digs in and Grove says, "I'm going to throw him a curve ball." So the Babe swings for a fast ball, and he missed it THAT FAR. The fans got excited and booed him again; he dug in again and said, "I've got to get the fast ball this time." Grove says, "He's looking for a fast ball, so I'm going to throw him a change-of-pace." That's a slow pitch, a dirty pitch; that change-of-pace. He threw him a change, and the Babe was way out front, lost his balance, and sat right down on home plate. Now the fans really got on him. The Babe stood up, dusted himself off and dug in again. The fans really booed him. Grove said, "I've thrown him the curve, and the change, I'm going to throw a fast ball right by him." Babe says, "He's thrown me a curve ball, and the change -- I'll bet he's going to try and throw a fast ball right by me." So he dug in, looked for the fast ball, got the fast ball, and he not only made contact but he hit the ball up on the building across the street.

Well, as the Babe started down toward first base with that funny little waddle he had, there wasn't a sound in the ball park, not a sound. As he went around first base some guy in the bleachers tapped another guy and said, "He's pretty good," and then he started to clap. Now when the Babe crossed home plate, there was a thunderous ovation. "We knew you could do it, Babe; we knew you could do it." The Babe just tipped his hat, smiled, and took a drink at the fountain. -Excerpts from a talk by Glen Tuckett-

A father asked his son (who was on the football team) why they had been beaten so badly. His son said "Dad, haven't you heard that we have a drug problem?" The father exclaimed "A drug problem?!"

"Yes," said the son. "The other team <u>drug</u> our butts up the field one way and then <u>drug</u> 'em down the field the other way."

O.J. SIMPSON

In 1959, the great Jim Brown had just finished another remarkable football game for the Cleveland Browns. Jim was acclaimed, in his day, to be the greatest football player to ever play the game. In the vernacular of the day he was awesome. As he ran into the tunnel leading to the locker room, he met a skinny little kid, suffering from rickets, who had been waiting patiently to get his autograph.

The boy stopped Jim Brown and said, "Mr. Brown, could I please have your autograph?" Being the kind of individual who loved youngsters, Jim stopped and signed the boy's autograph book and started toward the locker room, but the boy was not finished. He tugged on Jim's jersey and said,

"Mr. Brown, I want you to know that I am 12 years old and I am going to play little league football this fall and you're my hero."

The great Jim Brown smiled at the boy, and took the boy's scrawney little hand in his big hand. Then he turned and started again for the locker room, but the boy was not finished. Again he tugged on the jersey and said,

"Mr. Brown, I want you to know that I am going to break all of your football records." Now this stopped Jim in his tracks and he knelt down by the boy and talked to him for a second. "Son, what is your name?" he asked.

"It's Orenthal James Simpson, but my friends call me O.J."

And break records he did. Although as a youth he had suffered from rickets and was not overly impressive in high school, he played Jr. College football and later became the Heisman trophey winner at USC. Eventually, although he cut his career somewhat short in the NFL, he broke all but three of the great Jim Brown's records.

Certainly, I believe in excercise.
I do 15 minutes every morning,

That is unless I do it fast
Then it takes less time.

Bishop: Church athletics is a ZOO!
Athletic Director: No it's a JUNGLE! It isn't well enough
    organized to be considered a ZOO!

"Every boy in his heart, would rather steal second base than an automobile."

"I don't go into a ball game just hoping to play a good ball game. I go into the ball game to try to win. They still keep score, don't they? As long as they keep score, someone is anxious to know how it is going to come out, and I am one of those anxious people."

-Adolph Rupp–University of Kentucky–

IT COULDN'T BE DONE
-Edgar A. Guest-

Somebody said that it couldn't be done.
But he with a chuckle replied,
That "maybe it couldn't," but he would be one
Who wouldn't say so till he tried.
So he buckled right in with the trace of a grin
On his face. If he worried he hid it.
He started to sing as he tackled the thing
That couldn't be done, and he did it.

Somebody scoffed: "Oh, you'll never do that;
At least no one ever has done it."
But he took off his coat and he took off his hat,
And the first thing we knew he'd begun it.
With a lift of his chin and a bit of a grin,
Without any doubting or quiddit,
He started to sing as he tackled the thing
That couldn't be done, and he did it!

There are thousands to tell you it cannot be done.
There are thousands to prophesy failure;
There are thousands to point out to you, one by one,
The dangers that wait to assail you.
But just buckle in with a bit of a grin,
Just take off your coat and go to it;
Just start to sing as you tackle the thing
That "cannot be done", and you'll do it.

After the Stake President tried for the fourth time to drive out of a sand trap with no success, he picked up his golf club and broke it, but didn't say a word. Then he picked up the golf bag and threw it into the lake, but still he didn't say one bad word. Then he took the golf balls that had fallen on the ground and threw them into the rough. Still not a bad word. Finally he muttered in disgust, "I'm going to have to give it up!"

"Give up golf?" asked the young priest who was his caddie.

"No!" he replied. The Church!!!!"

BUCKLE IN

You've failed, you say, my boy?
Ah well,
The world will still be bright.
The strongest scrapper of them all
Must sometimes lose a fight.

The fastest horse that ever ran
Sees times when he can't win.
You've failed, you say, boy?
Ah well,
Just smile and buckle in.

The man who wins success must fail,
Not once, but often, lad.
All victories that come to one,
In failures must be clad.

The fellow who's ahead has seen
The times he didn't win.
He's had his setbacks--lots of them,
So smile and buckle in.

Hard work will do most anything,
If you'll but keep it up.
And in the end 'twill let you, lad
Drink from good fortune's cup.
You've failed, you say, my boy?

Ah well,
Greet failure with a grin
Keep pluggin' and you'll land on top
Get busy, buckle in!

☺☺☺

Mark Twain, the famous American humorist, puts it this way:
"If at first you don't succeed, Fail, Fail, Again."

☺☺☺

My doctor says he doesn't believe in unnecessary surgery --
He won't operate unless he really needs the money!

☺☺☺

Two cheerleaders were comparing notes on their respective boy friends. "He kissed my hand," complained one.

"That's the way a man with experience kisses," said the other.

"Oh yeh," returned the first, "you'd think a guy with experience would have better aim.

" GOOD, THE KIDS HAVE T.P.-ED THEIR SEMINARY
TEACHER. THAT MEANS THEY ARE STARTING TO LIKE HIM."

TEENAGERS

A suburban father read that a middle-aged man should not shovel wet snow because he could have a heart attack. So he called in his teenager and said, "Son, a middle-aged man should not shovel wet snow because he could have a heart attack, so would you do it for me?" The son said "Yes" and the father had a heart attack.

☺☺☺

Our teenage son complained of excruciating pains in his stomach, so fearing appendicitis we rushed him to the doctor. "What did you eat?" the doctor asked. "I had a piece of angel food cake." "Angel food cake shouldn't make a healthy lad like you sick," the doctor exclaimed.

"Well, Doc," my boy continued, "last night we had this swell birthday party. I drank plenty of punch, ate peanuts and pretzels. The chip and dip were good, but the sour pickles and hot peppers were my favorites. When dinner finally came we had choices of Kentucky Fried Chicken, hamburgers, hot dogs and pizza....naturally I had plenty of all four. After dinner they served the best homemade ice cream and apple pie...I must have had at least four servings and loved it. Then we went swimming and I still felt fine...but when I came home, I ate that lousy piece of angel food cake and it made me sick!"

☺☺☺

One sure way of keeping a teenage daughter out of hot water
is to put some dirty dishes in it.

☺☺☺

A teenager's essay on Quakers

"Quakers are very meek, quiet people who never fight or answer back.
My father is a Quaker, but my mother is something else!"

☺☺☺

A man and his wife were on their way out after giving instructions to the baby-sitter. The telephone rang so the husband returned to answer it. "How on earth should I know?" he said. "Why don't you call the Coast Guard?!" Then disgustedly he hung up and started toward the door with his wife.

"Who was that, dear," inquired his wife. "I haven't the faintest idea," replied the unsuspecting husband. "Some stupid teenager who wanted to know if the coast was clear."

☺☺☺

"Isn't it amazing how fast the teenager who can't learn to run a vacuum cleaner or lawnmower learns to drive the family car?"

One day when I got home from work my teenage daughter was crying. "What's the matter?" I asked. "My dog ate the pie I had made for you," she said, wiping away some tears. "Don't worry, honey," I said, "I'll buy you another dog."

☺☺☺

Boy on receiving an invitation to a stake dance, ask his mother, "Do I have to wear a suit and tie, or can I wear my own clothes?"

☺☺☺

Mother: "I had a frank discussion with our teenage daughter today about the facts of life."
Father: "Did you learn anything?"

☺☺☺

Teenage girl to saleslady in boutique: I need shoes for the dance. They've got to bring me up to Jimmy's shoulder, but not past Roger's head!

☺☺☺

A young man turned to his father after fast and testimony meeting and said, "Well, let's go home and celebrate the feast of the fast over."

☺☺☺

Seminary teacher: "Did you read the Bible?"
Student: "No, I saw the movie."

☺☺☺

You can tell that a child is growing up when he stops asking where he came from and quits telling you where he's going!

☺☺☺

Mama kept the Bible read
Daddy kept the family fed

And somewhere in between
I must have grown.

☺☺☺

Insanity is hereditary...
We inherit it from our children.

☺☺☺

Mother: "Every time you do something wrong I get another gray hair.
Daughter:"Is that why grandma's hair is so gray?"

There would be fewer problems with children today if they had to chop wood to keep the TV going.

☺☺☺

The best way to keep teenagers at home is to make the home atmosphere pleasant--and hide the car keys!

☺☺☺

A young man wanted a part-time job. He spotted a help wanted ad, placed by an exclusive restaurant, which read: "Parking attendant---Experience Preferred." Since he was barely old enough to drive, he had never worked as a parking attendant. However, he replied to the advertisement and listed his experience as: "Member of a four-car family with a one lane driveway." He got the job.

☺☺☺

Four high school boys, afflicted with spring fever, skipped morning classes. After lunch, they reported to the teacher that their car had had a flat tire. Much to their relief, she smiled and said: "Well, you missed a test this morning, so take your seats apart from one another and get out your notebooks." Still smiling, she waited for them to settle down. Then she said, "First question: Which tire was flat?"

☺☺☺

Definition of a teenager
A Human Gimmie Pig!

☺☺☺

You can lock me up in jail, you can throw the key away
But you can't stop my face from breaking out!
- A Country Western Song -

☺☺☺

When girls leave for summer camp it can be a highly emotional experience. My daughter cried her eyes out when she suddenly realized that she was leaving those nearest and dearest to her in all the world...the phone, the TV and the refrigerator.

☺☺☺

We originally put him in charge of refreshments...but it didn't work out. He flunked Kool-Aid. He couldn't figure out how to get a quart of water into that little envelope.

☺☺☺

Note left by teenage boy:
"Mom, I came home with a very bad headache and stomach ache.
I've taken two aspirins, a glass of milk and I've gone out to play football."

NOTE FROM MOM

Daughter of the universe,   May I ask one thing of you
Child of the atom age,   Before I have to screem?
Goddess of Aquarius,   Gymnast, jumper, acrobat,
Dancer on the stage,   Gazer on the moon,
Daffodil or buttercup,   Would you mind so terribly
Chaser of a dream,   To PLEASE CLEAN UP YOUR ROOM!

-Toledo Blade-

☺☺☺

Father: "Get a job, my boy. Work! Save your money. Soon you'll have enough money to stop working."
Son: "I'm not working now!"

☺☺☺

A father took his teenage daughter, who had been visiting his office, to an elegant restaurant for lunch. She ordered a hamburger. "Why not order something different or unusual?" urged her father. "But Daddy," she said, "I have never eaten a $5.00 hamburger before!"

☺☺☺

The Laurels and priests were having an old-fashioned sleigh ride. Everyone was having a wonderful time except one girl, who felt left out.
"What's the matter," asked one of the priests.
"Nobody loves me," whispered the young lady. "And my hands are cold."
"That's all right," he whispered comfortingly. "I'm sure your mother loves you, and you can sit on your hands."

☺☺☺

The main trouble with being a parent is that by the time you are experienced, you're suddenly unemployed.

☺☺☺

The Sunday School teacher was trying to teach the students the value of repetition. "You have my assurance, that if you repeat anything seven to ten times, it will be yours forever." On the back row one of the young girls sighed and whispered, "Donny, Donny, Donny....."

☺☺☺

Son: Father, how many gods are there?
Father: Hmmm, I don't really know.
Son: What does heaven look like?
Father: I don't know, son.
Son: I'm not bothering you, am I, Dad?"
Father: Not at all, my boy. You don't learn anything if you don't ask.

1916 BEEHIVE REQUIREMENTS
–Juvenile Instructor–

In 1916 every female over fourteen was a Beehive girl until she entered Relief Society. There were no Mia Maids, or Laurels. The following are twenty out of the three-hundred seventy-three requirements possible for a Beehive girl to earn her individual award:

1. Care successfully for a hive of bees for one season, and know their habits.
2. Give the distinguishing characteristics of 6 varieties of hen and cattle and tell the good and weak points of each.
3. Exterminate the mosquitos over an area of 1/2 mile square by pouring a little kerosene on the surface of all standing pools of water twice each month during April, May, or June. Six girls may do this and each receive an award, or one girl can receive six awards.
4. Make two articles of underwear by hand.
5. Cover 25 miles on snowshoes in any six days.

6. Learn to float in Great Salt Lake and propel yourself 50 feet.
7. During three consecutive months, abstain from candy, ice cream, commercially manufactured beverages and chewing gum.
8. For one month, masticate (chew) your food so thoroughly that it slips down without any visible effort at swallowing it.
9. Successfully put a new washer on a faucet.
10. Care for at least two kerosene lamps daily.

11. For three months, take care of milk and cream from at least one cow and see that the pails, pans, strainer, and separator are thoroughly cleansed.
12. During two weeks, keep the house free from flies or destroy at least 25 flies daily.
13. Have your toilet moved to an isolated place in the garden. Have a frame of chicken wire built about three feet away and plant quick-growing vines such as cucumber or morning glories to screen it from observation.
14. Whitewash your toilet inside and out.
15. Know and describe three cries of a baby.

16. Without help or advice, care for and harness a team at least five times; drive fifty miles during one season.
17. During 2 summer months, clean ice chest thoroughly twice a week.
18. Discover ten reasons why the Columbine should be made the national flower.
19. Clear sagebrush, etc. off of one-half acre of land.
20. Know 6 blazes used by Indians.

In a lesson on marriage, the teacher tried to explain to the young people the significance of the color white. "White," she explained, "stands for joy. That is why the bridal gown is white. Her wedding day should be the most joyous occasion of a young lady's life."

"Why, then," asked one of the boys, "do the men wear black?"

Teenage Daughter: Dad, the Bishop wants me to give a 15 minute talk
      in Sacrament meeting next week.
Father: That's wonderful.
Daughter: I can't talk for 15 minutes!
Father: Perhaps the Bishop would let you could take the phone to the podium
with you.

☺☺☺

When there is a bad storm, my kids think nothing of shoveling two feet of snow
from our driveway....at least, I guess that is why they don't do it!

☺☺☺

Many a teenager is the kind of kid
His mother wouldn't want him to play with.

☺☺☺

Definition of a Chaperone

One who could never make the team,
But is still in there intercepting passes.

☺☺☺

Physically, most teenagers are like a house on moving day
-- A temporary mess.

☺☺☺

Learn from the mistakes of others,
You'll never live long enough to make them all yourself.

☺☺☺

"That rug looks terrible. Sweep it under the dirt!"

☺☺☺

Sunday School teacher: "What happens when a body is immersed in water?"
Teenager: "The telephone rings."

☺☺☺

Mr. Blank: "She's a girl with a great deal of faith."

Mrs. Blank: "I've never noticed. What makes you think that?"

Mr. Blank: "She believes she can fit a size 9 body in a size 7 dress."

☺☺☺

"Youth is a wonderful thing. Too bad we waste it on teenagers."

We have five children...
Three are living... Two are teenagers!

☺☺☺

Teenage daughter: "What's good for biting nails?"
Mother: "Sharp teeth!"

☺☺☺

I climbed the door and shut off the stairs
I said my shoes and took off my prayers

I brushed my makeup and took off my teeth
I pulled down my alarm and set my sheets

I shut off the bed and climbed into the light
And all because he kissed me goodnight!

☺☺☺

A friend asked what is it like to raise a teenager? I said, remember what your two year old was like when he went through the "terrible twos"?

Well....just multiply that by eight and add a drivers license!

☺☺☺

Juvenile Delinquent
A minor
Who is a
Major Problem

☺☺☺

I thought I'd rather have a blister,
Than be cursed with another sister.
I said if I could have my druther,
She'd have been my little brother.

Yes, I'd like to have a brother,
But, now he'll have to be another.
One thing's for sure and I tell you mister.
No one's greater than little sister.

☺☺☺

Parents of teenagers worry about their children's eyesight
It seems that their daughter can't find anything to wear in a closet full of clothes and the son can't find anything to eat in a refrigerator full of food.

☺☺☺

A modern gentleman is one who insists that his wife should not touch the heavy chores as long as she can get the children to do them!

WEALTH
and
POVERTY

While attending graduate school, money was a scarce commodity at our house. One evening when my wife came home from work she was wearing a new dress. Cautiously she approached me and said: "Now don't get mad, just tell me how you like it." I had to admit, it did look nice. But you know you have to be firm with a new wife, so I said, "Honey, why did you buy that? You know we can't afford it."

At this she started to cry, "I don't know, the Devil must have tempted me." So I said, "You have heard in Sunday School, Seminary, etc., that when the Devil tempts you, you should say, 'Get thee behind me Satan.'"

"I did," she sobbed. "What did he say?" I asked. He said, "Boy, it sure looks good from the back."

☺☺☺

One year I gave my wife a $10 gift certificate on her birthday.
To my surprise, she used it as a down payment on a $2000 fur coat.

☺☺☺

Charity is like a good pair of underwear.
It is a good thing to make you feel warm inside,
But it is not something you should display in public.

☺☺☺

During a long spell of hot, dry weather in Utah, an old Pioneer remarked, "I'll tell you why we haven't had any thunderstorms. The good Lord can't afford the electricity rates."

☺☺☺

One day our teenage daughter dropped her contact lens in a wastebasket, which was full of trash. She looked through the trash for a moment, but in vain. After a minute she quit looking. I searched through the trash and found the lens.

"How on earth did you find it?" she asked. "Well," I explained, "You were only looking for a small piece of plastic, but I was looking for $150.00!!!"

☺☺☺

A friend in need -- Is a friend to feed!

Generations of great thinkers have dreamed
Of a moneyless society somewhere in the future.

As far as my family is concerned,
We're already ahead of our time.

☺☺☺

A recession is when your neighbor loses his job.
A depression is when you lose your job;
A panic is when your wife loses her job.

☺☺☺

The next time you feel like complaining, remember that your garbage disposal probably eats better than 50 percent of the people in the world.

☺☺☺

The easiest way to figure the cost of living
Is to take your income and add ten percent.

☺☺☺

An Irishman, down on his luck, was panhandling on Fifth Avenue before the annual St. Patrick's Day parade got under way in New York City. As a couple strolled by, he called out: "May the blessing of the Lord, which brings love and joy and wealth and a fine family, follow you all the days of your life." There was a pause as the couple passed his outstretched hand without contributing. Then he shouted after them, "And never catch up to you!"

☺☺☺

We think we're all born free
Until the bill from the doctor comes.

☺☺☺

When you get your hospital bill,
You understand why surgeons wear masks in the operating room.

☺☺☺

A burglar entered the chapel late one night and to his surprise ran right into the bishop who had just turned off the lights to go home. Drawing his knife, the burglar said: "If you say anything you're a dead man. I'm hunting for money." "Let me turn on the lights," said the Bishop, "and I'll look with you."

☺☺☺

Two youngsters were discussing the subject of piggy banks. "I think it's a childish way to save money," little Lori declared. "Me too," replied Annie. "It encourages children to become misers." "And that's not the worst of it," added Lori, "it turns parents into bank robbers."

267

"What's a million dollars to you, who is all-powerful?" a man asked the Lord.
"Hardly a penny," the Lord replied.
"What's twenty years to the Lord," asked the man.
"Hardly a second," said the Lord.
"Then, O Lord, please loan me a penny for a second," begged the man.
"OK," said the Lord, "but you'll have to wait just a minute."

A Sermon on the Amount:

Render unto Caesar that which is Caesars'
And unto God that which is God's----
But remember that that which you render unto God
Is deductible.

"Some people's only idea of exercise is letting bills run."

"Some people think they are worth a lot of money simply because they have it."

Money won't buy happiness.
But it's a lot easier to cope with depression
In a Rolls Royce than in a Ford Pinto.

A very elegant socialite died and arrived at the gates of Heaven.
"Welcome, come right in." St. Peter said.
"Absolutely not," she said, "anyplace where a stranger can enter without a reservation is not my idea of heaven."

A rich oil man in Dallas had finished off a huge mansion-type ranch house, similar to those on the T.V. shows. It the back he had a full olympic-size swimming pool. He invited all of his friends over for a big Texas Barbecue and a chance to "christen" the swimming pool. To his friend's surprise, he had filled the swimming pool full of hungry alligators. As he started the evening he said, "You all know I'm a wealthy man, and I know all of you would like to be as wealthy as I am. I agree to share with anyone who dares swim the length of this pool, one-half of my fortune!"

Everyone was crowded around the pool and suddenly they all let out a gasp! There was a large splash and one guy just flew the length of the pool, and when he got out on the other side he was hardly wet! "I can't believe that you would risk your life like that for money and wealth," the rich man said. "The swimmer replied, "I can't believe it either!....and I'd like to find the guy who pushed me in!"

After the Teton Dam broke and many Mormon families were virtually washed away in the upper Snake River Valley, my father-in-law and another farmer sat dejectedly looking at what had once been their beautiful farms. My father-in-law turned to the other farmer, who had recently been offered a reasonable sum of money for the purchase of his property, and said, "You know, I really should have sold you that farm a few months back."

The farmer reached in his pocket and he said, "Well, I've got 17 cents. How about selling it now?" To which my father-in-law added, "Naw, I wouldn't want to over charge you."

☺☺☺

The rich lady of the house was interviewing an applicant for a job on her household staff.
"Do you know how to serve company?" she asked.
"Yes, madam. Both ways," was the reply.
"Just what do you mean, both ways?"
"So's they'll come back or so's they won't."

☺☺☺

Man, after evaluating how much it would cost if his wife redecorated his house as she intended: "Honey, instead of redoing the walls, why don't we just paper them with dollar bills and bank the difference."

☺☺☺

If you have plenty of money, you'll have hair.

☺☺☺

A poor man will walk a mile to save a buck;
A rich man will walk five.

☺☺☺

If your outflow exceeds your income --
Then your upkeep will be your downfall.

☺☺☺

Would you like to live with ease?
Then do what you ought, and not what you please.

-Benjamin Franklin-

☺☺☺

He started as poor as a proverbial church mouse twenty years ago. He has now retired with a fortune of $1,000,000.00.

This money was acquired through economy, conscientious effort to give full value, indomitable perseverance, and the death of an uncle who left him $999,999.50.

As the Stake President, I have the opportunity to talk with missionaries as they return from their missions. They share their testimonies, their spiritual experiences--some their humorous experiences. One the other day was most interesting.

The young missionary said, "I had a dream that was as real as real. I dreamed that I died and went to Heaven. I got up there and it was everything people told me about--pearly gates and streets and a large parking lot paved with gold. St Peter met me and explained, "In Heaven you are rewarded a vehicle according to how good you were on earth. That Rolls Royce over there for example, belongs to Joseph Smith while the Mercedes coupe is Brigham Young's."

Well, the missionary couldn't wait to see what kind of car he would get. He felt he had been a pretty good guy on earth. But to his surprise St. Peter brought out a little Honda mo-ped and said, "This is yours."

"A mo-ped! I was a pretty good guy on earth; why only a mo-ped?" St. Peter paused and said, "You may think you deserve more, but my records show you earned the mo-ped. Try it for a few days and I think you will feel quite comfortable."

A few days later St. Peter bumped into the missionary and noticed that he was much happier. "See, I told you the day would come when you would feel comfortable on the mo-ped."

"Well, I don't know that I feel more comfortable," the missionary said, "but I feel better about it since I saw President Briggs go by on a skateboard."

SUCCESS COMES FROM LEARNING HOW TO SET PRIORITIES

Last year in the Uintah mountains, a deer hunter returned to base camp carrying a large six-point buck. After everyone admired his prize buck, someone asked, "Didn't you go hunting with George?"

"Oh, I almost forgot," commented the successful hunter. "About five miles down the canyon, just after I shot his beautiful six-point buck, George had a heart attack and died. I had to make a tough decision , I could either carry George or the buck. Then I realized NOBODY would steal George!"

"The glow of one warm thought is to me worth more than money."
-Thomas Jefferson-

Christopher Columbus is the father of modern financial success.

He set a goal.
When he achieved it he wasn't sure where he was,
Nor did he know how he got there,
But he was able to do it totally on borrowed money!

Harold worked as a painters helper. He was an excellent worker, although he never had much to say. The painter felt fortunate to have such a dedicated helper.

One day the painter got sick and had to stay home. He decided to see if Harold could manage to paint the house on his own. A couple of days later, when the painter felt better, he decided to drive over to see how Harold was doing.

To his surprise, he found Harold lounging under a tree, drinking a beer. Several empty bottles were lying in the grass around him. Up on the ladders were two young high school boys painting the house.

"What's going on here?" asked the astonished painter.

"Oh," said Harold nonchalantly, "I hired me a couple of helpers. Paying 'em five bucks an hour."

"Five dollars an hour! How can you afford that? I only pay you $7.00!"

"Yeah, I know," replied Harold. "But for me it's worth it, just to be the boss for once in my life."

☺☺☺

THE SECRET OF THE WORTHLESS ZERO

"Son, BIG things are just like LITTLE things; only BIG things have more ZEROS after them. If you are RIGHT in the SMALL things, you can multiply them by ten, by a hundred, or by a million, and they will still be RIGHT.

But if you are WRONG in the SMALL things, you can't make them RIGHT by adding ZEROS. A BIG man is one who learns how to do the LITTLE things RIGHT, so that when he faces a BIG job, all he has to do is add the ZEROS.

A key chain is a wonderful gadget
That allows us to lose several keys at the same time.

My father worked for many years in a big grain elevator. The elevator was the roosting area for many pigeons. During one period of time when farmers were losing their farms and struggling to make ends meet. He shared with me this bit of farm town wisdom:

"Son," He asked. "What is the difference between a farmer and a pigeon?"

"The pigeon can still make a small deposit on a big tractor."

When we were young, life in the Briggs' home was somewhat of a struggle. Our parents tried to teach us the value of provident living. Over the old coal stove was a little needle work wall-hanging that expressed beautifully the pioneer philosophy of our family:

EAT IT UP; WEAR IT OUT;
MAKE IT DO, OR DO WITHOUT!!

☺☺☺

A person with one watch knows the time.
A person with two watches is never sure.

☺☺☺

A socialist once came to see Andrew Carnegie and soon was railing against the injustice of Carnegie having so much money. In his view, wealth was meant to be divided equally.

Carnegie asked his secretary for an assessment of everything he owned and at the same time, looked up the figures on world population. He did a little arithmetic on a pad and then said to his secretary,

"Give this gentleman 16 cents. That's his share of my wealth."

☺☺☺

A shrewd Maine farmer was approached by a stranger one day and asked how much he thought his prize Jersey cow was worth.

The farmer thought for a moment, looked the stranger over, then said, "Are you the Tax Assessor or has she been killed by your car?"

☺☺☺

Last year at the Primary Penny Parade I spoke for hours...
But ended up giving them a penny anyway!

☺☺☺

"Remember last year when I was broke, and you helped me out. I said I'd never forget you." "Well, I'm broke again."

☺☺☺

Astronaut: "Studies have yet to find another planet that is able to support life."
Father: "It isn't exactly easy on this planet either."

☺☺☺

College age daughter to father: "All right, I'll admit I like to spend money. But just name one other extravagance."

"WE'RE STILL REHEARSING, SWEETHEART. YOUR SUPPER IS IN THE OVEN."

WOMEN
MOTHERS
WIVES

THE FELLER YOUR MOMMY THINKS YOU ARE

While walking down the street one day,
I heard a little urchin to his comrade turn and say:
"Say, Jimmy, let me tell you I would be happy as a clam,
If I were only the feller my mommy thinks I am."

"She thinks I am a wonder and she knows her little lad
Would never mix with nothing that is is ugly, mean or bad.
Oh, lots of times I sit and think how nice it would be, gee whiz,
If the feller was the feller his mommy thinks he is."

My friends, be yours a life of pain or one of undiluted joy,
You still may learn a lesson from this small unlettered boy.
Don't try to be an earthly saint with eyes fixed on a star;
Just try to be the feller your mommy thinks you are.

The husband and wife were having a polite difference of opinion. "It's obvious that I must be right and you must be wrong," said the wife. "God created woman after man...therefore, it stands to reason that we are an improvement over the original model."

"Not at all," suggested the husband. "God had a very good reason for making woman after he made man. He didn't want any advice."

Doctor:	Your husband must have absolute rest and quiet. Here are some sleeping tablets.
Patient's wife:	When must I give them to him?
Doctor:	Oh, they're not for him, they're for you.

Impatient husband:	Mary, for the last time, if you don't hurry we're going to be late for Church!
Wife:	Be patient! I've told you for the last hour that I'll be down in a minute!

"I have just invented a new machine that does the work of at least fifty men."
"What is it?"
"Ten women."

☺☺☺

I've decided on a name for the baby," said the expectant mother. "Let's call her Hazel."

The young husband didn't care much for her selection, but being a tactful fellow, he was too wise to object. "Fine," he agreed. "That's a beautiful name. Why, the first girl I ever really loved was called Hazel, and the mention of her name revives for me many happy memories."

There was a brief moment of silence. "I've changed my mind," she said. "I think we should call her Jennifer...that's much better, don't you agree?"

☺☺☺

"She told me," the woman complained to her friend, "that you told her the secret I told you not to tell her."

"Well," replied her friend in a hurt tone, "I told her not to tell you I told her."

"Oh, dear," sighed the woman, "well, don't tell her I told you that she told me."

☺☺☺

The three sisters sat down in Sunday School to read the ward bulletin. Each put on a pair of glasses. "Of course, I only need mine for close reading," remarked the first.

"I only wear mine when the light is poor," explained the second. The third was much more frank..."I rarely wear mine," she declared, "except when I want to see."

☺☺☺

Being a woman is a terribly difficult trade,
Since it consists principally of dealing with men.

☺☺☺

She doesn't mind him talking in his sleep
...But it bothers her when he chuckles.

☺☺☺

Woman at perfume counter:
"Is there one that means some other time?"

☺☺☺

"I'll meet you half way," said my wife during an argument. "I'll admit I'm right if you'll admit you're wrong."

The leaders of Women's Liberation went to a minister and said, "When are you going to start saying "Ah women" instead of "amen?"

He answered, "When we start singing "hers" instead of "hymns.""

☺☺☺

As my wife opened the Christmas present I gave her, she chuckled and then with a smile said, "Oh, you angel! This is just what I need to exchange for what I want!"

☺☺☺

Mrs. Jones already had five children aged 12 to 24, and when the doctor told her she was going to have another baby, she shrieked, "Oh, no!"

The doctor said, "Don't take it so hard, you're a young woman and your children are at an age where they can be of considerable help to you."

"It's not that, doctor," cried Mrs. Jones, "I just can't bear the thought of having to attend another PTA meeting!"

☺☺☺

My friend and I often spend a few free afternoons together. She called the other day and said: "I have a friend I want to invite over this afternoon, but I must get some house cleaning done before my husband gets home from work. How can I tell her to come over for just half an hour?"

"Well, if she is a true friend," I told her, "she wouldn't be offended if you just told her straight out." "Okay," she replied, "Would you like to come over for just half an hour?"

☺☺☺

My wife and I took an evening class at the University on the "religions of the world." One night the professor asked us to discuss the theory of reincarnation. Most of us thought the idea would be great if we could come back as actresses, company presidents, lawyers, etc.

My wife, however, calmly declared: "Not me; I would like to come back as a bear." "Why?" asked the professor. "I would finally get a nice fur coat, I could sleep all winter, and I wouldn't have to worry about my waistline."

☺☺☺

Sure, man was created before woman,
But you always make a rough draft before the final masterpiece.

☺☺☺

School days can become the happiest days of your life,
Provided your children are old enough to go.

A secretary came up to her boss and announced that she was quitting. He said "You can't quit, I really need you!" But she wouldn't change her mind, so he asked her to put in writing a good reason why she should leave.

She typed the following: "The reason for my leaving will soon be apparent, and so will I."

☺☺☺

A small boy ran into the house. "Mom," he yelled, "there's a dog out in the yard as big as a horse!" "Now, now," said his mother. "If I've told you once, I've told you a million times....don't exaggerate!"

☺☺☺

My friend, Ann, has a jewel of a cleaning woman. Every Wednesday morning, right after Ann's husband and three children have left for the day, Mrs. Olson appears and cheerfully plunges into her tasks until three....just before the children return to a sparkling, clean home. Ann's husband and the children are enchanted by the stories Ann tells of the warm, homely philosophies of Mrs. Olson. She has practically become an unseen member of the family.

As a matter of fact, she is just that. Every Wednesday afternoon at three, Mrs. Olson removes her cleaning clothes, collects the $15 Ann's husband has left for her and regains her own identity: that of a young housewife and mother, $15 richer, named Ann.

☺☺☺

Three mothers were bragging about their sons. "My son is a wealthy lawyer," said one. "For my birthday he gave me this fur coat." Said the second: "My son is a medical doctor and last winter he gave me a vacation in Miami Beach."

The third thought for a moment then blurted out, "My son sees a psychiatrist each week. He pays the psychiatrist $50 an hour. and who do you think he spends his time talking about-------me!!!"

☺☺☺

A mother sent a note to her son's teacher: "Georgie is very sensitive. If he needs disciplining, please do not slap him. Slap the boy next to him and this will frighten Georgie into doing right."

☺☺☺

She's very proud of the fact that she and her daughter are often mistaken for sisters. Oldest looking daughter you've ever seen!

☺☺☺

A woman was filling out an accident report. She had dented the fender of a parked car while trying to park her own. One question on the report was: "What could the operator of the other vehicle have done to avoid the accident?" She wrote: "He could have parked somewhere else."

After listening to a women's lib rally, two elderly ladies decided that they had been inhibited all of their lives. So to prove they were no longer subject to the old laws, they decided to "streak" through the lobby of the hotel.

As they went running through the lobby, two men were watching. One turned to the other and said: "What were those ladies wearing?" "I don't know," said the other, "but whatever it was sure needed ironing."

"Doctor," the lady said loudly as she bounced into the room and talked to the young man in a white jacket, "I want you to say frankly what's wrong with me."

He surveyed her from head to foot. "Madam," he said at length, "I have just three things to tell you. First, you should lose fifty pounds. Second, you can improve your looks if you'd use about one tenth as much rouge and lipstick. And third, I'm an artist, the doctor's office is just down the hall."

Last week the Sunday School lesson was entitled, "The Rich Young Man," and the reading assignment was "One Thing Thou Lackest."

The teacher asked anyone in the class if they could remember what they had studied. One young lady in the class quickly repeated, "One Thing Thou Lackest, A Rich Young Man."

Young lady: Officer, this man is annoying me.
Officer: But ma'am, he isn't even looking at you.
Young lady: I know, that's what's so annoying.

One woman told her psychiatrist:
The telephone drives me crazy...it never rings."

A little girl was about to say a part in an old-fashioned children's day program. When she got in front of the crowd, the sight of hundreds of curious eyes focused upon her threw her into a panic. Every line that she had rehearsed so carefully faded from her mind and she stood there frozen in her tracks, unable to utter a single syllable.

In the front row her mother was almost as frantic as the little girl. She gestured, she screwed up her lips as though to form the words to be spoken, but to no avail.

Finally in desperation the mother whispered the opening phrase. "I am the light of the world." Instantly the child's face relaxed, a smile appeared where there had been clouds before, and with supreme confidence she began--"My mother is the light of the world."

WHAT ARE MOTHERS MADE OF?
– Cheryl Briggs–
What are Mothers made of?
It's very plain to see––
Lots and lots of yummy things,
'Cause they're as sweet as they can be!

I think they're made of snickers
To keep a laugh and smile,
While getting through the rough days,
The ones that are a trial!

At times they're made of lemons
When they get sour and mad––
Just cause we scribble on the wall––
They think we're really bad!

They could be made of marshmallows––
So tender, soft and puffy.
'Cause sometimes they'll give in to you,
Instead of getting huffy!

Perhaps they're made of chocolate bars,
Melting in the sun.
Especially when you tell them,
"Mom, you're my favorite one!"

They could be made of onions––
When at times they start to cry.
And if you ask the reason––
They really don't know why!

Sometimes I think they're made of rocks
So strong and firm and set!
You try so hard to change their mind––
And couldn't on a bet!

I think they're made of Mr. Clean
Always putting things away––
Making sure we do our chores
Before we can go and play!

They must be made of medicine––
They always have the cure.
No matter what the pain and ache
They fix us up for sure!
I know they're made of honey––
So gooey and so sweet.
With hugs and kisses and "I love you,"
Which they constantly repeat!

I guess they're made of all these things––
And even so much more––
They teach us, love us, help us through,
'Cause that's what Moms are for!

BLESSED ART THOU MOTHER

Blessed art thou woman, for thou shalt be called Mother.
Yea, and thy chores and thy tasks shall follow thee all the days of thy life. And thou shalt eat the bread of thine own baking, and thou shalt dwell forever in a dirty house if thou dost not choose to clean it thyself.

Thou shalt arise before the cock croweth, and thou shalt say unto thine self, "Where are the offspring which were given me? Yea, the sun has risen high in the sky and the hour is getting late; wherefore I have been long at my labors."

And thou shalt go and find thy offspring upon their cots. And thou shalt say unto them "Haste, arise and shine, for I have many labors for thee to perform, wherefore I have been many hours already preparing the way."

And thine offspring shall linger in sleep and shall say unto thee, "Thou dids't not watch the late, late, late show as I did last night, and mine eyes are heavy and mine loins acheth."

And thou shalt say unto thy offspring, "Get thee up from thy cot ere I lay my hand upon thee, and go ye hither and scrub a sparkling tub, for thou hast left black rings upon its sides."

And thy offspring shall say unto thee, "I will go and do thy bidding in a minute." And thy rage shall know no end, and thou shalt weep and wail and gnash thy teeth mightily. Nevertheless; thou shalt scrub a sparkling tub thyself, and glory shall be added unto thee, for thou dids't not strike the lazy beast.

Thou art blessed above all others and thy descendants shall call thee blessed, for thou preparest a table before them. Thou cookest meat and all manner of tasty vittles, and they shall sit at the table with thee, and partake with thee.

And they shall add glory to thy crown for they shall let thee also wash the dishes, if thou wilt. And when the night falleth, thou shalt be pooped; and thy offspring shall say of thee, "She is an old woman, wherefore she neither goes dancing, nor does she watch the late, late, late show."

Thy art and thy craft shall make thee called one, and thou shalt labor at many tasks in the kingdom for whosoever asketh, thou do his bidding.

Thy back shall ache with arthritis; thy cane and thy husband shall be thy support. Thy veins shall be varicose in thy aching legs, but thou shalt do thy labors with a smile; neither shalt thou gripe, for in the day that thou doest, thy name shall be mud.

Nevertheless, thou art blessed, for thou art crowned with the angels on the second Sunday of May on each and every year. Therefore, thou shalt be blessed above all others, for thou art Mother, and thou shalt find peace and joy in thy offspring forever and ever....if thou endureth to the end!

-Author unknown
-Taken from the files of Hazel Briggs-

Adam, Cain, and Abel were out working in the field one day. It was extremely hot and dusty, the weeds were tall and the work was hard. For a break the boys convinced their father, Adam, to climb a small hill with them to see if there was a little breeze.

From the top of the hill, the boys saw for the first time, the Garden of Eden. It was beautiful with tall green trees, fruit and melons, and a waterfall of crystal clear water. The boys were excited and asked Adam what it was. Adam explained that it was a beautiful garden where there were no weeds, and fruit and melons grew naturally, without needing care.

The boys were astounded at its beauty and asked, "Why, don't we live there?"

To which Adam responded, "Your mother and I used to live there, until your mother ate us out of house and home."

After studying magnets in the science class at Olympus Junior High the teacher asked in a test: "What begins with M and picks things up?"

More than one-third of the students answered the question: "MOTHER".

I once asked my mother if she had ever had a dream or seen a vision and her reply was simply:

"Yes, I had a dream, and in my dream the kitchen was a mess, as usual. The boy's bedrooms were a mess, as usual. I looked out the window and the garden was full of weeds, as usual. The radio was so loud I could hardly think, as usual. The neighbor kids were running in and out, as usual.

In my dream, I dreamed I died and went down below...and the sad part was, it took me three days to realize that I'd left home!"

There is no such thing as a non-working mother.

God made the earth and rested.
God made man and rested.

God made WOMAN...
and since,
Neither God nor man has rested!

In my house I always have the last word...

YES, DEAR!

Home is the warm feeling you get when you walk into the house
And everybody ignores you.

☺☺☺

If you want to forget all of your troubles,
Wear tight shoes.

☺☺☺

"The world doesn't want to hear about the labor pains.
It only wants to see the baby!"

☺☺☺

One day when the repairman were working in the school cafeteria, the cooks handed out peanut butter and honey sandwiches instead of serving a hot meal.

After lunch, a satisfied youngester said, "Finally, they gave us a good home cooked meal!"

☺☺☺

Teacher: Now that we have completed our study of the Constitution, who can tell me how the principal of checks and balance works in the American Society?

Student: In my house it's easy. Mom writes the checks and Dad struggles to keep them in balance.

☺☺☺

All anybody needs to know about prizes
Is that Mozart never won one.
–Henry Mitchell–

☺☺☺

Discipline is like broccoli. We may not care for it ourselves,
but feel sure it would be good for everybody else.
–Bill Vaughan–

☺☺☺

Friends are those who even though they know you...
still like you!

☺☺☺

Trying to squash a rumor is like trying to unring a bell.
–Shana Alexander–

☺☺☺

Our faults irritate us most when we see them in others.
–Pennsylvania Dutch Proverb–

"SOMEDAY MRS. SPACKLE, YOU'LL THANK US FOR TAKING YOUR CIGARETTES."

WORD OF WISDOM

Old Mrs. Wilson loved to hear a firey sermon. She would ensconce her comfortable bulk in the pew, rock back and forth in time to the minister's cadences, take a dip of snuff and cry "A-a-a-men," at every piece of ministerial denunciation.

When the minister spoke harshly of sex, drinking, smoking, and drug-taking, she approved heartily, taking snuff at each item and emitting her rolling "A-a-a-men."

Finally the minister began, "And now let me talk about another vicious habit that, fortunately, is going increasingly out of fashion. I refer to the deplorable practice of snuff-dipping..."
Whereupon Mrs. Wilson sat bolt upright and muttered under her breath, "Wouldn't you know? He's stopped preachin' and commenced to meddlin'!"

☺☺☺

Tobacco is a filthy weed.
It's the devil that sows the seed.

It stains your fingers and stinks your clothes,
and makes a stove pipe of your nose.

☺☺☺

Groom in the hotel dining room: "Science says that what we eat, we become."

Bride, seizing menu: "Good! Let's order something rich!"

☺☺☺

A fellow found face down in the gutter was rushed to a hospital. Pinned to his shirt was a note which read:

"To members of the Medical profession: I'm only drunk. Please don't remove my gall bladder--You've already taken it out twice."

☺☺☺

There is so much that is bad in the best of us,
And so much that is good in the worst of us,

That it doesn't behoove any of us,
To talk about the rest of us.

☺☺☺

Dignity and self respect can't be preserved in alcohol.

One day in Sunday School our teacher got a little over-enthusiastic about why we should eat natural foods. The preservatives in store-bought foods, he claimed, were against the Word of Wisdom.

At this, one of the older sisters in the ward raised her hand and said: "I'm at the age when I'll have nothing to do with natural foods. I need all the preservatives I can get."

☺☺☺

Traveling with one of the brethren, and feeling the need of a little stimulant, J. Golden whispered to the waiter as his companion's head was turned, "Put a little coffee in my postum this morning, and don't say anything."

The waiter returned with the postum, but left his discretion in the kitchen. For he blurted out in a voice audible to both, "Which one of you gentlemen ordered coffee in his postum?"

☺☺☺

In pioneer days, whiskey was considered a good
antidote for snake bite.

That's why many of the wagons crossing the plains
carried a case of Scotch.

☺☺☺

You're past the point where medicine will be of any help to you," the doctor told the elderly patient. "What you need is a complete rest and a change of living. Why don't you get away to some quiet country place for a month. Try going to bed early, eat more roast beef, drink plenty of good, rich milk and smoke just one cigar a day."

A month later the patient walked into the doctor's office. Indeed, he did look like a new man and the doctor felt like telling him so.

"Yes, doctor," said the elderly gentleman, "your advice certainly did the business. I went to bed early and did all the other things you told me.

But let me tell you, doctor, that one cigar a day almost killed me at first. It's no joke to start smoking at my age."

☺☺☺

News item in the Rexburg Journal, Rexburg, Idaho:

Local police are puzzled over the finding of a car parked outside of the First Ward Chapel, containing a full case of Scotch whiskey. So far they have found no trace of the owner but Bishop Ricks is diligently working on the case.

☺☺☺

In former times people who committed adultery were usually stoned.
Today, it is usually the other way around.

Bishop: If I understand it correctly, at her request you gave up drinking?
Young Convert: Yes
Bishop: Did you stop smoking for the same reason?
Convert: I did.
Bishop: And it was for her that you gave up gambling and playing cards?
Convert: That's correct.
Bishop: Then why don't you marry her?
Convert: Well, after I did all that reforming, I decided I could do better.

"In conclusion," said the seminary teacher, "I would like to give you a demonstration on the evils of tequila. I have here two glasses, one filled with water, the other filled with tequila. I will now place a worm in each glass. Notice how the worm in the water squirms and gyrates, while the worm in the tequila dies in agony. Now, students, what is the moral of this story?"

Young Seminary student: "If you don't want worms, drink tequila."

Two hobos who had had a little bit too much to drink were walking down the railroad tracks late one evening. One said to the other, "These long stairs sure do get to me."

"It's not the stairs that bother me," replied the second, "it's these blasted low banisters!"

Judge: Tell me, young man, how on earth did you come to get so completely intoxicated?

Young Man: Well, it's like this, your honor. I got into bad company. There were four of us. I had a bottle of whiskey and the other three refused to touch the stuff.

A regular customer at a certain bar always ordered two whiskeys, both of which he drank. At first, the bartender asked him why he didn't order a double whiskey. "You don't understand," was the reply. "One is for me and one's for my friend who's out of town. We always drink together."

One day the customer, looking very depressed, ordered a single whiskey. The bartender asked sympathetically, "Has your friend passed away?" "No," the man sighed. "My doctor ordered me to give up drinking."

Mark Twain was a great believer in moderation

"I make it a point," he said, "never to smoke more than one cigar at a time."

Daughter: "Guess what Dad, I smoke."

Dad: "No, darling, you don't smoke. The cigarette smokes. You're just the sucker."

☺☺☺

A man was driving along a highway when he was stopped by a traffic cop. "You were speeding," said the policeman politely. "I will have to give you a ticket." "But I wasn't speeding," the man protested. "I was only doing forty." "I'm sorry sir," said the policeman. "You were doing fifty in a forty-mile zone."

"Now look here," said the man belligerently, "I know I was only doing forty." The argument continued briefly until the man's wife interrupted. "You're wasting your breath, officer," she said. "You can't argue with my husband when he's been drinking."

☺☺☺

At a country auction, a farmer watched with unbelief as a lady antique collector bid $43 for a hand-blown whiskey bottle. As she carried the bottle back to her seat, the farmer got a close look at it.

"Holy smokes, Martha," he said to his wife, "that there jug is empty!"

☺☺☺

A man was bothered with continual ringing in his ears, bulging eyes and a flushed face. Over a period of three years he went to doctor after doctor. One took out his tonsils, one his appendix, another pulled all his teeth---he even tried a goat gland treatment in Switzerland---all to no avail. Finally, one doctor told him there was no hope, he had six months to live.

The poor fellow quit his job, sold all his belongings and decided to live it up in the time he had left. He went to his tailor and ordered several suits and shirts. The tailor measured his neck and wrote down 16 1/2. The man corrected him: 15 1/2. The tailor measured again: 16 1/2. But the man insisted that he'd always worn a size 15 1/2.

"Well, all right," said the tailor, "but don't come back here complaining to me if you have ringing ears, a flushed face and bulging eyes!"

☺☺☺

An English poet visited Florida for the first time.
Asked by reporters what his impressions were, he said,

"All the women appear slim and trim and all the men pregnant."

☺☺☺

Remember the good old days when a juvenile delinquent
Was a boy who hid back of the barn and tried to smoke corn silks?

The missionaries were out business contacting, and stopped a smart-looking businessman on the street corner who was standing there smoking a cigar.
"How many cigars to you smoke a day?" asked the missionary.
"About ten," responded the businessman.
"What do they cost you?"
"Twenty cents a piece."
"My, that's two dollars a day. How long have you been smoking?"
"Thirty years."
"Two dollars a day for thirty years. That's a lot of money."
"Yes, it is."
"Do you see that office building on the corner?"
"Yes."
"If you'd never smoked in your life, you might own that fine building."
Business contact: "Do you smoke?"
Missionary: "No, never did."
Contact: "Do you own that building?"
Missionary: "No."
Contact. "Well, I do!"

☺☺☺

There is a story about a Tennessee accountant making his first visit to Washington as a guest of an old friend from army days. For three days he was wined and dined by his host and hostess, and then the last night they said, "Sorry, we have an office function, but you go to the Swedish Embassy and they'll take good care of you. They are having a cocktail party."

The Tennessee accountant had never been to one of these fancy parties before. Every five minutes a waiter was offering him a drink, and he felt obliged to take one. So after a time he really was "blind." The music started to play and he felt very much like dancing. He saw ahead of him a figure in a long red dress. So he went over and said, "Will you dance with me?"

The person responded very haughtily, "For three reasons my answer is no. One, you're intolerably drunk. Two, they're playing the national anthem. And three, I'm a Cardinal in the Catholic Church!"

☺☺☺

Doctor to portly patient
"We'll make your diet real simple---if it tastes good, spit it out."

☺☺☺

You talk vitamins A, B, C,
And some vitamins D, E, and G.
You see that the children get these is true,
But they don't get enough of the vitamins Y, O, U!

☺☺☺

"Ignorance ain't knowin' nothin'
It's knowin' too much that ain't so!"

One evening two meetings were scheduled side by side in a large hotel, but the groups were quite different. One was the twenty-fifth reunion of fraternity brothers from a large university. The other was a meeting of the local Relief Society organization with their husbands. The manager of the hotel was very concerned, because the menus of the two groups was totally different. The fraternity brothers wanted everything bathed in booze, hors d'oeuvres in beer batter, the entre' in wine sauce and for dessert—spiked watermellon. While the Relief Society and their husbands had requested a nice salad and a weight watchers dessert.

The kitchen was in the basement and the meals were served on the top floor in the sky room with the two groups separated by a large sound partition. The bus boys took everything up the elevator while the manager fretted back and forth from the kitchen to the skyroom trying to make sure everything made it into the right room.

All went well, until the dessert. The bus boy mistakenly took the spiked watermellon to the wrong room. Unknowingly the waiter served the spiked watermellon to the Relief Society and their husbands. When he discovered the error, the manager was irate. How could such a error be made? Not wanting to be seen, but wanting to know what was being said, he asked the waiter to go back in and determine how upset everyone was.

When the waiter returned, the manager, eager to know what was happening asked, "What are they saying?" "Well," said the waiter, there are a few ladies who are not eating their dessert, but I noticed that their husbands are saving the watermellon seeds."

Most of us don't realize how hectic it is for the Angel who, after we die, must decide whether we go to Spirit Prison or to Paradise.

Well, one holiday weekend was unusually busy and the Angel had both St. Peter and the Devil booked solid. Both were complaining that they couldn't handle another spirit, when suddenly there appeared three more, a Monk, from St. Martins Vinyards; the Mayor of Milwaukee; and a Mormon Bishop, from Salt Lake City.

First, the Angel tried to send them to St. Peter, but there was no more room. So, after some persuasion, Satan agreed if they would be patient he could handle them. Satan first interviewed the Monk. After listening for a while he said, "Take these forms down the hall to the third door on the left, there you'll find a refrigerator full of fine wine. Just take your time and fill out the forms, I'll call you when I have time."

Next, he interviewed the Mayor of Milwaukee. After listening for a while he said, "Take these forms down the hall to the third door on the right, there you'll find a refrigerator full of beer. Just take your time, fill out the forms, and when I have time I'll come and get you."

Finally, he interviewed the third person. When he found out that it was a Mormon Bishop from Salt Lake City, the Devil became all upset and called the Angel in charge. Over the phone he yelled, "I'm upset, I told you that I was busy... You knew I didn't have time to make punch and cookies."

BACKGROUND TO THE RECEPTION OF THE WORD OF WISDOM

"I think I am as well acquainted with the circumstances which led to the giving of the Word of Wisdom as any man in the Church, although I was not present at the time to witness them. The first school of the prophets was held in a small room situated over the Prophet Joseph's kitchen, in a house which belonged to Bishop (Newel K.) Whitney, and which was attached to his store, which store probably might be about fifteen feet square. In the rear of this building was a kitchen, probably ten by fourteen feet, containing rooms and pantries. Over this kitchen was situated the room in which the Prophet received revelations and in which he instructed his brethren.

The brethren came to that place for hundreds of miles to attend school in a little room probably no larger than eleven by fourteen. When they assembled together in this room after breakfast, the first thing they did was to light their pipes, and while smoking, talk about the great things of the kingdom, and spit all over the room, for as soon as the pipe was out of their mouths, a large chew of tobacco would then be taken. Often when the Prophet entered the room to give the school instructions, he would find himself in a cloud of tobacco smoke. This, and the complaints of his wife at having to clean so filthy a floor, made the Prophet think upon the matter, and he inquired of the Lord relating to the conduct of the Elders in using tobacco, and the revelation known as the Word of Wisdom was the result of his inquiry."
–Brigham Young––Journal of Discourses, 12:158–

The preacher walked into the saloon and ordered milk. By mistake the bartender served him some "milk punch."
After taking a good long drink, the holy man lifted his eyes to heaven and was heard to say, "Oh, Lord. What a cow!"

There are three great American Parties
Democrat, Republican, and Cocktail.

I kissed my first woman and smoked my first cigarette on the same day.
I have never had time for tobacco since.
–Mark Twain–

Pollution in Salt Lake is so bad this winter,
That I put air in my tires and two of them died!

Winston Churchill was having a running battle with Lady Aster, who wanted prohibition in England. Churchill loved to go to the pub for a drink. One day Lady Aster said, "Winston, you are disgusting! You are drunk!" Winston smiled and replied, "Lady Aster, you are absolutely right, I am drunk. But you are ugly. The beauty of it is that tommorrow, I shall be sober."

"COME ON, BROTHER YOUNG. WHERE'S YOUR STRONG PIONEER STOCK?"

WORK

Many of us live our lives the way we watch television. Even though the program isn't as good as we would like it to be, we are too lazy to get up and change it.

☺☺☺

Work will win while willy-wally wishing won't!

☺☺☺

A pig and a chicken were walking down the street one day when they passed a billboard advertising "America needs a good breakfast." The picture shown was of two eggs over easy with several beautiful strips of bacon.

The chicken said, "Doesn't that make you proud to see that we contribute daily to a better America." The pig thought for a moment, then slowly commented,

"Well, that's easy for you to say. For you it is just a contribution, but for me it requires a total commitment!"

☺☺☺

Wanted: Man to assemble Nuclear Fissionable Isotopes, Molecular Reactivity Counters and Three-Phase Cyclotronic Uranium Photosynthesizers. No experience necessary.

☺☺☺

To err is human, but to really louse things up
takes a computer.

☺☺☺

During the power failure many people complained of having gotten stuck for hours on escalators.

☺☺☺

Farmer Brown's chickens refused to go all out to improve their egg laying. One day a football was accidentally kicked into the yard.

The rooster, thinking it was an egg, said to the hens, "I'm not complaining, but look at the work they are turning out next door."

☺☺☺

You are more successful if you OWE a million dollars than you are if you OWN a million dollars. The latter shows that at least two people have faith in you.

Results of fifty dollar computer aptitude test:

"Your vocational aptitude test indicates your best opportunities lie in a field where your father holds an influential position."

☺☺☺

An employee who had been shorted ten dollars in his pay envelope came storming into his boss and complained bitterly about his shortage. "You know," said the boss, "I took your case as an example. I overpaid you ten dollars last week, and you didn't object. This week I underpaid you ten dollars and you complained bitterly."

"I know," said the employee. "I can overlook one mistake, but when it happens the second time, I think it's time to complain!"

☺☺☺

A secretary was having a tough time getting up mornings, so her boss recommended that she go to a doctor, which she did. He prescribed a pill. She took the pill, slept well, and awoke before the alarm.

She dressed, ate a good breakfast, drove to the office and strolled up to her boss and said, "Boy, I feel so much better. I didn't have a bit of trouble getting up this morning."

"Fantastic," replied the boss. "But where were you yesterday?"

☺☺☺

Most times when we cast our bread upon the waters --
It comes back buttered.

☺☺☺

Our lawn mower had broken down and I had been working fruitlessly for two hours trying to get it back together. Suddenly my new neighbor appeared with a kit full of tools. "Can I give you a hand?" he asked.

In twenty minutes he had the mower functioning beautifully. "Thanks a million," I told him. "Say, what do you make with such a fine kit of tools?" "Mostly friends," he smiled. "I'm available any time."

☺☺☺

A man wrote his congressman that he'd like to be an inventor, but didn't want to waste his time on things already invented. "Will you please go down to the patent office," his letter read, "and get me a list of things that haven't been invented yet. Get me the answer by return mail, as I am eager to get to work."

☺☺☺

There are certain signs that tell you when you're under too much stress. For instance, when you realize that things are so far out of control, only the boss can handle it--and then you remember that you're the boss!

<u>Chinese proverb</u>

Man who say it cannot be done.
Should not interrupt man doing it.

☺☺☺

A committee is an arrangement enabling one to share the blame with others.

☺☺☺

The brain is an organ that starts working the moment you get up in the morning and does not stop until you get into the office.

☺☺☺

To frown, we exercise 87 muscles; to smile,
we exercise only 13. Why work overtime?

☺☺☺

<u>Sign in a small store in Southeast Idaho</u>
We sell nothing on Sunday--and D _ _ _ little through the week!

☺☺☺

If you want to soar with the eagles, don't act like a turkey!

☺☺☺

Robert Frost once observed that if a man works faithfully eight hours a day, eventually he may get to be a boss and work twelve hours a day.

☺☺☺

Truman said: "If you can't stand the heat, get out of the kitchen."

☺☺☺

Everything cometh to him who WAITETH,
So long as he who WAITETH, WORKETH like crazy while he WAITETH!

☺☺☺

Do the best you can and you will generally find that's bad enough.

☺☺☺

Don't worry if your job is small and your rewards are few.
Remember that the mighty oak was once a nut like you.

☺☺☺

Yesterday is a cancelled check; tomorrow is a promissory note;
Today is ready cash -- spend it wisely.

An entrepreneur is the kind of person
Who will work 16 hours a day
Just to avoid having to work 8 hours a day for someone else.

☺☺☺

Some people treat life like a slot machine. They try to get as much as possible out of it, while putting in as little as possible. Some people spend life always looking for the jackpot.

☺☺☺

There's no traffic jam on the extra mile.

☺☺☺

A management consultant makes the following observation:
"Be the first in the office every morning, be the last to leave every night, never take a day off, slave through the lunch hours, and the inevitable day will come when the boss will summon you to his office and say, "I've been watching your work very carefully, Jackson. Just what the devil are you up to, anyhow?"

☺☺☺

IDLENESS

He wasn't much for stirring around
Such wasn't his desire.
In cold weather he was always found
Just sitting by the fire.

Same old habits everyday,
He never seemed to tire
While others worked and drew their pay
He kept sitting by the fire.

And when he died by slow degrees
Some said he had gone higher
But if he's doing now, what he was doing then,
He's still sitting by the fire.

☺☺☺

Variety may be the spice of life,
But it's monotony that brings home the groceries.

☺☺☺

Two gardeners for wealthy estates on Long Island met one day at the local hardware store. "I hear you're working for that banker fellow now," said one.

"You've got it all wrong," replied the other. "He gets up at five thirty every morning to get aboard an over-crowded, rickety train to commute to the hot city so he can keep up his estate and pay us all our weekly wages. No....I'm not working for him, he's working for me."

Experience is what you got
When you were expecting something else.

☺☺☺

Monday is a hard way to spend one-seventh of your life.

☺☺☺

A new joke is making the rounds in Moscow. It's about two workmen with shovels, one of whom is observed stopping every 20 feet to dig a hole along the street. As soon as the hole is dug, his companion fills it and the process is repeated.

Comrades! shouts the observer. What are you doing? You accomplish nothing. We're wasting money paying you!!

You don't understand, one of the workers replies. Usually we work with a third fellow, Mikhail, but he's home drunk today. I dig the hole, Mikhail sticks in the tree, and Dimitri here puts the dirt back in the hole. Just because Mikhail is drunk doesn't mean that Dimitri and I have to stop working!

☺☺☺

Fortune Cookie message of the month

If man too busy making fortune,
Somebody may steal his cookie.

☺☺☺

Actress Molly Picon heard some performers complaining about accommodations on tour.

"I never complain about such things," she said, "my grandmother raised eleven children in four rooms."

"How did she manage?" someone asked. "Easy," Miss Picon replied. "She took in boarders."

☺☺☺

After a lengthy examination, the doctor told the tired businessman the answer to his illness.

"The best thing for you," said the doctor, "is to give up drinking and smoking, get up early in the morning and go to bed earlier at night."

The tired businessman thought about the doctor's recommendations for a moment and said, "Doc, perhaps I don't deserve the best. What's second best?"

☺☺☺

They mistook activity for accomplishment.
They meant well---but they got no place.

There was a dedicated, hardworking cowboy who had been out on the range in the dust and hot sun, branding and rounding up cattle. He could hardly stay awake in his saddle as he brought in the 1st of the herd to the ranch. He couldn't wait to eat a hot meal, take a bath and head for the bunkhouse.

He was just about to get down from his horse when the ranch owner came up to him and told him that some more cattle had been spotted up a canyon not too far from the ranch. The owner asked him to go out and bring down everything in the canyon. Without a word he turned his horse around and headed for the mountains.

This cowboy was so dedicated to his work that when he was told to bring in everything in the canyon, that's what he did. The next morning the whole ranch was awakened by a terrible noise coming from the corral.

When they went to investigate they found 65 head of cattle, 20 sheep, 16 deer, 10 coyote, 3 mountain lions, 2 badgers and a wood chuck. And what's more, they were all wearing brands.

☺☺☺

All of his life Sam Hankins had been a handyman doing odd jobs around town. One day a mill owner offered him a full-time job guarding the mill's dam from muskrats.

Sam was delighted. It was the first steady job he'd ever had, and after all the years of eaking out a living, he kinda figured he deserved it. There in the lovely spring weather Sam sat on the grassy bank, his gun across his knees, a contented look on his face. Finding him one morning, a friend, who'd not heard about his new job, asked him what he was doing.

"Guarding the dam," Sam replied. "Paid to shoot them pesky muskrats." The friend looked out at the dam just as a muskrat appeared. "There's one now," exclaimed the man. "Get him, Sam--shoot him!"

Sam continued puffing quietly on his pipe. "Sam," said the man, after the muskrat had disappeared, "why didn't you shoot him?" "Shoot him, you darned fool? You think I want to lose my job?"

☺☺☺

When the Lord asks you to put your shoulder to the wheel
Don't start looking around for a tow truck.

☺☺☺

Some people have insomnia; they can't even sleep when it's time to get up.

☺☺☺

A new employee was habitually late. Finally, the foreman called him in. "Don't you know the time we go to work here?" he shouted.

"No, sir," was the reply. "I haven't been able to figure it out yet, because when I get here in the morning the rest of you are already here!"

A business executive in Los Angeles has given up trying to get neat, correctly spelled letters from his secretary. Instead, according to the Paul Harvey report, he bought a rubber stamp which he stamps on every piece of correspondence.

It says: "She can't type, but she's beautiful."

☺☺☺

Secretaries slogan: Seek and ye shall file.

☺☺☺

Committee: The unwilling, recruited from the unfit, to do the unnecessary.

☺☺☺

Isn't it strange
That princes and kings
And clowns that caper
In sawdust rings
And common people
Like you and me
Are builders for eternity?

Each is given a bag of tools
A shapeless mass
A book of rules
And each must make
Ere life has flown
A stumbling block
Or a stepping-stone.

☺☺☺

Genius is one percent inspiration --
And ninety-nine percent perspiration.

-Thomas Edison-

☺☺☺

Everything comes to him who hustles while he waits.

-Thomas Edison-

☺☺☺

"Are you looking for work."
"Not necessarily--but I would like a job."

☺☺☺

"Inch by Inch, it's a Cinch,
Yard by Yard, it's Hard!

"We are not going to help the caboose catch up to the engine
by stopping the train."
–Jay Van Andal–
(A founder of Amway Corp)

Plan ahead...
Remember it wasn't raining when Noah built the Ark.

Cooperation is doing with a smile what you have to do anyhow.

Stick to your task 'til it sticks to you;
Beginners are many, but enders are few.

Honor, power, place, and praise
Will come, in time, to the one who stays.

Stick to your task 'til it sticks to you;
Bend at it, sweat at it, smile at it too;

For out of the bend and the sweat and the smile,
Will come life's victories, after awhile.

A word from the coach:

I'm just a plowhand from Arkansas, but I have learned how to hold a
team together. How to lift some men up, how to calm down others,
until finally they've got one heartbeat together, a team. There's just
three things I'd ever say:

If anything goes bad, I did it.

If anything goes semi–good, then we did it.

If anything goes real good, then you did it.

That's all it takes to get people to win football games for you.

–Bear Bryant–

Question for sports group

How many of you are golfers? (Ask for a raise of hands)
Now how many of you have a set of golf clubs? (Ask for a raise of hands)
Oh, many more own clubs than will profess to be golfers. You know why don't
you? It's because you're Americans, that means you can buy better than you
can play!

MR. MEANT-TO

Mr. Meant-to has a comrade,
And his name is Didn't-do.
Have you ever chanced to meet them?
Did they ever call on you?

These two fellows live together
In the house of Never-win,
And I'm told that it is haunted
By the ghost of Might-have-been.

☺☺☺

"You can't do today's work on yesterdays successes --
If you expect to be in business tomorrow."

☺☺☺

As the rescue boat sped away to pick up survivors of the shipwreck of the Titanic a signalman on shore flashed to it the following message: "Good Luck!"

The captain had his signalman reply: "Thanks. but actually, we rely on skill."

☺☺☺

MONEY
-Richard Armour-

Workers earn it,
Spendthrifts burn it,
Bankers lend it,
Women spend it,
Forgers fake it,
Taxes take it,
Dying leave it,
Heirs receive it,
Thrifty save it,
Misers crave it,
Robbers seize it,
Rich increase it,
Gamblers lose it,
I COULD USE IT!

☺☺☺

"Everyone is born with an EQUAL chance to become
Just as UNEQUAL as he or she possibly can."

☺☺☺

The man who deals in sunshine,
Is the one who gets the crowds;
He does a lot more business
Than the one that peddles clouds!

PUT-OFF TOWN

Did you ever go to Put-Off Town
    where the houses are old and tumbled down,
And everything tarries and everything drags
    with dirty streets and people in rags.

On the street called Slow lives old man Wait
    and his two little boys named Linger and Late.
With unclean hands and tossled hair
    and a naughty sister named I Don't Care.

Did you ever go to Put-Off Town
    and play with the little girls named Fret and Frown,
Or go to the house of old man Wait
    and whistle for his boys to come to the gate,

To play ball all day on Tarry Street,
    leaving your errands for other feet.
To stop or shirk or linger or frown
    is the nearest way to this Put-Off Town.

JUST BECAUSE IT HAS BEEN DONE THAT WAY FOR YEARS DOESN'T MAKE IT RIGHT!

HISTORY OF THE TYPEWRITER KEYBOARD

The standard typewriter keyboard was designed with one idea in mind—to slow down typists. The typewriter, as invented in 1872 by Christopher Sholes, had a serious flaw: Whenever typists worked up any speed, the keys would jam.

To remedy this, Sholes rearranged the keyboard, positioning frequently used letter combinations as far from each other as possible and assigning a disproportionate amount of work to the weakest fingers.

His "improvements" slowed typists down to a crawl but largely eliminated the jammed-key problem. Thus was born the modern "QWERTYUIOP" keyboard.

Since then, many persons have tried to introduce more conveniently designed keyboards. None of these designs has gained acceptance, although that of a University of Washington professor, August Dvorak, came close in 1932.

He reworked the standard keyboard, putting the often-used letters where the typist could get at them most easily and easing the burden on the weakest fingers. Dvorak said his refinements would speed typing by thirty-five percent, but they never replaced Sholes' mishmash, which remains the standard throughout the world—for computers as well as typewriters.

I love my job...
It's the work I hate!

BEWARE OF USING A MIDDLE-MAN!

Pedro robbed a bank in Texas and crossed the border into Mexico to escape. Normally the law doesn't cross borders, but this big fat-bellied sheriff in a little Texas town was not about to be cheated by any squirrely little guy named Pedro.

So he crossed the border and caught him. The only trouble in his broken Spanish he couldn't communicate well enough to get Pedro to tell him where he had hid the money. So he grabbed a local bartender, who fortunately spoke Spanish and English, to translate.

The Mexican bartender asked Pedro, "Where's the money?" "I don't know," Pedro said. "He's got the wrong man!" So the bartender tells the Texas sheriff, "He says he doesn't know where the money is."

This enfuriated the Texas sheriff, so he grabbed Pedro, whipped him with his pistol several times, stuck the gun in his ear and told the bartender translator to tell him if he didn't tell him where he had hid the money, he would shoot him in the head!

So the bartender looks Pedro in the eye, and says, "Say man, this sheriff is serious, if you don't tell him where you hid the money, he is going to shoot you dead!"

Well, this finally scared Pedro so bad that he cried, "Don't let him kill me! I'll tell! . . . I'll tell! . . . The money is in the back of the piano."

The translator turned to the fat-bellied Texas sheriff and said, "He says he doesn't care if you kill him. He refuses to tell a fat Texan where he hid the money. He's ready to die, so go ahead and shoot. "

☺☺☺

Too error is human,
But to forgive is against company policy.

☺☺☺

The wages of sin are high!
Unless you can find someone who will do it for nothing.

☺☺☺

A secretary burst into the office of an executive on May 21, 1927, and cried, "Mr. Smith, a man, Charles Lindberg, has just flown from New York to Paris all by himself!"

When Mr. Smith continued to work calmly, she cried out, "Don't you understand? A man has just flown the Atlantic all by himself!"

Mr. Smith looked up, and calmly said, "All by himself, a man can do anything. When a committee flies the Atlantic, let me know."

The world is full of men looking for better jobs...
But unwilling to do better work!

☺☺☺

The world is filled with willing people --
Those willing to work and those willing to let them!

☺☺☺

Hard work, when mixed with a keen interest in your job --
Is the yeast that raises the "DOUGH."

☺☺☺

The best place to find a helping hand
Is at the end of your own arm.

☺☺☺

A large aircraft carrier was moving quickly through the fog, when in the distance the captain saw the light of what appeared to be another ship coming towards them. The captain on the deck requested the signal man to send a message: "Move aside we are coming through!"

Back came a most unusual message, "You move aside."

Startled by the rude reply of the other ship, the captain said, "Perhaps he does not realize that he is talking to the captain of the largest aircraft carrier in the fleet and that we have the admiral aboard. Tell him, that we demand he move aside because we are coming through!

So in a quick, abrupt fashion, the signal man sent, "We are coming through. Now move aside!"

Quick as flash, the message returned. "No, you move aside!"

So the captain sent for the admiral. After he explained what the problem was, the admiral, who had been a signal man once himself, grabbed the signal light and sent: "I am the admiral of this fleet, and this the largest aircraft carrier in this part of the world, and I personally demand that you move aside. We are coming through!

There was a pause. Then the message. "Admiral, I am just a lowly seaman, but you better move aside. I am in a lighthouse!"

☺☺☺

Blessed is he who expects nothing
For he shall rarely be disappointed!

☺☺☺

It's not the ups and downs in life that bother us,
It's the "JERKS."

JUST A TINY LITTLE MINUTE

Just a tiny little minute, just 60 seconds in it,
    Forced upon me -- can't refuse it,

Didn't choose it, but it is up to me to use it,
    Give account if I abuse it.

The tiny little minute, but eternity is in it.

☺☺☺

It matters not if you try and fail,
    And try and fail again.

It matters much if you try and fail,
    And fail to try again.

☺☺☺

The Wall Street Journal had an interesting article the other day, entitled "A Secret on How to Make a Small Fortune in the Stock Market."

The article was short, but the answer was prophetic: "Begin with a Big Fortune!"

☺☺☺

Bishop: "Which of the parables do you like best?"

Ralph: "The parable of the man who loafs and fishes."

☺☺☺

For those who are discouraged, we quote from the unwritten scriptures of Briggs Chapter 10: verse 1: "THIS TOO SHALL PASS."

We substantiate this from the famous Book of Mormon scripture: It came to pass. It doesn't say, It came to stay!

☺☺☺

Perhaps you enjoy as I do the wonderful comic strip, "SNOOPY."

Recently, they had a cartoon showing Lucy, giving advise for a dime to her friend Charlie Brown. After listening to Charlie's problems she said, "Charlie, some people's life is like a folding chair on a great cruise ship. Some people prefer to face backward to see where they have been. Others prefer to face foreward to see where they are going."

"Now, Charlie, which way do you like to face your folding chair?"

Charlie's profound statement expresses how many of us feel about our own feeble efforts in life. He said, "I don't know. I've never been able to get mine unfolded!"

WARNING!

This publication may contain material which will make even the most sour reader snicker and smile. Realizing the danger this may have on your disposition, we have included a complaint form.

Please feel free to express all your frustrations on the form provided below. If the space provided is not adequate, we express our regrets.

Only material received on the official complaint form will be accepted by the Briggs family.

- -

COMPLAINT FORM

Please write your complaints
in the space provided below.

(write legibly)

- -

ADDITONAL COPIES MAY BE OBTAINED FROM

A TIME TO LAUGH
BOX 17375
SLC, UTAH
84117
Retail Price $9.95

(Please include $1.50 for Postage and Handling)